THUNDER AND TRUMPETS

American Academy of Religion
Studies in Religion
edited by
Charley Hardwick
James O. Duke

THUNDER AND TRUMPETS
Millerites and Dissenting Religion
In Upstate New York, 1800–1850

DAVID L. ROWE

Scholars Press
Chico, California

THUNDER AND TRUMPETS
Millerites and Dissenting Religion
in Upstate New York, 1800–1850

David L. Rowe

BX
6115
.R69
1985

©1985
American Academy of Religion

Library of Congress Cataloging in Publication Data

Rowe, David, 1947–
  Thunder and trumpets.

  (Studies in religion . American Academy of Religion ;
no. 38)
  Bibliography: p.
  1. Adventists—New York (State)—History—19th
century. 2. New York (State)—Church history. I. Title.
II. Series: Studies in religion (American Academy of
Religion) ; no. 38.
BX6115.R69   1984   286.7'747   84–13923
ISBN 0–89130–770–2
ISBN 0–89130–769–9 (pbk.)

Printed in the United States of America
on acid-free paper

To Dad and Mom

CONTENTS

Preface

On October 22, 1844, hundreds of New Yorkers throughout the state watched the skies expectantly for the Second Coming of Christ. A scoffing public had called these people Millerites for William Miller, the Low Hampton, New York, farmer who had sparked this excitement with his lectures on the approaching end of the world. But they called themselves adventists,[1] often capitalizing the label to brandish before unbelievers their self-conscious identity as people who were separate from other professing Christians, superior to them in faith and understanding of the Bible. Like other "watchers on the walls of Zion" in New England, Pennsylvania, Canada, Ohio, and the farther west, they believed that at any moment the Son of Man would descend to Earth from Heaven through clouds ablaze with lightning and reverberating with the crash of thunder and the compelling call of celestial trumpets. Then, an enraged God would shower purifying fire upon the corrupt earth, shatter cities and topple thrones with earthquakes, put an end to the reign of churches and governments, and send the wicked to the punishment they deserved. Only true Christians, those who were now watching for His coming, praying for it, yearning for the rewards Christ would mete out to the saints, were to taste the joys of paradise in the New Jerusalem.[2]

These seemingly bizarre and simplistic beliefs had earned the Millerites a public reputation as fools, cranks, and lunatics, but the adventists cited this very simplicity as proof that they were of God's Elect. They described themselves as the humble, the poor, and the virtuous, soldiers in the army of the Lord defending Truth in the Latter Days against the attack of the educated, the rich, and the wicked. Both images have stuck to the Millerites ever since. Today, they provide us with a certain "comic relief" as historical characters in the otherwise complex and tragic play of events from Jacksonian Democracy to civil war. Stories of Millerites climbing to the tops of hills and the roofs of barns to be closer to Jesus when He appeared, of them making and wearing ascension robes in which they expected to rise in the air to meet God, of ardent adventists refusing to

---

[1] I do not capitalize the first letter of *adventist* when applying the word to the Millerites because Millerism was the non-formalized phase of the Adventist movement. But I do capitalize the *a* when applying it to the movement after 1844, when denominationalization provided Adventism with a formal theology and structure.

[2] Discussions of historiography are reserved for the bibliographical essay.

plant or harvest crops in anticipation of the event and then starving in the winter that followed their tragic disappointment have long "instructed" us about the naiveté of the human character. We have always assumed these stories to be true, the only "facts" about the Millerites worth knowing.

Of course, Adventist historians have tried to correct and improve their theological forebears' unfortunate reputation. In doing so, however, they have often erred in the opposite extreme. For the apologists, the Millerites were saints who, having received Truth from God, had become martyrs in their attempt to convey that Truth to others. So in their interpretations, William Miller often becomes a strong leader, a messenger of God, a 19th century Noah building the latter-day ark of salvation aboard which so many Adventists have since climbed.

It became obvious as research and interpretation of resources progressed that both views are flawed, that the truth about Millerism lies somewhere between the lurid descriptions of scoffers and the hagiographics of defenders. Not so obvious was the real nature of the movement. The traditional assumption that Millerites all believed the world would end on a particular day in 1844, though seemingly reasonable, is not correct. Certainly common threads ran through the crusade—a belief in the literal return of Christ to judge the world and create the New Jerusalem, hostility to worldly sins of all kinds, rejection of human institutions and human authority. But Millerites varied greatly. Millerism was many things to many people, with little consensus of belief or practice, a "movement" rife with disputes and contradictions. No coherent Millerite personality existed at all.

The challenge was to select a method of presenting Millerism that would not only reveal this variegation but also explain it. In fact, causation became a more important determinant of methodology as the work developed. Describing Millerism in all its complexity, a fairly simple task, might have required a book that studied the movement nation-wide, if that was the sole objective. But as the reasons for Millerism became clear, so too did the inadequacy of a macroscopic assessment to reveal why such a phenomenon arose at that particular time. Scholars usually cite the general cultural ferment of the period, Jacksonian Democracy, and revivalism as reasons for its development, but by placing Millerism in a national context they have left unconsidered more parochial cultural, institutional, and social reasons behind the movement. They have also neglected the role of personal motivation, for becoming a Millerite was not entirely a collective decision. Individuals found themselves attracted to Miller's message for their own reasons, they interpreted the message according to their own religious and social needs, and they acted on the basis of this interpretation in highly individualized ways.

The only way to project this more complex picture of the movement was to look at its regional development. Choosing the region, upstate

New York, was natural. It was there that Miller lived and first preached his theory, and it was there that Millerism achieved probably its strongest support. There, too, were all the elements necessary to illustrate the crusade's multifaceted personality—cultural ferment, fragmentation of the churches, regional varieties of Millerite belief, local leaders who took adventists into directions national Millerite leaders deplored, radical reactions to disappointment, the drive to create a specific and separate Adventist sect. Of course, regional developments often followed national developments, so where necessary the focus broadens. But the primarily regional approach allows for a thorough and in-depth description of how and why Millerism arose.

Upstate New York's sobriquet as the "burned-over district" implies a second methodological quality. The region earned that nickname for its widespread religious peculiarity, what Whitney R. Cross, whose monumental history of the region is titled *The Burned-over District*, called "ultraism." The commonly held impression has been that the area was particularly conducive to religious innovation of which Millerism was but one example. Whether the area burned more hotly than any other is debatable, and this study does not answer the question, nor can it for reasons that will become clear. Indeed, that is not an important question at all, though some thoughts about the nature of the burned-over district will appear in the epilogue. It is more helpful to accept the presence of many innovative religious groups in the region and then to ask what they had in common. What was it about the life of people there that caused them to turn to sects; did these sects share attitudes or perspectives; in what ways did they differ? Cross suggested that ultraism resulted from maturation, the transformation of the region from a frontier outpost to a settled locale. In other words, it was the product of a social process, the causes of which he leaves unexplained. A regional study of Millerism comparing it with similar movements suggests that ultraism was itself a process, and it also provides one model of how that process operated. Finally, by focusing on Millerism specifically rather than attempting a formal comparative view of millenarianism or innovative religion in general the study attempts to avoid the overgeneralization that often mars more intentionally comparative works.

Both the institutional character of Millerism and the culture that gave it birth are readily discoverable. Early nineteenth-century New Yorkers left hundreds of apocalyptic statements in letters, diaries, newspaper articles, poems, and many other forms, and this rich literature allowed for a close examination of apocalypticism as a theme in popular culture and religion. Also, Millerites left a vast number of letters and reports in Millerite newspapers, published books and tracts, and surprisingly complete collections of correspondence, so it is possible to gauge the geographic distribution of the movement in upstate New York and to describe its structure. These sources also permit an inter-disciplinary examination of Millerism drawing on literature, sociology, and popular culture as well as more traditional tools of religious and social history. In order to impart the flavor of this culture, I have chosen to insert quotations as they appear in the original documents, misspellings and all. Because of the frequency of spelling error, I have omitted the editorial *sic*, but if the error is sufficiently egregious that the word's meaning is obscured, the correct spelling is inserted in brackets.

Years of research and writing have created many obligations that I happily acknowledge. This book began as a doctoral dissertation at the University of Virginia, where it benefited from the careful and critical reading of Josef Barton, Merrill Peterson, and L. Baird Tipson. I was able to produce the final manuscript in part with a grant from the Seminar for Community and Family History of the Newberry Library, Chicago. Several scholars generously donated their spareless time to read the manuscript or otherwise to give invaluable advice. My gratitude is extended to Milton L. Klein, L. Baird Tipson, Donald J. Grout, David T. Arthur, Judith Wellman, W. Barton McCash, and Fred S. Rolater.

Many libraries and historical societies generously assisted my research. This is especially true of the late Doris Colby and the staff of Aurora College, Aurora, Illinois, which made the Second Advent Collection available, and Gould Coleman and the staff of the Local and Regional History Collection of Cornell University. I thank also the Manuscript Division, Rush Rhees Library, University of Rochester; the Manuscripts Room, Bird Library, Syracuse University; the Massachusetts Historical Association, which xeroxed many letters for me from the Joshua V. Himes Collection; the New York Historical Society; the American Baptist Historical Society, Andover-Crozier Theological Seminary, Rochester; the public libraries of Buffalo, Rochester, and Syracuse; the Pickering-Beach Historical Society, Sackets Harbor; and the literally dozens of local historians across New York who kindly supplied information about archive sources in their communities. With all these I eagerly share any credit for the good things in this book while greedily clutching any faults to myself.

Middle Tennessee State University provided a grant to have the final manuscript edited and typed. Kathleen R. Ferris served expertly and gallantly as editor of this manuscript; Mrs. George Burns typed it at short notice, and Shirley Reed and Wilma Barrett assisted with previous drafts; Roberta Brown was an indefatigable proofreader. My colleagues in the Department of History, Middle Tennessee State University, should know how much their intellectual support has meant to me.

Some research material in this book has appeared in three articles I authored from 1975 to 1978: "Elon Galusha and the Millerite Movement," *Foundations: A Baptist Journal of History and Theology*, VIII (July–September 1975): 252–60; "Comets and Eclipses: The Millerites,

Nature, and the Apocalypse," *Adventist Heritage: A Magazine of Adventist History* III (Winter, 1976): 10–19; "A New Perspective on the Burned-over District: The Millerites in Upstate New York," *Church History* (December 1978): 408–20.

Finally, to my "nuclear" family and to the "extended" family of friends who bore me through difficult years, I pray this book will justify your encouragement and faith. As I am yours, I give it to you.

Chapter 1
PROFILE OF A PROPHET

The speaker stared at the congregation fearful of what the next hours would bring. William Miller had never lectured before, and he worried that his advanced age of nearly fifty years and short uninspiring stature might make him an ineffective orator. To be sure, he had often read prepared sermons to his home Baptist congregation in Low Hampton, New York, when the preacher was absent, but today was different. These Baptists in Dresden had called Miller from his farm to travel the sixteen miles up Lake Champlain on this August sabbath, 1831, to preach a sermon of his own composition, to explain his own views. That was the real source of anxiety—his views. This would-be preacher was about to say that in twelve years, sometime in 1843, Christ would return to earth in person, and on that awful day the "world and all the wicked will be burnt up." For all he knew, this would make him the laughing-stock of Washington County. Even more terrifying, perhaps these people would accept his notions and spend years preparing for the end of the world only to find, too late, that their "prophet" had been wrong. No wonder that he paused, hesitating to begin.[1]

The congregation too was restless. They knew Miller—he enjoyed a county-wide reputation as a leader of his community and church. A captain of artillery in the Vermont militia and the United States army during the War of 1812, he later had been elected town sheriff and was now completing a third term as Supervisor of Hampton Township. He was a member of the local Masonic lodge. An ardent Baptist, Miller had helped lead a subscription campaign to rebuild the Low Hampton church in 1828 after a fire had destroyed the old meetinghouse, and he

---

[1] Allen Corey, in his *Gazetteer of the County of Washington, N. Y.* (Schuylerville, 1850), 249, describes Dresden as so "difficult of access that it is almost impossible to get to it, except by way of the Lakes." The quote is from William Miller to his sister Emily Atwood, June 14, 1831, Miller Papers, Jenks Adventual Collection, Aurora College (since all Miller letters cited in this book come from this collection, I will hereafter dispense with reference to the Miller Papers, Second Advent Collection). Miller described his own frame of mind at the time of this meeting in his autobiography, collected and edited by Sylvester Bliss and published as *Memoirs of William Miller: Generally Known as a Lecturer on the Prophecies, and the Second Coming of Christ* (Boston, 1853), 80–84, 92–93.

had served as Sunday School teacher and as an exhorter in times of religious revival. Furthermore, Silas Guilford and his wife, Dresden Baptists
who had opened their home to host this meeting, were Miller's brother-
in-law and sister.[2]

The audience almost certainly knew already what the topic of
Miller's talk would be. If Guilford had not told them about his views
they must have heard about them from others, for although Miller had
never spoken publicly about the approaching end of the world, in the
ten years since he first came to believe it he had discussed the notion
privately with relatives and friends, warning loved-ones to get their
spiritual affairs in order. In the rural society of which Miller was such an
important member word of his ideas had spread, giving him "no little
celebrity in his denomination in all that region." Not all of the comments
about him "were flattering to his sanity"; a local doctor had loudly proclaimed the man a "monomaniac."[3] But professing Christians were used
to being called insane by the less pious public. Revivalism was sweeping
the region, and the Dresden Baptists had been undergoing a religious
refreshing for several months. In such a time of spiritual excitement the
congregation was probably already prepared to give Miller a
sympathetic hearing. Why else would they have invited him?

Unaware of any inherent support from his audience, Miller began
his talk tremulously, describing in detail the terrifying events of that
awful day so rapidly approaching. While his words are nowhere re-
corded they could not have differed greatly from warnings he wrote to
family members in 1831 and 1832. First, Christ would appear in the sky
and raise the dead saints to everlasting life. Simultaneously, "I see children of God who are alive then, will be changed and caught up to meet
the Lord in the air where they will be married to him." After this "first
resurrection" unto salvation would commence the horrible work of destruction and purification with God raining down lightning and fire on
the wicked and hurling the forces of nature against sinners. "Behold,"
went Miller's vision, "the heavens grow black with clouds; the sun has
veiled himself; the moon, pale and forsaken, hangs in middle air; the
hail descends, the seven trumpets utter loud their voices; the lightnings
send their vivid gleams of sulphurous flames abroad; and the great city
of the nation falls to rise no more forever and forever." Only after God
had cleansed the world of sin would Christ actually descend to earth to
inaugurate the Millennium, His thousand years' reign of peace and joy.
The final act would take place at the end of that blissful period when
God will raise the wicked dead, judge them, and then send their souls to

---

[2] Corey, 190–91; Bliss, 83–84.
[3] Bliss, 95–96.

everlasting punishment in the lake of fire prepared to consume them.[4]

Caught up with the "greatness of the subject," Miller lost his "diffidence and embarrassment." Having captured the Baptists' rapt attention he finished the lecture confidently with a strong firm voice. Far from jeering at him, the audience was so taken with his views that they invited him to remain for the week to give additional lectures outlining in greater detail the approach of the end of the world. Miller accepted, perhaps suspecting this was only the first of many such invitations. Indeed, during that same week a letter arrived at his farm asking Miller to lecture in Poultney, Vermont.[5] The crusade had begun.

The opening scene of the Millerite movement, like so much of Miller's life, is projected to us through an opaque lens. In the 1840s Miller dictated a memoir of his life, and a few letters to family members written before 1832 survive. But while they reveal the outline of images, features are obscure. The memoir was a religious testimonial and even promotional literature, notable as much for its omissions as for its revelations, and the letters are widely separated chronologically. Still, we learn much about the man from them.

On the one hand Miller made a most unlikely missionary. In younger years he had been an agnostic, and even after a conversion experience in 1815 he continued to require unquestionable proof of God's existence. A lengthy study of the Bible revealed sufficient evidence to satisfy him, and also produced the scriptural analysis that formed the basis of his eschatology. Even so, fearing public ridicule, he remained silent about his apocalyptic beliefs until God cunningly tricked him into undertaking a campaign to warn sinners of their peril.

On the other hand, Miller's entire religious development, heavily influenced by his family relationships, led him ineluctably to this high level of commitment. He was born at Pittsfield, Massachusetts, in 1782, the first of sixteen children, on the farm his grandfather had settled thirty-five years earlier. In 1786 his father, like so many other Yankees, entered the stream of migrants to Low Hampton where he built the farmhouse that was to be young William's home for the next eighteen years.[6] Family concern for the boy's salvation was intense. William's pious mother took personal responsibility for her son's growth in godliness, and his maternal grandfather, Elnathan Phelps, and paternal uncle, Elisha Miller, both Baptist preachers who had founded the Low Hampton Church,[7] were frequently present to exhort him. William's father, a professing but unenthusiastic Christian,

---

[4] Miller to Truman Hendryx (hereafter cited as Hendryx), March 26, 1832; Miller to Emily Atwood, June 14, 1831.

[5] Bliss, 97–98.

[6] Ibid., 2–4.

[7] *History and Biography of Washington County and the Town of Queensbury, New York* (New York, 1894), 135; Bliss, 28.

offered his home for sabbath services. The Bible was William's first primer, and a family hymnal and prayer book were in frequent use. So at an early age Miller learned the hard Calvinist lessons of religious life—the perseverence of sin, necessity for vigilance, and inevitability of the Last Judgment. This last provided particularly fertile ground for a child's imagination, and it was undoubtedly fears of damnation that moved him during a religious awakening at the age of ten to promise God he would be "a good boy." Years later, continued longing for salvation is evident in a poem he wrote:

> Come, blest religion, with thy angel's face,
> Dispel this gloom, and brighten all the place;
> Drive this destructive passion from my breast;
> Compass my sorrows, and repose my rest;
> Show me the path that Christian heroes trod,
> Wean me from earth, and raise my soul to God![8]

But, still only a child, William could not appreciate the spiritual power of religion or focus his attention for very long on glum thoughts of vigilance against sin. Besides, another ambition had captured his dreams. A thirst for knowledge struck Miller at an early age, and it grew into such a craving, he later recalled, that an education became "almost essential to existence." He attended school during winter months between fall harvest and spring planting when work on the farm was not so pressing, but the rest of the year he had to study on his own by reading borrowed books in stolen hours. Neighbors with private libraries made their books available to the aspiring young scholar. Many nights, after the family had retired, he would creep silently to the fireplace to read for hours by the light of burning pine knots. Such makeshift efforts could hardly quench his longing, however. The realization that a formal education was financially unobtainable frustrated his hopes to such an extent that his yearning "approached to agony."[9]

Miller never did receive the kind of formal education about which he dreamed, but in 1804 he found a congenial atmosphere and greater opportunities for pursuing his literary ambitions. That year he married Lucy Smith of Poultney, Vermont, and moved from his childhood home the few miles across the border to set up his own household near his in-laws. In contrast to the isolation and relative cultural deprivation of Low Hampton, this new environment provided rich nourishment for a hungry mind. Not only did Poultney have a public library, but several

---

[8] James White, *Sketches of the Christian Life and Public Labors of William Miller* (Battle Creek, 1875), 28–29. This book consists of a reediting and annotation of Bliss's *Memoirs.* Much of Bliss's work is quoted at length, but there are additional anecdotes by participants in the Millerite movement.

[9] Bliss, 14–15.

townspeople had book collections of their own which they made available to their personable new neighbor.

Among these helpful lenders was Matthew Lyon, the Revolutionary War firebrand and friend of Ethan Allen, a founder of Vermont statehood, and the district's Congressional Representative. Around Lyon circled a clique of politicians loyal to the Democratic-Republican Party of Thomas Jefferson, and it was not long before Miller became a leading personality in the group. Within five years after moving to Poultney he ran for sheriff and won, after a campaign conducted so uprightly that he earned praise from his defeated Federalist opponent as "the only honest Democrat" he knew. Popular figures socially, the Millers achieved prominence; their home became a "place of common resort" for the young, and they achieved a status as the "central unit which drew them together and kept all in motion."[10]

It would be difficult to imagine a more dramatic change from his childhood environment. Twenty-two years old when he married, Miller was independent with a farm, family, and friends of his own. Low Hampton was just a few miles to the west, but the seat of his adolescent catechisms might as well have been on the other side of the moon. Miller responded to his new-found independence the way many young people do who have just loosened tight apron strings; he rebelled against his family and their orthodox religiosity.

Poultney neighbors provided him with an intellectual whip to flail family and faith. Matthew Lyon was an infamous agnostic, as disreputable to the professing mind as Ethan Allen. He and his Jeffersonian compatriots subscribed to the Deism and skepticism that had recently made Tom Paine anathema. According to their Rationalist view of the cosmos, the Bible was a history of the ancient world, a guide to proper ethical conduct, but no revealed word of the Omnipotent First Cause. Their God was a *deus absconditus*, the Great Clockmaker who had retreated from the universe after creating its parts and setting them in motion. Among these new friends, adherents of "skeptical principles and deistical theories," Miller first came in contact with Rationalism, and, as he later stated, out of a desire to be popular with them he proclaimed himself a Deist. The Bible was not the revealed word of God, he now averred, and belief to the contrary was nothing but rank superstition.[11]

The way that Miller trumpeted his new philosophy indicates that Deism met personal as well as philosophical or social needs, for he used it as a whiplash to flail the religious teachings of his childhood and to chastise his family. Belief in a personal God was superstition, he now

---

[10] Ibid., 18–22.
[11] Ibid., 22–28. For a history of deism see Herbert Montfort Morais, *Deism in Eighteenth Century America* (New York, 1943).

said, and he derided the Millers' faith in the divine revelation of the
Bible. He singled out his preacher grandfather and uncle for special
abuse. In their presence Miller mocked them by mimicking their pulpit
styles, caricaturing their "words, tones of voice, gestures, fervency" with
the "most ludicrous gravity." Such antics hurt his family terribly, especially his mother, who felt William's behavior "as the bitterness of
death."[12]

More than simple rebellion, Miller embraced Deism out of deep-
seated cynicism that caused him not only to reject religion but to conclude gloomily from his study of history that mankind was totally
depraved. (Ironically, the Calvinism he now rejected would have
agreed!) "The more I read," he wrote in his memoirs, "the more dread-
fully corrupt did the character of man appear. I could discern no bright
spot in the history of the past. Those conquerors of the world, and heroes
of history, were apparently but demons in human form. All the sorrow,
suffering, and misery in the world seemed to be increased in proportion
to the power they obtained over their fellows. I began to feel very dis-
trustful of all men." In 1814, in a letter to his wife and children, Miller
advised them not to place "too much dependence on human favor, for
there are but few who walk the narrow path." He added bitterly,
"Remember my children, that your father has vainly sought the friendship of men, and never could he discover any friendship only where
there was a dependence."[13] This from one of the most popular men in
Poultney!

So in spite of his stunning conquest of Poultney society he was
"morose and ill natured," a contradiction that is difficult to understand.
What seemed to be developing here, as later events would verify, was an
external projection of an inner tension between the two incongruous
parts of his life—his strict religious family and upbringing in Low
Hampton on the one hand, and on the other his flamboyant social life,
relationships, and philosophy in Poultney. Miller paid for his rebellion
against his family with a severely guilty conscience that eventually
forced him to resolve his dilemma. According to his own testimony, this
sense of guilt would be the catalyst that would transform him from a
protestor into a prophet and undoubtedly made him a receptive vessel
for apocalypticism.

Fear of death gradually wrought this transformation. From 1812 to
1815 death surrounded him. First, his father died in 1812.[14] Then, when

[12] White, 32.

[13] Bliss, 23; Miller to Lucy Miller, November 11, 1814.

[14] There is some confusion about the circumstances of the elder Miller's death. It is not
clear whether he joined the militia in 1812 and died during the cholera epidemic at
Burlington where the militia was bivouaced or whether he died in his home before the
war broke out.

the United States declared war with England that year, Miller volunteered for service in the Vermont militia and soon received a commission as a captain in the regular American army. The principal enemy was not immediately the British but spotted fever that swept the Green Mountains in 1813, carrying off an estimated 6,000 persons. The disease struck at Burlington where Miller and hundreds of other militiamen were encamped, and he was among those stricken. His wife Lucy and grandfather Phelps showed up in camp to nurse him. Although William recovered, Phelps caught the fever and died. Somewhat later Miller fell from the back of a wagon, hit his head, and was unconscious so long that his companions thought him dead. In September of 1814, he saw armed conflict at the Battle of Plattsburgh. With so much death around him, he felt, how could he escape it? In November, he wrote a long doleful letter to his wife and children. Lucy had not written as often as she had promised, and he chastised her with a sarcasm that became a hallmark of his letters. Lucy must have died, he wrote, so he addressed to his children a long testament on life because he did not expect to live much longer himself. "Dear Children," he wrote, "You have lost your Mother, but a little while and your father must follow, perhaps before you receive this he will be no more. . . . Remember the lives of your parents were short, and you know not the hour you will be called for."[15]

Miller was feeling sorry for himself, but he was also deeply concerned about the question of death and immortality. His loudly proclaimed Deism, he now felt, tended to "the denial of a future existence." With death all around him lately, such a cold doctrine offered no solace. Discussing the death of a comrade from wounds received at the Battle of Plattsburgh, Miller wrote, "What a short time and, like Spencer, I shall be no more. It is a solemn thought. Yet, could I be sure of one other life, there would be nothing terrific; but to go out like an extinguished taper, is unsupportable—the thought is doleful. No! rather let me cling to that hope which warrants a never ending existence; a future spring where troubles shall cease, and tears find no conveyance; where never ending spring shall flourish, and love, pure as the driven snow, rests in every breast."[16]

One wartime episode reveals in Miller a budding religious renewal. Learning that a sergeant had been up all night praying with his men, Miller, as a practical joke, accused him of spending the night gambling. The sergeant was embarrassed to say what he had really been doing, but the captain's jibes forced the admission from him. Rather than feeling amused, however, Miller was ashamed of the shabby way he had treated the sergeant's piety.[17]

[15] Bliss, 31–52; Miller to Lucy Miller, November 11, 1814.
[16] Miller to Lucy Miller, October 28, 1814.
[17] Bliss, 57.

The key to understanding both Miller's deep depression and his increasingly renewed religiosity was the death of his father in 1812. The extent to which this event had affected him became apparent only in 1815 when he wrote to his mother for the first time after leaving for the war. He could not write to her earlier, he said, "because this subject would intrude." He wrote sadly, "Alas, I never can think of my mother but the image of my father presents itself to my view. The death of him whom I ardently loved, can never be forgotten. It has ever seemed since to me like a dream. I think the peculiar state I was in at that time, has ever rendered my feelings more poignant, and was to me more distressing. Often, yes, often have I almost taken my pen in hand to write my father, before I could reflect that my father was no more. How has he visited me in my nightly dreams, how often in my imaginations have I seen him . . . it is more cutting now than the first moment I experienced the loss."[18]

Miller and his father seem to have had a warm relationship, but in his memoirs Miller devoted considerable space to a disagreement between them. The elder Miller did not appreciate his son's yearnings for an education, and he disliked William's nocturnal studies because they might make him unfit for work. He laid down the law finally—William was to go to bed when the rest of the family retired—but William continued to sneak as many late night hours by the fire "as he dared to." The father's attitudes may have mellowed over the years, for when he built a new frame house, William received a room of his own where he could read in peace. Later, though, without his father's knowledge or permission, the boy wrote to a local doctor to ask for a loan so he could attend a formal school. Before he could send the letter, his father found it and read it. His first reaction must have been one of anger—Miller later remembered his father became "somewhat disturbed for a moment"—but after thinking the matter over he began to appreciate the depth of the boy's longings, and he felt ashamed and sad that he could not afford to satisfy them. Happily, the incident produced a change in his father's attitude so that afterward, although formal education remained financially impossible, he "rather encouraged than hindered" William's studies.[19]

In view of Miller's craving for an education, the obstacle his father placed in his path may have caused considerable resentment, conceivably inspiring the youth's later rebellion against his family after he left Low Hampton for the literary circles of Poultney. Certainly available information does not warrant a psychohistorical interpretation of the development of Miller's adventism. What is clear is that by 1815 Miller

[18] Miller to Paulina Phelps Miller, May 21, 1815.
[19] Bliss, 18–25.

was anxious to assuage his nagging conscience by reconciling himself with his family. The first step was to apotheosize his father, who now became a role model for William both as a man and a father. "I am led to believe," he said, "that my conduct, through the world, where there is so much example for vice, would have been more reprehensible had I not the spirit of my father, and his example continually before me, to lead me in the path of rectitude. Oh! that I could teach my children to love and revere me, as I did my Parrent who is gone forever."[20] The next step was to leave Poultney and return to Low Hampton to be near his mother. His rebellion, he felt, had made him and Lucy unfit to be parents. He could no longer trust the rearing of his children to "the blind partiality of their Parrents and Grand Parrents [the Smiths]" because that would "prove to be productive of the greatest evil. [Their] young and tender minds would imbibe feelings that when they come into the world they would, on the first rub in life, loose their spirits, and would thereafter be unfit for society." They must see "enough of the world, to be aware of the intrigues, and deceptions, made use of to decoy the artless lad unsuspecting into the snares of vice." He and the family would move back to Low Hampton so that his mother could "by example and good advice work much good in the first place. . . . I flatter myself that your experience in life, will cause you to give Lucy and myself such advice as will be for the happiness of both."[21] So later that year he turned his back on Poultney and bought a farm close to his childhood home, where his mother and brother Solomon still lived.

Having reconciled himself to home and hearth, Miller also took tentative steps toward submitting himself once again to God and the Baptist Church. At first he tried to compromise revealed religion and Deism by loudly proclaiming the latter but attending church and allowing his farm to become the "headquarters of the denomination in Low Hampton," a position remarkably similar to his father's. Such an uneasy alliance between skepticism and grudging acceptance of the forms of religion could not endure for long. The rather off-handed way he obtained an important church role illustrates its gradual disintegration. In the absence of the preacher, it was customary for the deacon to read a sermon from one of the many homilies then in circulation. On such occasions Miller absented himself because, he said, he did not like the deacon's reading style. To assure his continued interest, the Baptists voted to allow Miller to read sermons himself, even though he was not a deacon, an invitation that his loudly trumpeted Deism did not prevent him from accepting.[22]

[20] Miller to Paulina Phelps Miller, May 21, 1815.
[21] Ibid.
[22] Bliss, 65.

With revivalism flaring in the region once again after the War of 1812, and with his mother, brothers, and sisters all encouraging Miller openly to renew his faith in Christ, a crisis was sure to develop. One day he took the name of the Lord in vain and felt a wave of deep shame engulf him. Contemplations of death continued to plague him, doubts and fears leaving him exhausted and depressed. "The heavens were as brass over my head," he recalled, "and the earth as iron under my feet. *Eternity!—what is it? And death—why was it?*" In this state of mind he attended a special church service commemorating the anniversary of the Battle of Plattsburgh. Although he went admittedly "more from curiosity than from any other actuating cause," the sermon troubled him deeply, recalling memories of the scene of battle and of his depression at that time. Despondent and uncommunicative, Miller would not attend the ball planned for the evening. His personal gloom seeped through the town producing a "time of searching," and prayer meetings "took the place of mirth and the dance."[23]

His emotional crisis reached a climax soon afterwards when the congregation called upon him to read a sermon on "the importance of Parental Duties." Suddenly Miller found his "deistical principles" to be an "almost insurmountable difficulty" and the nature of the topic focused directly on his personal guilt. Faith could no longer coexist with skepticism. In a state of intense anxiety, he could not finish the presentation. Then a conversion experience shattered his gloom and lifted the penitent above the tension that had troubled him so long. "The character of a Saviour was vividly impressed upon my mind," he remembered. "It seemed that there might be a Being so good and compassionate as to himself atone for our transgressions, and thereby save me from suffering the penalty of sin. I immediately felt how lovely such a Being must be." Comforted by faith, released from tormenting contradictions, Miller quickly became the "ornament and pillar in the church" less than a year after returning to Low Hampton.[24] Reconciled first with his family, he was now reconciled with his God.

Now that he was a professing Christian, Miller argued with his Deist friends in favor of revealed religion. The problem was that he was still enough of a Rationalist to feel that "to believe in [the] Saviour without evidence would be visionary in the extreme." Now he searched for an empirical verification for faith, and he found it through hermeneutics. Like his contemporary Alexander Campbell, founder of the Disciples of Christ, Miller decided that the scriptures themselves held the key to their validity and that by studying the Bible in a scientific way, he could provide evidence of its divine origin. By the end of 1816 he had devised his

[23] Ibid., 66.
[24] Ibid., 65–67.

method. If he could reconcile all the apparent contradictions in the scriptures, he would show the Bible to be consistent, and as a consistent document, he reasoned, it must have had only one author—God. God alone could have revealed so much information consistently.

The greatest challenge this method posed was to "distinguish between the Bible and all the peculiar and partisan interpretations of it." The common assumption of the day was that the prophets' words have both a figurative and a literal meaning, and exegetes (Bible interpreters) interpreted these figures differently. To illustrate the Bible's consistency, Miller decided to "lay aside all commentaries" and find a natural way of determining the true message the Lord wished to impart by referring solely to the Bible. Here Miller's principal question inadvertently became an assumption underlying the procedure he developed. Because the scriptures *were* consistent any word used figuratively in one verse would symbolize the same idea or object throughout the Bible. He could define and interpret these figures by isolating a particular word, finding the same word in other verses with the help of a concordance, interpreting it in the light of these other passages, and then applying the definition to the word in the original phrase. For instance, he chanced upon a passage in which the word "beast" *seemed* to symbolize something other than an animal. He searched for the word throughout the scriptures until he came upon Daniel 7:17, "These great beasts, which are four, are four kings, which shall arise out of the earth." So the word "beasts" when used figuratively in the Bible meant kings or kingdoms. Beginning with the book of Genesis, Miller followed this arduous exegesis for two years until by 1818 he had decoded the entire Bible. He concluded gleefully that "the Bible is a system of revealed truths, so clearly and simply given that the 'way-faring man, though a fool, need not err therein!'"[25]

Unexpectedly these labors produced some startling revelations. Translations of the prophecies in Isaiah, Joel, Daniel, Matthew, and Revelation relating to the end of the world seemed to present a coherent chronology of events leading inexorably to the Apocalypse. There, translated from symbolic language, were the rise and fall of empires and the tribulations of the Saints. By comparing these predictions with actual history, he discovered that most of the predictions had already been fulfilled. Three of Daniel's four kingdoms—Babylon, Persia, and Greece—were gone. Only the fourth, Rome and the Roman Catholic Church, remained to taste the vengeance of the Lord of Hosts! There, too, was revealed the order of events on the Last Day: Christ's appearance in person, the resurrection of the righteous and transfiguration of the living saints, the purification of the world by fire and destruction of the old earth, the creation of a New Heaven and New Earth, the establishment of the

[25] Ibid., 71–74.

Millennium, and the resurrection and damnation of sinners.

Finally, by applying the day-year formula, the idea that the prophetic "day" was a year of actual time, Miller computed when all these events were to take place. The prophet Daniel had written that 2,300 "days" would elapse between the fall of the Persian Empire and the fall of the fourth "beast" and that the fourth empire would reign for 1,260 "days." By consulting historical chronologies, Miller found that most exegetes and historians agreed the persian Empire fell in 457 B.C. and the Roman Catholic Church (the fourth beast) began its reign in A.D. 583. Subtracting 457 from 2,300, Miller found the year when the fourth beast would fall. And adding 1,260 and 583 he computed the year when the Catholic Church's reign would end. Both calculations pointed to the same year—1843. Sometime that year, he concluded, God would destroy the fourth beast by shattering the Catholic Church in the long-awaited cosmic event that would complete prophetic history.[26]

This exegesis was probably Miller's own, but other interpreters undoubtedly influenced it. Throughout the centuries since Christ's death and resurrection, hundreds of scholars had searched the prohecies for hidden information about the Apocalypse, the Second Coming of Christ (or Parousia), and the beginning of the Millennium.[27] Most likely Miller was familiar with this literature. The fact that he decided to "lay aside all commentaries" meant he must have read some of them, and he knew that the day-year formula accorded "with the opinions of all the standard commentators."[28] Certainly, none of his principal points—that Christ would return to earth personally, that the Millennium would soon begin, and that the world was coming to an end—was new. All were long-lived Christian traditions. Even his prediction that all would come to pass in 1843 would not have been shocking to anyone steeped in formal apocalyptic. One compilation of prophetic timetables lists nineteen British and American exegetes from 1768 to 1831 who published predictions that 1843 would be a critical year (though they did not agree on *what* would happen).[29] In view of Miller's love of reading, it is possible he had encountered at least one of these published theories. If so, we can still treat his theory as his own. He never cited any other work to support his chronology, as he might reasonably have done, and he took sole responsibility for predicting the year, though in self-defense he could have pointed to other interpreters who had also focused on 1843. And clearly Miller was intelligent enough to have calculated the year quite on his own.

[26] Ibid.

[27] A fuller discussion of formal apocalyptic and Millerism's relationship to it appears in chapter 4.

[28] Bliss, 68; White, 56.

[29] Leroy Edwin Froom, *The Prophetic Faith of Our Fathers* (Washington, 1946–1954), III, 404–5.

Miller's contribution to formal apocalyptic was to delineate in a new way the relationship among the principal events of the Last Day. Historians of prophetic interpretation traditionally distinguish two types of theories about Last Things.[30] One is postmillennialism, the belief that Christ will return to judge the world and create the New Heaven and New Earth at the *end* of the Millennium. That thousand-year period of peace and happiness will be a time of spiritual renewal when the Bible will guide human affairs. Humanity is responsible for creating the Millennium (through the grace of God) by evangelizing the Christian message around the world. The second type, premillenialism, emphasizes God's central role in creating the Millenium. Only Christ has sufficient power to purify the world of sin and thus create the Millennium, so millenarians preach that He must return *before* the Millennium begins. Even they, though, generally believe that the end of the world and Final Judgment would occur at the end of the Millennium, even though the Parousia precedes it.[31] Miller was related intellectually to this millenarian tradition, but he added a new dimension to apocalyptic. He preached that all the events of the Last Days would occur simultaneously. In 1843 Christ would return, separate the wicked from the just, destroy the Earth, create the New Heavens and New Earth, and introduce the Millennium. The only event left to occur at the end of the Millennium would be the actual damnation of the wicked dead, which would destroy all sin and inaugurate eternal righteousness.

In attempting to reconcile faith and Rationalism Miller had revealed to himself meanings of passages and books of scripture that had previously been shrouded in mystery. Now the Bible was a new book. "It was indeed a feast of reason. All that was dark, mystical or obscure, to me, in its teachings, had been dissipated from my mind before the clear light that now dawned from its sacred pages." The fact that his hermeneutic pointed to the imminent destruction of the world did not frighten him, for he anticipated the "delightful prospect" of the "joys of the redeemed" in the rapidly approaching Millennium.[32] If reason pointed to the terrors of the approaching Apocalypse, faith pointed to the bright hope of the New Jerusalem.

Now Miller faced a dilemma. He knew that if "the end was so near, it was important the world should know about it" and that if he did not

---

[30] I briefly discuss this traditional morphology of millennialism, founded on a consideration of its intellectual structure, at this point simply to introduce the terms *postmillennial* and *premillennial*, terms that Miller and his contemporaries knew and used. In a later chapter I will suggest limitations of this approach.

[31] The distinction between pre- and postmillennialism is so common that one can find it in any of the works discussed in the section of the bibliographical essay labeled "Millennialism."

[32] Bliss, 76.

awaken sinners to their peril "their blood might be required at my hand."[33] But he did nothing. In the first place, he was shy. Once, when the people of Poultney planned a Fourth of July celebration, in honor of the occasion Miller composed lyrics that the celebrants could sing to an old melody. But he was too shy to volunteer his work openly. So he went to the home of the master of ceremonies, reached through an open window, and left his poem on a table. When the celebrants gathered, they all received copies of the anonymous anthem, wondering who had written it. Unfortunately for Miller, his visible embarrassment when receiving his copy answered the riddle of its authorship, and the abashed poetaster had to accept blushingly his neighbors' plaudits.[34]

He was cautious, too. Miller wanted to be certain that his views were correct before broadcasting them over the countryside. So for five years, from 1818 to 1823, he weighed "the various objections which were being presented to my mind" against their reasonableness. Perhaps this insecurity was why he mentioned only briefly his startling apocalyptic beliefs in the "statement of Faith" he wrote in 1822. In most particulars it resembled any other private covenant, confession, or religious testimony common in that day. Only in article fifteen did he attest, "I believe that the second coming of Jesus Christ is near, even at the door, even within twenty-one years—on or before 1843." But Miller himself later confessed that all this circumspection was little more than procrastination—he had "managed to evade" his felt duty so long as he "could find the shadow of an objection remaining against its truth."[35]

The real reason he would not preach his ideas was his fear of public ridicule. When that nagging voice demanded commitment Miller would argue that he was "very diffident, and feared to go before the world," that no one would "believe me or hearken to my voice." After all, those to whom he had "thrown out occasional hints" about his apocalyptic beliefs had treated them "as an idle tale." If even among his family and friends there were "very few who listened with any interest," would strangers pay him heed?[36]

Gradually, though, courage conquered caution. In 1826, he later claimed, he had a dream that convinced him God would bless and support a crusade to warn the world. In this dream Miller wandered lost in a barren land. Guides gave him directions out of the desert, but they led him onto crooked paths and into danger. (Later he would identify these guides as false prophets and sectarians.) Then he chanced upon a crossroads where a broad highway filled with wayfarers converged with a

[33] White, 70.
[34] Ibid., 20.
[35] Manuscript Sheriff's Book, September 5, 1822, Jenks Adventual Collection.
[36] Bliss, 92.

narrow, almost untraveled path. A mysterious voice told him to take the latter, and he was led to several mystical tableaux, allegories of the Christian life. Once blood dropped on him like rain. This was the blood of Christ, Miller reasoned, a sign of God's grace. "My mind, which all along had been more or less troubled, by fears and doubts, now became calm." Finally the wanderer climbed a stairway to a huge, light-filled, upper room[37] where he found a multitude singing joyfully. Here were "persons of all denominations of Christians, yet all distinctions were taken away." In this upper chamber universal love was the rule, and Miller felt elevated, released from worldly troubles. "I felt myself free from every clog, and all my soul was swallowed up in the celestial throng. I then thought it was a dream—a slight and disagreeable feeling passed over my mind, to think I must return and experience again the woes of life."[38] So, reluctantly, he awoke.

Miller described this dream only in his memoirs, twenty-two years after it happened. Probably it was less a prognostication of things to come than an allegorical memoir of things that had happened to him during the Millerite movement. But, like Jacob, he likely did have a dream—not his last—that convinced him he had a special relationship with God. Belief in the prophetic nature of dreams was common, and by including this story in his memoirs, Miller was at least offering justification for later actions in a form people would understand and appreciate.

The dream was still not enough to force him into preaching. About that time, however, he "began to speak more clearly my opinions to my neighbors, to ministers, and others," and religious revival in the area made people listen more attentively. During a sabbath meeting in 1828, many Low Hampton Baptists found themselves "in tears or labouring under solemn convictions for sin." Miller said of this refreshing, "I never lived in a refformation so general, so solemn, and so little noise." Again in 1831 the Baptists gave vent to "a great deal of sobing and crying," producing "an union of prayer" in which conviction and conversion were common. The religious exercises accompanying revivals frequently convinced enthusiastic converts that God was pouring grace on the world to prepare it to receive the Millennium, and the Low Hampton refreshing reinforced Miller's conviction: "These are the last times truly."[39] Since he was an exhorter at these revivals, he possibly encouraged the notion. Whatever the reason, others felt the same way, for it was in the midst of this excitement that the Dresden Baptists invited Miller to speak to them.

---

[37] Miller was a Mason, and since Masons met in an upstairs chamber this may account for this interesting symbolism.
[38] Bliss, 89–90.
[39] Miller to unidentified, March 12, 1828.

The request took him completely unawares, but in spite of his long-felt reluctance to preach, he was no longer in a position to demur. Just an hour before the invitation arrived an unusually powerful impression to "go and tell it to the world" had suddenly seized his mind. Not doubting this was a direct command from God, he had slyly promised to do so if God would provide the opportunity, a safe bargain, he thought, since no one had ever yet called on him to preach his views. Within the hour his nephew arrived with the Dresden invitation. Stunned that the Lord had called his bet so soon, the frightened man ran to a nearby grove and pleaded with his creditor to release him—but to no avail. "I finally submitted, and promised the Lord that, if he would sustain me, I would go, trusting in him to give me grace and ability to perform all he should require of me."[40] There would be no turning back.

Because we must rely almost exclusively upon Miller's own recollection of these events, we will never know how accurate they are. The fact that he delivered his first apocalyptic lectures in the home of his sister and brother-in-law suggests that Miller played a more direct hand in arranging it than he would have us believe. But later events would show Miller to be truly as careful and even as reluctant as his memoirs portray him. At any rate, the encouragement he received from the Dresden Baptists steeled him for what became a fourteen-year crusade of preaching and writing about the end of the world. Miller did not become a new man, however. His message would remain a mixture of orthodox evangelical theology and empirical methodology. Doubts about his capacity to raise his own children to righteousness were multiplied into almost constant insecurity about his role as a spiritual father to thousands. For long unwilling to disseminate his views, he would remain a most reluctant prophet. But if Miller and God together had partnered the movement that would bear Miller's name, there was also a third party to the arrangement. As much as anything else, the congregation in Dresden called the Millerite movement into existence, and throughout the Northeast thousands of worried Christians would sustain it and propel Miller and his message into a public role that he could not have imagined possible in 1831. Together, the prophet and the congregation would go and tell it to the world.

[40] White, 80.

Chapter 2
REAPING THE HARVEST

Miller's crusade to warn the world seems to have received an enthusiastic initiation in Dresden in 1831. After finishing a series of lectures there, he spoke on the end of the world in Poultney and Pawlet, Vermont. But the following year his momentum slowed. Self-doubts and fears once again assailed him. He was "too old, too wicked, too proud" to carry on an adventist crusade. The pastor of the Low Hampton Baptist Church had left, and there was no one to preach to the congregation but Miller, "the *old man* with the Concordance," as he described himself. "And he is so shunned, with his cold, dull, lifeless performance, that I have strong doubts whether he will attempt it again." Discouraging, too, was the disappearance of the religious enthusiasm of 1831. Whereas "one short year ago and Zion was rejoicing with her multiplied converts," now she was "down by the cold waters of Babylon."[1]

Even his leadership of the Low Hampton Baptists was in jeopardy. The congregation was seeking a new preacher, and Miller disagreed with many of his brethren about what kind of preacher to hire. A new breed of revivalist was appearing in the evangelical denominations in the early 1830s, New School preachers who emulated the enthusiastic methods of Charles Grandison Finney. Finney, the founder of modern revivalism, had sparked a wave of revivals in 1826 that swept across New York and the Northeast producing thousands of converts to Christ and members for the evangelical churches—the Methodists, Baptists, Presbyterians, Congregationalists, and Christians. The key to the New School's success was a series of spectacular "new measures"—hell-fire-and-brimstone preaching, wailing benches where individual exhorters could work on penitent sinners, home visitations, women praying in public with men.[2] More conservative Old School Calvinists found these new measures embarrassing. They charged that the new revivalists were mere technocrats, men who knew how to rant but who cared little for the quality of the sinner's conversion. Miller, a loudly outspoken and old-fashioned

---

[1] Miller to Hendryx, February 8, April 10, and March 1833.

[2] A variety of books discusses the Second Great Awakening, and many are listed in the bibliographical essay. A good work to begin studying this awakening is William G. McGloughlin, *Modern Revivalism* (New York, 1959).

Calvinist, had alienated many in the Low Hampton congregation with his theological conservatism and his "old schoolman's" suspicions of New School revivalism. His disagreement with others in the congregation focused on the selection of the new preacher. Some of the brethren wanted "a quick gab," wrote Miller, but he wanted a man with " a quick understanding," who was well versed in the scriptures and could preach good Calvinist doctrine.[3]

Masonry split the church even more seriously. A Canandaigua Mason named William Morgan had threatened to publish a book revealing the secrets of the Masonic rites. Before he could do so, a Batavia sheriff arrested him on debt charges and threw him into jail. One night men invaded the jail, kidnapped Morgan, and rode off with him in a carriage. No one ever saw Morgan again. His disappearance and probable murder provoked popular resentment against the Masons, a secret society that many believed had perpetrated the deed. When investigations of the kidnapping failed to produce arrests or convictions, resentment turned into suspicion that highly placed Masons in the courts and government had subverted justice to protect their organization. The hostility these events ignited across New York and New England from 1826 to 1834 forced the revocation of lodge charters in hundreds of communities, and it often split congregations into pro-Masonic and anti-Masonic factions. The dispute raged so fiercely in Miller's own Washington Baptist Association that it split into a weak pro-Masonic Washington Association and a strong Bottskill Anti-Masonic Association. The movement must have been strong in the Low Hampton church, for three Anti-Masonic Baptists obtained letters of dismission with no difficulty even though, according to Miller, "these brethren said at the same time they could not and would not walk with the Ch[urch]." Miller was a Mason, and his membership in the local lodge could not have escaped notice. It was probably attacks against his affiliation with the lodge that evoked his strong defense, "I never said—nor practiced, anything knowingly to injure my country, the Ch. of Christ—or my fellow creatures. Therefore, if I sinned it was against God, and to him I am accountable and to him I am bound to co;,fess."[4]

Furthermore, Miller's apocalyptic views had begun to attract the kind of criticism he had always feared. People "who ought to have taught the same things," in other words preachers, were giving him "much opposition." Isaac Sawyer, a local Baptist preacher who had adopted many of Miller's ideas, jokingly revealed the nature of these criticisms in a letter to Miller intended to caricature the adventist's detractors. He "chastised" the aging man for his "wretched and *strange perversion* of the right 'laws of

---

[3] Miller to Hendryx, November 17, 1832.
[4] Ibid., April 10, 1833.

Biblical exegesis,' your 'bigotry' and 'overweening dogmatism' which are discoverable in your labor'd commentary."[5] Sawyer's use of single quotes may indicate that a review of Miller's spoken lectures had actually appeared in print.

Miller's discouragement was understandable. Once again he reverted to warning people privately that "the wrath of God is to be poured on our world." One day a young preacher (Truman Hendryx) arrived at the Miller farm to "save Brother Miller if possible from going down to the grave" with erroneous views weighing down his soul. But Miller defended adventism so well that the visitor asked to "let him come and board with me two or three months to study Bible."[6] He also tried to cajole local preachers into spreading the warning so that he would not have to, but his success was disappointing. Hendryx showed much interest in the Second Coming of Christ but seemed little inclined to preach it, so Miller chided him irritably, "Have you been ridiculed out of your belief or not?" Isaac Sawyer was going in the right direction, Miller thought, but he had "some fetters on" and had not "improved [as] much in Bible knowledge as he might, if he were not afraid of being a 'Millerite.'" Isaac Fuller, former Baptist pastor of Poultney, openly advocated the Second Coming and was preaching it through his new home in Chautauqua County, but Anti-Masonic disputes there divided the churches and prevented significant success in propagating the message.[7]

Miller did take one important step in 1832 when he published a series of eight lectures on the Second Coming of Christ in a Baptist newspaper in Brandon, Vermont, called the *Vermont Telegraph*. Hardly a bold move, this allowed Miller to spread the doctrine without appearing in public. Even so he requested that the articles appear anonymously, but when the editor refused, Miller reluctantly agreed to have them appear with his initials at the bottom.[8] If his plan was to fulfill his responsibility with as little publicity as possible the plan backfired, for the articles gave him wider, more immediate renown than preaching alone could have accomplished. Soon afterwards, the Dresden and Poultney Baptists asked him to repeat his course of lectures, and new invitations to preach arrived from Putnam and Wrentham, Vermont. The public responded so enthusiastically to the articles that in 1833 the *Telegraph* printed them in pamphlet form.[9]

[5] Ibid., March 26, May 20, 1832; Isaac Sawyer to Miller, May 10, 1833.
[6] Miller to Hendryx, March 26, 1832.
[7] Ibid., January 25, 1832; April 10, 1833.
[8] Bliss, 99–100.
[9] William Miller, *Evidence From Scripture and History of the Second Coming of Christ, About the Year 1843* (Brandon, VT, 1833). A copy of this pamphlet, the first of several editions of Miller's lectures, is available in the Second Advent Collection at Aurora College.

Almost immediately the pamphlet caught the eye of Henry Jones, an itinerant reformer who journeyed around New England and New York selling subscriptions to various reform journals. In December of 1832, he was in Vermont working in behalf of temperance when he found the *Telegraph* articles, and they so impressed him, he wrote to Miller, that they inspired him to "read over and over the whole book of 'Rev.'" At first he was skeptical. Other interpreters had thought the idea of a literal personal Second Coming of Christ was "too vain, childish or idle, to call for any notice by way of refutation." Particularly difficult to accept was Miller's claim that the Apocalypse would occur in 1843. To be sure, Jones wrote, he had wondered so much about the *"nature* of the [Millenium]" that there had been "little or no opportunity to examine for the *time* when it may *commence.*" The notion surely would cause people to think Miller fanatical, wrote Jones, and as far as he could tell "you are truly so, and running wild." For self-protection Jones prayed the Lord to prevent him "from imbibing dangerous, or delusive notions." Nevertheless, his mind was "in a state of suspense, open to conviction of truth." Jones never did accept Miller's predicted date, but he was sufficiently impressed with the rest of his eschatology that he began to speak about the Second Coming of Christ on his own. In September of 1833, he wrote to Miller that he had been lecturing on that theme "before small and unlearned congregations," and soon afterwards he published his own pamphlet defending Miller's views.[10] He thus became the first principal convert to take up the burden and help disseminate adventism quite independently of Miller.

In 1833, too, the brethren in Miller's church decided to give him a license to preach, a formality that simply would recognize Miller's ability as a speaker but without necessarily endorsing his views. Licensing and formal ordination were the two methods of appointing Baptist preachers, and the former worked particularly well since that church traditionally emphasized a lay, uneducated clergy. Strangely enough the congregation approved the license in February but did not deliver it until September. Continued Anti-Masonic friction in the congregation may explain the delay, but also Miller hesitated to accept the license. He confessed his typical diffidence in a letter to Truman Hendryx. "I wish I had the tongue of an Apollos," he wrote, "the powers of mind of a Paul; what a field might I not explore, and what powerful arguments might not be brought to prove the authenticity of the Scriptures, but I want one thing more than either, the Spirit of Christ and of God."[11] In spite of his doubts, he eventually did accept the license.

By the end of 1833, through private conversation, correspondence,

[10] Henry Jones to Miller, December 27, 1832, and September 1, 1833.
[11] Miller to Hendryx, February 8, 1833.

publishing, and lecturing Miller had acquired the services of five men—to one extent or another—and had taken hesitant action to complete his bargain with the Lord. It seemed that in return the Lord provided a spectacular exhibition of what the end of the world would be like, for on the night of November 13, 1833, the skies erupted in a dazzling display of meteors. Falling at a rate of one or two every minute, they seemed to one observer to be a "constant succession of fire balls," a sight so spectacular, declared another, that "those who saw it must have lost their taste for earthly fireworks." This Shower of Stars seemed to many a dire prediction, filling their imaginations with "an apprehension that the stars of heaven were falling to leave the firmament desolate." Many turned to the prophecies of Revelation for an explanation and found there God's promise that in the latter days the stars of heaven would fall to earth "even as a fig tree casteth her untimely figs, when she is shaken of a mighty wind." The meteor storm thus became a portent of the "wreck of matter and the crush of worlds." Said one newspaper editor, "Even the bold bosom might be excused should an involuntary tremor disturb its equanimity." The editor of the *Old Countryman* declared the "raining fire" to be "a sure *forerunner*—a merciful sign of that great and dreadful Day which the inhabitants of earth will witness when the SIXTH SEAL SHALL BE OPENED." It was a vivid fulfillment of the Revelation image of "*a fig tree casting its leaves when blown by a mighty wind.*" Skeptics may call this idea "enthusiastic" and consider him "fanatic and *Mad*," nevertheless the earnest editor warned everyone "to turn to the LORD, while YET he is near."[12]

There is no clear connection between the Shower of Stars and increased interest in adventism, but the tempo of the movement did accelerate in 1834. In March Isaac Sawyer, a Baptist preacher in Stillwater, New York, told Miller that there was "a wide field to occupy and almost destitute of reapers" and urged him to conduct a lecture tour of the Champlain Valley. That spring Miller visited towns along the west shore of the lake—Jay, Keene, Mooer's Forks, Keeseville, and Peru. In October he retraced the route, speaking again in many of the same towns, and then crossed the lake to preach throughout western Vermont. By February of 1835, he had received invitations to lecture in Schroon, Ticonderoga, Moriah, Essex, Chazy, Champlain, Plattsburgh, Peru, Moorstown, Canton, Potsdam, Hopkinton, Stockholm, Parishville, and other towns in New York's northern neck.[13] His fame was increasing, as

[12] *Plattsburgh Republican*, November 30, 1833; *Oswego Palladium*, November 15, 1833; *Albany Argus*, November 15, 1833; the *Old Countryman* commentary was reprinted in the *Plattsburgh Republican* on November 20, 1833; the Bible text is Revelation 6:13.
[13] Isaac Sawyer to Miller, March 5, 1834. Miller kept a record of his itinerary and the biblical texts he used in lectures in his "text books" consisting of two manuscript volumes,

were the sales of his pamphlet. Hendryx had sold many copies, and a
Robert Brisbin, whom Miller had met at a Baptist associational meeting
in 1834, reported to Miller that during a recent tour of western New
York he had been "instrumental in exciting some interest in the subject
of your pamphlets" and had sold several copies in Sherburne, Chenango
County. Miller was justified in declaring to Hendryx in 1835 that his
views were "making no small stir in these regions." In March of that year
forty-three Baptist ministers from towns where Miller had lectured
signed an affidavit attesting that they had heard Miller's views and that
they were "worthy to be read and known of all men."[14]

The following year, 1836, a whole new field of labor opened for
Miller in the Hudson and Mohawk valleys. Emerson Andrews, a New
Measure revivalist in Lansingburgh (today a part of Troy), invited him
to preach to his congregation. Here Miller realized his most significant
success to date, when in June he and Andrews preached together at a
camp meeting in "Bog Meadow." Miller's lectures on the Second Coming
of Christ struck the community so deeply, wrote Andrews, that many
who felt "the soul reviving benefit of your lectures" had become "'zeal-
ously Engaged'" in religion. Predictably, the enthusiasts' first reaction
was one of fear, Andrews complaining that they were "more desirous of
Escape than *Preparation*." He wanted to evoke from them an active
piety, but they "*say* and do *not—confess* but *forsake* not." Andrews left
Lansingburgh for a pulpit in Rome shortly afterwards, but under the
nurture of three other ministers, Isaac Wescott from Stillwater and
Charles Cole and E. B. Crandall of Lansingburgh—all Baptists—the
revival blazed. Cole told Miller in October that his lectures had caused
"trembling in some and [in] others something of a fearful looking forward to the Judgment." The most exciting event was the dramatic conversion of a die-hard sinner who "prayed in public for the first time."
Said Cole, "The heavens appeared to open, he [seized] upon the horn of
the Altar, and the moral elements contaminated with sin, appeared to
flee—as the darkness pursued by the Light of day; terrible and awful did
it appear when the victory was gained, his enemies fleeing and he comforted by the promise of God." Religious enthusiasm burned so hotly
that even the staid Episcopal minister declared Miller's pamphlet to be
"the best work he has ever seen."[15]

---

included in the Miller papers. Volume I covers his tours up to 1840. Also, scattered
through his correspondence are dozens of invitations asking him to preach in congregations across the Northeast.

[14] Miller to Hendryx, February 8, 1833; Robert C. Brisbin to Miller, June 4, 1834; Miller
to Hendryx, March 6, 1835; Affidavit and Recommendation, 1834.

[15] Emerson Andrews to Miller, July 20, 1836; Charles Cole to Miller, October 25, 1836.
According to a letter from an unidentified person to Cornelia Brockway written in Lansingburgh on December 14, 1835, a certain "Brother C" had initiated a revival there

The revival flared sporadically throughout 1836 and 1837. The Baptist Churh claimed twenty-four new members by November of 1837, a total of one hundred thirty since Miller's lectures, and Cole said he had "never seen so powerful an effect in any place as in this upon all who heard. I am of the opinion that not less than 100 who were of Infidel sentiments are brought to believe the Bible.— *Infidelity* is dumb in this place, as if *frightened*." As late as March the fervor remained so intense that Cole could write again, "There has never been such a time in this region, as at the present." Then John G. McMurray, a prominent local philanthropist and owner of a brush factory, capped the excitement when he endorsed Miller's book. "The most violent opposers are broken down. You can imagine the present state of this community."[16]

The Lansingburgh revivals were critically important to Miller and his crusade. Two of the revivalists, Cole and Wescott, became an informal steering committee for the dissemination of Miller's ideas providing imaginative and energetic innovations that the still-reluctant Miller could not match. Wescott suggested and arranged for a second edition of his pamphlet lectures and then negotiated with a Troy printer for its publication in 1836 in an expanded form as a book. Cole and Wescott served as agents for the sale of the book, and Cole reported to Miller's son in 1836 that he had distributed "all the books your father sent me and would have sold 50 or an 100 more." It was to Cole that local preachers went to arrange for a visit by Miller and to him that one church sent a delegation to find out why Miller had failed to keep an appointment. The two preachers decided independently of Miller on a venture which, had they executed it, would have changed the course of the movement. In March of 1837, Cole recommended to Miller that they publish a newspaper "devoted to the subject and object of Christ's second coming," believing that this would be "the most effectual way to enlighten and save souls." A newspaper would take adventism to "thousands who would not otherwise have heard of the 2d coming," and they were sure that "all most any number of subscribers might be obtained." The next month Cole called for a meeting with Miller to discuss the proposal. Wescott volunteered to contribute one-tenth of the newspaper's costs and Cole promised at least to match that amount.[17] The success later of the advent journals in Boston, New York City, and elsewhere attests to the soundness of their idea, but for some reason it never reached fruition. Perhaps there was some hint this early that Wescott could not be trusted. But at least Miller had finally found preachers who

---

before Miller arrived. This must have been either Cole or Crandall. See Brockway Family Papers, Syracuse University.

[16] E. B. Crandall to Miller, November 23, 1837; Cole to William S. Miller (William Miller's son), January 7 and March 19, 1839; Cole to Miller, June 19, 1838.

[17] Cole to Miller, March 27, 1837; Cole and Wescott to Miller, April 5, 1837.

were willing to devote themselves wholeheartedly to his crusade.

The Lansingburgh revivals had the further effect of circulating Miller's reputation in the Hudson-Mohawk region so that after 1837 he received invitations to preach in Troy, West Troy, and Rome (probably to Andrews's congregation). Again his lectures produced revivals. "Of the second coming of the Lord," wrote one preacher, "much is said." A Catholic in Rome complained of Miller's harsh treatment of his church but confessed that Miller had "by the extraordinary character of your preaching, created considerable excitement among the people."[18]

These revivals of the mid-1830s illuminate the union between Millerism and revivalism in these early years of the movement—a union so close that adventism hardly had an identity of its own. Miller gained his initial reputation as much for his ability to spark revivals as for his adventist notions. The Second Great Awakening and Finney revivals of the 1820s and early 1830s had made revivalism the chief form of religious expression among evangelicals and the principal path to salvation. The New Measures personalized sin and conversion and brought penitents along a well-marked path to repentence. Preachers who used these new techniques successfully became famous and were in great demand, roaming from one camp meeting to another and from church to church. They kept careful tabulations of the number of conversions they achieved, and more often than not their reputation was made on the basis of this scorecard. Indications are that many, if not most, of the preachers who invited Miller to lecture viewed him as one of these New School revivalists, adventism as but his particular measure. The Finney revivals had otherwise died down by 1834, and Miller's successes promised a whole new wave of religious fervor. After all, awesome warnings of the coming Judgment were frequent at camp meetings. Daniel Nash, Finney's theological mentor, had formulated a theory very similar to Miller's message. Sometimes preachers were more interested in the effects of Miller's lectures than in their content. One wrote bluntly that he disagreed with Miller's views, but he believed "that more Souls [will be] converted to god in six months under the influence of your sentiments, than would be under those I embrace in six years, *even* if these were so extensively circulated as yours. My heart Rejoices to know that Souls are converted to god, I care not by what means, if true penitence, producing true piety is clearly manifested in their fruits." Emerson Andrews said, "I am not fixed so firmly on the time as on other points, but I believe it will hurt no one to be ready for Christ's Coming Today—Now! but I think it consummate folly to live in sin—and sleep without oil in their lamps."[19] Two Baptist preachers who had signed the

18 John Blakeney to Miller, undated; Emerson Andrews to Miller, March 20, 1838.
19 Unidentified to Miller, undated; Emerson Andrews to Miller, March 20, 1838.

1835 affidavit attesting that Miller's views were "worthy to be read and known of all men" were concerned that this statement was too innocuous, reflecting the caution of the majority of the signers. They added a more direct recommendation: "Having heard the above mentioned lectures, I see no way to avoid the conclusion that the Coming of Christ will be as soon as 1843."[20] Others apparently would not go so far.

The marriage between revivalism and adventism was advantageous to both. Miller kept revival fires burning, and in turn he received publicity and a platform for spreading his views. Because camp meetings were always interdenominational, he was able to reach out beyond what had previously been an almost exclusively Baptist audience.[21] But this union also confronted Miller with a dilemma. Though he seemed to be very much a part of the New School, at least identified with it in the public mind, he was in reality opposed to its principal tendencies and tenets. Accompanying and justifying the New Measures was a New School theology of which Finney was the principal formulator. The New School theology with its individualistic methodology seemed to be homocentric. A preacher could convince the sinner of his or her sinfulness, cajole the sinner to throw himself or herself on the mercy of God, and persuade the penitent to choose righteousness over sin. Because Christ's blood atoned for the sins of all people, salvation was available to anyone who accepted God and would consecrate himself or herself to the Lord. Such ideas were anathema to Old School Calvinists. Their view of conversion was theocentric—God chooses particular individuals for salvation, and it is the power of God's grace that produces the conversion experience. To them, Christ's blood atoned only for the sins of the Elect; all others were damned, and no matter how sorry they might be for their sins no one could reverse Divine judgment. The disagreement cut across denominational lines and affected all the evangelical, revivalistic churches. It forced a division of the Presbyterian Church in 1836 and an Old School secession of two Baptist associations in New York in the mid-1830s. The doctrine of the General Atonement was also the focus of Old School evangelicals' hatred and fear of Universalists who preached universal salvation. So conservatives often felt themselves besieged from without and betrayed from within evangelicalism.[22]

Miller was caught in the middle. He deplored the intradenominational wrangling, for he felt that "both parties carry their sentiments too

[20] Affidavit and Recommendation.
[21] See for instance Cole to Miller, March 27, 1837; B. Collins to Miller, April 15, 1837; Parke to Miller, March 1839.
[22] Fascinating contemporary discussions appear in Lewis Cheeseman, *Differences Between Old and New School Presbyterians* (Rochester, 1848), on the Old School side, and from the New School perspective, Calvin Colton, *History and Character of American Revivals of Religion* (London, 1832).

far." But he also deplored the liberalizing tendencies of New School theology. He once complained, "Our churches as well as ministers have all departed from the Calvinistic creed, and to mention '*Election*' would in a public congregation produce about as much effect as an electric battery with the whole congregation hold of the conductor." New Measure revivalists with their emphasis on means over sanctification seemed to Miller either to be "awfully ignorant of their Bibles, or are favoring secretly the plan of *universal salvation*." He had carried out a long and heated correspondence with a brother-in-law who had gone over to the Universalists, and he hated to see the virus of free will invade the body of evangelicalism. Naturally, wrote Miller, he preferred the Old School Calvinists. "I love their piety and doctrine. Yes, and my heart inclines more towards them than toward the new school baptists." The problem was that among the New School evangelicals he was scoring successes, while the others remained aloof. "Old school Baptists, believe in the personal reign," he wrote, "but are not many of them on the time as I know of. But I think they would be, if they would come to the light." Most distressing of all, one of the sects particularly drawn to his views was the Free Will Baptists![23]

Though Miller could count hundreds of converts to God coming out of his adventist lectures, commitment specifically to adventism—his views—was weak. While revivalists were busy tallying the number of new church members, Miller was enumerating the number of people who accepted adventism wholely, and the score was dismal. He found only a handful of preachers who accepted adventism and preached it, and even among those only a few accepted the date. More numerous were "those who believe but dare not preach it," while the number of opponents was large and increasing. Even his own children and neighbors were not in the fold. "Why will they not believe?" he asked in consternation. "Why will they not hear? Why not be wise? Oh God do awake the people of God in Hampton and those who are sleeping over the vulcano of Gods wrath."[24]

A crisis occurred among his followers, too. Isaac Wescott was arranging with a Troy, New York, printer for the publication of a new edition of Miller's lectures, and Cole warned Miller that Westcott's object had nothing to do with "the glory of God." Cole had been present when Wescott told the printer high-handedly that "he could prove the copy right is his" and that Miller had no rights in its disposal or use. Apparently Wescott was planning to acquire the profits from the second edition, or perhaps even print it under his own name. There was considerable money to be made.

[23] Miller to Hendryx, April 2, 1836; November 28, 1834.
[24] Miller to Hendryx, April 2, 1836; Miller to his son (otherwise unidentified), November 17, 1838.

Printers of the first edition had expected to make "little or nothing from the work," but volunteer distributors had quickly disposed of their stocks, and at least one printer volunteered to publish the second edition, expecting to make "considerable sale." Wescott showed great interest in the sales of the book, encouraging Miller to sell copies on commission in towns where he preached and to accept particular invitations to lecture because "you could also no doubt sell many books there." Now Wescott said he had not sold many copies and did not have enough money to pay off the printer. Possibly he had simply kept the money from the sales of the books. The problem so upset Miller that he refused to answer Wescott's letters after hearing from Cole.[25]

If this were not trouble enough for the "old man," as he liked to call himself, increasing opposition to his views was making him irritable. In 1837 an Aaron Angier of Waterbury, Vermont, began publishing a series of articles in the *Vermont Telegraph* in which he said that Miller had misinterpreted the prophecies. Angier's primary objective in analyzing Miller's ideas, he said, was to discover truth, and he commented to Miller soothingly, "I do not come now as your *antagonist*. If you are wrong, I doubt not you wish to know it. If right, we all should believe it. . . . Let us pray for the 'spirit to *guide us into all truth*.'" Miller's response was of a different temper. When Angier commented reasonably that if Miller was wrong his error would harm Christianity's reputation among unbelievers Miller retorted, "If brother Angier has no better arguments than this one, I do beg of him for the love of truth to withhold altogether." As his critic's articles appeared week by week the adventist's patience stretched thinner. Angier had purposely distorted his meaning, Miller wrote. "It is always painful to correct the faults of others, especially when they appear to be done through design, or wilfulness." Angier, he claimed, was only the spokesman for others and was not expressing his own views honestly. "If you would follow your own feelings instead of a prompter, we should have had instead of ribaldry, ridicule, and darkness, sound sense, fair arguments and instruction." His own opinions would "rebound more to your credit."[26]

This irascibility resulted in part from Miller's belief that the stakes involved in a dispute over the end of the world were no less than an "eternity of happiness or misery," and he constantly tried to be "very careful that the blood of souls may not be found on our skirts." The truth of the approaching Apocalypse had so struck him that he could not understand why others could not see what the Bible so plainly revealed

[25] Cole to William S. Miller, May 8, 1838; Kemble and Hooker to Miller, July 20, 1836; B. Young to Miller, June 14, 1839; Wescott to Miller, July 25, 1838.
[26] *Vermont Telegraph*, November 1, 1837; November 29, 1837; February 21 and 28, 1838.

to him. But was it so plain? Even he had private doubts, and Angier's reasoned arguments probably forced Miller to confront them, thus producing his anger. "I sometimes feel as though I can do all things 'through Christ strengthening me,'" he wrote to Hendryx, "and sometimes the shaking of a leaf is terror to me." To his son Miller confessed, "[The] world do not know how weak I am, they think more much more of the old man than I think of him."[27]

At this low point in his personal and public life Miller received a welcome endorsement. Early in 1839 Joseph Marsh became the new editor of the *Christian Palladium*, the Christian Connexion's New York State journal published at New York Mills, outside of Utica, and he began to warn his readers about the imminent end of the world. The Christian Connexion was a loose confederation of independent Christian congregations that had formed during the Second Great Awakening. In other parts of the nation these congregations had united with the Campbellites to form the Disciples of Christ, but in New York they remained aloof from the union movement, thanks in large part to the opposition of the *Palladium* and Marsh's predecessor, Joseph Badger. Badger had paved the way for a sympathetic reporting of Millerism with editorials predicting "great and important events in the world, our country, and the Church of God." Political and social unrest were signs that "the scriptures are rapidly fulfilling—the great day for overturning the nations is at hand—the coming of the glorious Messiah is at the door." But notwithstanding this millenarian-like rhetoric, Badger really was a postmillennialist. Christ's rule over the world would be spiritual, not personal, for during the Millennium "the *Holy Bible*, and *holy spirit* will be the *rule*." He condemned prophets, and he might have had Miller among others in mind when he warned his readers that social ferment would temporarily make "*Infidels, Universalists*, and *fanatics*. . . . One Prophet speaks to us like an orator, and another like a logician. One endeavors by his eloquence to charm us, and another by his clear reasoning to convince our minds. One threatens, another promises. Here we have presented to our eyes a sceptre of divine love, and there our ears are arrested by the shrill voice of the warning trumpets. . . . One herald of salvation points us to the smoke of torment that ascendeth up for ever and ever, and another with tender accents of a Savior's love, cries out, 'turn ye, turn ye, why will ye die?'" The rationalists clearly were the Universalists, the fanatics the Millerites.[28]

By denigrating these radicals, Badger also gave them publicity, and

---

[27] Ibid., November 29, 1837; Miller to Hendryx, August 27, 1835; Miller to his son, November 17, 1838.
[28] *Christian Palladium*, V (January 2, 1837); December 1, 1836. Unfortunately, the Connexion has received little scholarly attention.

appeal for public acceptance of Millerism, only for fair play and an open
public hearing of Miller's views. "Believing you to be a friend of free
discussion," he wrote flatteringly, "we take the liberty to address you,
and solicit your aid in sustaining the *Signs of the Times*." Because none
of the public newspapers had "*fairly* presented the truth in relation to
[Miller] or his views," it was necessary to have a new paper "that will do
him justice; that will give him a chance to speak for himself, and at the
same time let his opponents speak in their own defense; thus giving all
their rights." Himes hired agents to travel throughout the North solicit-
ing subscriptions to the paper, a tried-and-true reformist technique, and
he persuaded other adventists to solicit subscriptions among their friends
and associates. These tactics were so successful that on July 27, 1840,
Himes boasted that the paper had acquired 950 subscribers and more
than enough money to meet all its expenses. He must have sighed with
relief when he reported to Miller, "I think we shall succeed with the
paper now, and save ourselves."[4]

Himes also published the works of other adventists who were now
coming out with their own pamphlets—Henry Jones, Josiah Litch,
Henry Dana Ward, even his own speeches and lectures. Eventually these
works, comprising the Second Advent Library, filled thirteen volumes.
He sent sets of these books along with copies of the paper and Miller's
Evidence from Scripture and History of the Second Coming of Christ
to "every town where it is practicable." These publications would surely
"make some noise about town, but one must let the light shine."[5]

His new position as Millerite manager, and particularly as editor of
the *Signs of the Times*, made Himes in effect Miller's proprietor. Miller
must supply particular articles for the *Times*, Himes insisted. Criticisms
of Miller's views from Alexander Campbell demanded a response, so
Miller had "to take care of him." A point of doctrine needed clarifica-
tion, so the adventist must "give an article for the next no." Increasingly,
requests resembled orders. "I want you . . . ," "There must be no mistake
about it." Himes also choreographed Miller's lecture itinerary to make
sure he reached as many people as possible. A certain "German Profes-
sor" in New York City who was "rather wild" believed Miller was correct
"*in the computation* 1843"; Miller should meet him. Miller must attend
a large Christian Union convention in Connecticut where his appearance
would "*do great good.*" The two of them would conduct an extensive
tour of the South. "*I will go with you,*" he assured his abolitionist friend,
"and attend to all the affairs, except the *Lectures—These you must*—the
rest I will attend to,—I want you to think of this." The editor, who now

[4] Himes to Miller, November 12, 1840 (written on the bottom of a flyer) and July 27,
1840.
[5] Himes to Miller, January 26, 1840.

called himself "Bishop" Himes, also had Miller write brief autobiographies and religious testimonies. He even went so far as to sign Miller's name without his permission to a call for a general conference of adventists in Boston, assuming "by all means you will act with us in this conference."[6]

High-handed though his conduct was, firmness was necessary in working with the timorous prophet, and the steps Himes took assured the wide dispersal of adventism. Himes was nevertheless sensitive to Miller's feelings, while maintaining a strict stewardship. He once wrote to Miller, "My position, you know, is a trying, and responsible one. My attachment to you, and the views you have given to us, are ardent, and stronger than any earthly considerations. I feel that I can live with you in Gloom or Glory—I look to you, as to a Father for support, and counsel, and aid to carry forward the work of God, in giving the Midnight Cry. You do not know my feelings when I am obliged to call upon you so often, and so much for help. I think of your age, and your infirmity, etc., and could I only help you, or do anything to lighten your care; how gladly I would do it. But you see how it is—and how I am placed, and will make allowances for me."[7] It is difficult to find much humility in these words. We might almost conclude from them that Himes felt the movement was his and that Miller's job was to help him! But considering Miller's weaknesses and Himes's enormous energy, one rather wonders that the two men could have achieved a working relationship so effective for both, which, over time, produced genuine affection between them.

Soon other reformers with well-established public reputations and clienteles engaged themselves as volunteers. Henry Dana Ward, a New York City abolitionist who had gained his first reformist experience as an Anti-Masonic publicist, would soon become Millerism's most temperate spokesperson. Nathaniel Southard, abolitionist, temperance advocate, and education reformer, would in 1843 become editor of a new adventist newspaper in New York City, the *Midnight Cry*.[8] Many new recruits, like Himes and Southard, were Christianites, and with members of the Connexion gaining influence in the movement, Christianite practices

---

[6] Ibid., November 24, 1843, November 3 and 26, 1840; August 24, 1840.

[7] Himes to Miller, November 26, 1840.

[8] Francis D. Nichol, *The Midnight Cry: A Defense of William Miller and the Millerites* (Washington, 1944), 174–76; Charles Fitch, *Slaveholding Weighed in the Balance of Truth* (Boston, 1837); Henry Dana Ward wrote an attack on Masonry in 1828, and David Bernard included it in his book *Light on Masonry: A Collection of all the Most Important Documents on the Subject of Speculative Free Masonry* (Utica, 1829). Bernard himself became a Millerite in 1843. Biographical sketches of many other leading Millerites appear in Isaac C. Wellcome, *History of the Second Advent Message* (Yarmouth, Maine, 1874). On October 21, 1840, Himes wrote to Miller that Jones, Litch, and Ward "with *yourself* will be constant *contributors* to the 'Signs of the times.'"

inevitably became Millerite practices. One of the most important of these was the use of local and regional conferences, which had the four-fold effect of mobilizing volunteers, planning strategy, bolstering the faithfuls' resolve, and disseminating adventism. From 1840 to 1845 hundreds of conferences took place in small towns and large cities across the Northeast. Himes institutionalized the practice by organizing what he called the General Conference of Believers in the Second Coming of Christ at the Door which held sessions fairly frequently. The first session took place in Boston in November of 1840, and subsequent sessions were held in Portland, Maine; Lowell, Massachusetts; New York City; and Low Hampton. Himes published the meetings' minutes, thereby taking advantage once again of the printed word.[9]

Himes's innovations aided the movement in New England, but they had little immediate impact on upstate New York. There, Miller's personal preaching remained for a year the principal method of spreading adventism, and its revivalist success continued to be Miller's major attraction to preachers.[10] Gradually, however, the leaders of the New England movement assumed control of the New York popular crusade so well established in the 1830s. Henry Jones joined the eastern leadership when he became associate editor of the *Signs of the Times*, E. B. Crandall became an agent for selling subscriptions to the paper in Lansing-burgh and Troy, and Himes worked directly with longtime adventists to arrange conferences and meetings. For instance, John G. McMurray, the converted brush manufacturer from Troy, agreed to publicize a local Millerite meeting "as directed by Br. Himes." New Englanders and New Yorkers met face to face for the first time at the General Conference session held in Low Hampton in November 1841, especially to assure the presence of Miller, who had not attended any of the previous sessions because of illness. It must have been an interesting meeting with the new Boston and New York City leaders of the movement interacting with longtime believers from all over eastern New York—Queensbury, Southbury, Fort Ann, Sandy Hill, Hartford, Granville, Minerva, Chester, and White Hall.[11] The session marked the ascendancy of the New England, Christianite phase of the movement over the New York, Baptist crusade of the 1830s. The popular crusade was now subsumed by the growing mass movement of the 1840s.

[9] *First Report of the General Conference of Christians Expecting the Advent of Our Lord Jesus Christ* (Boston, 1840); Nichol, 85–87, 91–93.
[10] See Jeremiah Murphy to Miller, December 18, 1841; Joshua Fletcher to Miller, February 4, 1842; William B. Curtis to Miller, March 12, 1842.
[11] Crandall to Miller, July 28, August 27, September 25, 1840; Seth Emery to Miller, December 18, 1841; John G. McMurray to Miller, December 10, 1842; *Signs of the Times*, December 1, 1841.

The Low Hampton conference set off sparks in neighboring communities. A regional conference, with Miller, Himes, and Litch in attendance, took place the following March in Sandy Hill. I. R. Gates of
Burnt Hills was so impressed with its effects that he organized another
conference for his home town that June, and another took place shortly
afterwards in Brockett's Bridge. These meetings institutionalized the
movement in New York State. Their formal structure with elected
moderators and special committees, set agendas, and sessions on educat-
ing the public, recruiting volunteers, and planning strategy provided a
recognizable leadership and course of action. How wonderful, said
Gates, to see the faithful "not only answering and refuting the arguments
and objections of the opposers, but in seeing *scores* of sinners, under the
influence of this doctrine (the *Advent* near) crying out what shall we do
to be saved." The meeting had left him "much refreshed and resolved to
buckle on the armor of righteousness . . . [to] go into the field and see
what could be done for poor sinners."[12] The enthusiasm these four conferences generated inevitably touched Albany. Calvin French, a New
England Millerite who had been preaching in eastern New York, went
there following the Burnt Hills conference, which he had helped to organize. There he met George Storrs, another New England Methodist minister with a local reputation as an abolitionist, who had been delivering
Second Advent lectures in Albany and Utica. Together they planned and
executed a conference for July that attracted such a huge audience,
French wrote to Himes, that they had to turn away "hundreds who were
anxious to hear."[13]

French may have exaggerated the number somewhat because he
wanted very much to get Himes to journey to Albany for a series of lectures. The Bostonian had been traveling in New Hampshire and Vermont
with a new public relations gimmick, a huge portable pavilion called
appropriately the Great Tent. Fifty-five feet high with a circumference of
three hundred feet, it could seat three or four thousand people. The Tent
attracted large crowds, and in August Himes was considering taking it to
Stillwater or Troy, long established Millerite towns. But when French
implored him to take the Tent to Albany to cap their conference with a
"full, and able illustration" of Millerism, Himes acquiesced "for the cause
sake." With only five days' notice of the Tent's arrival, French and Storrs
were hard pressed to find a site large enough to accommodate the mon-
strous canopy. A woman sympathetic to Millerism solved the problem by
donating the use of a plot of land on Arbor Hill. Then a steady downpour of
rain delayed the Tent's arrival and made the ground so soggy that raising it
became nearly impossible. On the morning of August 10, however, it

12 *Signs of the Times*, May 18, 1842; Calvin French, *Signs of the Times*, July 20, 1842.
13 Wellcome, 281; Nichol, 191; Calvin French, *Signs of the Times*, August 3, 1842.

finally rose like a gray cloud and immediately aroused public curiosity. Behind schedule, the Millerites had to cancel their first meeting, but the evening lecture drew hundreds of spectators. A revival developed, which attracted still more people—as many as six thousand, Storrs estimated. "We pretend not to *number* either the converts to Christ, or to the faith of his soon appearing 'in the clouds of heaven,'" he wrote to the *Signs of the Times*, "but, we believe there are *many* to both." Small wonder then that, in spite of the difficulties they had encountered, Himes felt the Tent would "answer our purposes in all respects."[14]

Having proved its value, the Great Tent would be instrumental in opening a vast new field of labor for the Millerites in New York State west of Rome, a region the adventists had so far ignored. There a few devoted disciples, some of them friends and relatives of Miller, had done what they could to disseminate the Second Advent message, principally by circulating Millerite publications. Generally it was by lending Miller's book to neighbors that people there first promulgated adventism. One man in Attica read a copy a neighbor had brought from Vermont. He wrote to Miller, "Your book has continually been from place to place and people seem to be much taken with it." William I. Lovegrove, who offered to sell books for Miller as he went about the state "Labouring in the Cause of Temperance," told him that he had lent Miller's book to one woman and "had to Borrow it again in order to lend it to another Brother and [he] has lent it to another." Other Millerite publications circulated in the same way. E. D. Spencer of Westernville "could not keep the papers you sent me long enough to read them until they had gone the rounds through the neighborhood; and some of them I have not read yet." A druggist in Clyde obtained copies of a Millerite pamphlet by Fitch and distributed them free of charge to his customers, and an unidentified Millerite in central New York spent over $100 on publications and set up a Second Advent Circulating Library.[15]

Some Millerite itinerants had already appeared in central and western New York. Isaac Fuller had early preached the Second Advent in Chautaqua County, and Truman Hendryx had visited many towns in

[14] Hiram Munger, *The Life and Religious Experiences of Hiram Munger* (Chicopee Falls and Boston, 1861), 48. According to Nichol, 114, a tentmaker of East Kingston, New Hampshire, made the Tent in 1842, and Himes first used it in Connecticut shortly after. See also Himes to Miller, August 5, 1842, Himes's reports in the *Signs of the Times* on August 11, 17, and 24, 1842.

[15] Among relatives of Miller were a nephew, Silas Guilford, whose parents had hosted Miller's first lectures (Guilford to Miller, January 6, 1841, and January 2, 1843). Guilford by the mid-1840's was living in New Haven, Oswego County. A personal friend of Miller was Jonathan Bellamy living in Clyde (Bellamy to Miller, December 4, 1843). See also Clark Flint to Miller, July 19, 1840; William I. Lovegrove to Miller, August 26, 1841; and John Corwin, *Signs of the Times*, May 1, 1841.

central New York during an evangelical tour of the early 1830s. In 1842 Augustus Beach, the first important Millerite itinerant in the region, and H. V. Teall, a Christianite preacher turned adventist, began separate campaigns to rouse the area, Beach in western New York and Teall throughout central New York.[16] Together they laid the groundwork for an intensive regional crusade. When the second principal advent journal, the *Midnight Cry*, began publication in New York City in 1843, Millerite leaders quickly awoke to the untapped zeal in the western portion of the state. Reports in the very first issues from Teall, Beach, and others stirred the leaders' yearning to make new converts. Letters to the editor told of the "great thirst . . . for light and truth" there, and one suggested that a region-wide campaign followed by a general conference "would benefit many thousands of souls." S. W. Paine of Warsaw wrote directly to Miller complaining, "While our eastern and other states have been flooded with light on this subject, western N. York has been almost entirely neglected, while *none* are more anxious to hear. No lecturer has been through here but brother Beach. And we heartily bless God for *one*." Wrote Justus Da Lee from Pittsford to Miller, "You are much more needed at the West than at the East."[17]

Now awake to the region's needs and the promise of much support there, the Millerites planned a full-scale assault on western New York. At a conference in New York City in 1843 the advent leaders called for measures to "present the claims of Christ's speedy coming" throughout central and western New York. Lecturers should "give the alarm throughout this whole field," and someone should establish an adventist newspaper and open a bookroom "at some important point," preferably at Rochester which they considered to be "most eligible" for the undertaking.[18] It was indeed. Rochester was the center of the business and cultural life of western New York with access to the north and the far west via the Great Lakes, to the east and south via the Erie Canal, Genesee River, and the Finger Lakes. Inevitably the city had become a center for printing and consequently for reform agitation, the town where the Anti-Masons had first published a journal and where their important spokesmen Thurlow Weed and William Henry Seward had enjoyed their start in publishing and politics.[19] There was no better site

---

[16] Reports of travels by Beach and Teall appear throughout the *Signs of the Times* and the *Midnight Cry* in 1842 and 1843. See also I. C. Bronson to Miller, January 11, 1843; S. W. Paine to Miller, April 15, 1843.

[17] E. E. Paine, *Midnight Cry*, April 13, 1843; L. P. Judson, *Midnight Cry*, May 11, 1843; Justus Da Lee to Miller, January 10, 1843.

[18] *Midnight Cry*, May 11, 1843; Justus Da Lee to Miller, January 10, 1843.

[19] Blake McKelvey, *Rochester, The Water Power City: 1812–1854* (Cambridge, 1945); Paul Johnson, *A Shopkeeper's Millennium: Society and Revivals in Rochester, New York, 1815–1837* (New York, 1978).

for beginning the evangelization of the west.

In June of 1843, Himes, Fitch, and a battery of volunteers took the Great Tent to Rochester and reared it on the east bank of the Genesee River. They held only one meeting in it though, when a furious gale brought the canvas down "on the heads of about 500 persons." Fortunately no one was injured, but Himes was ready to give up the Tent as a total loss. The incident, however, created publicity and aroused public sympathy. Rochesterians—including some who had "felt no interest or sympathy with us—but much to the contrary"—volunteered money and labor to repair the canvas. Within a few days it was standing again, and crowds flocked to see it. Wrote Himes, "All has turned out well to the furtherance of the good cause."[20] Himes assured that the cause would not languish once the Tent left by opening a bookroom where people could purchase and read adventist publications and by establishing a new newspaper called the *Glad Tidings of the Kingdom of God at Hand*, copies of which he distributed free of charge throughout the city. Also, after the Tent left Rochester, Fitch and several others stayed behind to keep stoking the fires. Thomas F. Barry remained in the city for two full years.[21]

Concerned that high winds would make use of the Tent in western New York impracticable, Himes considered returning with it to New England. But as the Rochester revivals had sparked intense interest throughout the region, he took it to Buffalo, western terminus of the Erie Canal and gateway to Ohio. The city more than repaid him for his trouble. So lively were the meetings there that lecturers rushed from the east to join him. At the end of their six-day August visit Himes proclaimed exuberantly, "The whole city is roused. The people are anxious for light. We have distributed publications by the thousands, and they are being read in every part of the city." All thought of returning to New England ended, and he packed up the Tent and took it even farther west to Ohio.[22] This "Western enterprise" as he called it was "a most important field of labor," and he urged other eastern lecturers to help out. In answer, Nathaniel Hervey rushed from Albany to join his schoolmate Asahel Chapin in spreading Millerism in Chautauqua County; a New York City businessman left his store and traveled throughout central New York lecturing; others worked in Cortland County, the Southern Tier, and Erie County. By the end of 1843 over two dozen itinerants were plying the highways and canals of the region spreading the call to repentance.[23]

---

[20] See Himes's reports from Rochester in the *Cry*, June 29, July 6, 13, and 30, 1843.

[21] Ibid., July 20, 1843.

[22] Ibid., July 13, 1843, and August 3, 17, and 24, 1843.

[23] Ibid., July 20, 1843; N. Hervey, ibid., July 13, 1843; anonymous, ibid., August 24, 1843; N. Pitcher, ibid., May 11, 1843.

Miller capped the crusade by personally touring the upstate region with Himes in November and December. His lectures began in Rochester where Himes counted scores of converts. He then moved west to Lockport, Buffalo, Lewiston, and Penfield, all providing large and enthusiastic crowds. A New York City itinerant who caught up with them in Rochester and helped deliver lectures there was amazed by the support he found. "O, when I see such an interest awakened in a little city," he cried out jealously, "containing less than 30,000 inhabitants, and then think of our own city containing almost half a million, with but few, if *any* more believers in the great leading truths of the Bible than there are here; my heart is pained within me for the condition of the people of New York." Miller cut his tour short. He had anticipated going to Auburn, Syracuse, and Utica on his way home, but he by-passed them all. Whitney Cross suspects that the lack of an already well-established Millerite presence in these towns was the reason, the tired man being unwilling to break new ground, wanting only to meet the already faithful.[24] This may be true, but more likely the trip simply wore him out.

All these eastern itinerants took advantage of travel time to evangelize. Calvin French lectured to passengers on an Erie Canal packet boat and sold books. H. V. Teall, while traveling to central New York on boats, stagecoaches, and packets, debated the depravity of the Catholic Church with a priest, overheard a conversation about the supposed effect of Millerism driving people insane, and initiated a conversation and debate about the end of the world among fellow passengers. Terminals were good places to leave promotional literature (just like today), and Himes made a point of distributing books "on canal boats, railroad cars, steam boats, vessels, etc."[25]

Himes had discontinued printing the *Glad Tidings*, but an experienced publisher moved to Rochester and put it on a permanent footing. Joseph Marsh received so much criticism for his preoccupation with the end of the world in his editorials that he resigned as editor of the *Christian Palladium* and moved to Albany, where he bought a press and began printing an adventist paper called the *Voice of Truth*. But he was aware of gains to be made in western New York because he had earlier toured the region for the Christian Connexion which had been planning to move *its* press there.[26] So Marsh packed up again, moved to Rochester, merged his paper with Himes's, and in March 1844 came out with his first issue of the

[24] See reports of the tour appearing in ibid., November and December 1843; see also Cross, 303–4.
[25] Calvin French, *Signs of the Times*, July 20, 1842; Teall, *Midnight Cry*, June 15, 1843, Himes, *Midnight Cry*, August 3, 1843.
[26] Editorials appearing in the *Palladium* following Marsh's resignation indicate the divorce was less than amicable. And there are hints that divergent theology was not the only source of complaint against him. Though never stated, charges may have been circulated that Marsh bought his Millerite press with Connexion money.

Voice of Truth and Glad Tidings of the Kingdom of God at Hand.[27] For the next months this paper would truly be the voice of the Millerites in western New York.

Like their eastern compatriots, Millerites of western and central New York used conferences and camp meetings. In fact, because high winds made use of the Great Tent inconvenient, Himes specifically recommended these devices as a substitute. In the spring of 1843 adventists held conferences in Oswego, Cooperstown, Jamestown, Westfield, and Rochester. Camp meetings caught on quite late in New York State generally, but Millerites to the west held them very early in that region's evangelization. The first took place in Plainville and Sennett, near Auburn, in June of 1843, and adventists held grove meetings in Geneva, Schroeppel, Albion, and Utica that year. Collective action again educated the public and spurred on the faithful, just as it had in the east.[28]

Perhaps gatherings like these helped soothe hurt feelings among small-town adventists who often felt neglected. Because the Millerites' goal was to gain large numbers of converts they concentrated their efforts on the large towns and cities where dense populations and good communications promised success. Himes had found the cost of shipping and erecting the Great Tent to be so high that he could take it only to prosperous cities "where the people will sustain it." Besides, wasn't the city the hotbed of sin and corruption? Regardless, adventists in small towns resented being by-passed. They were particularly upset when Miller left the region without making some of his scheduled stops. The thought that Miller would visit Syracuse "excited a great deal of interest in this region," wrote one disappointed adventist. But his failure to appear "to say the least, proved a very great disappointment to many hundreds of persons." Daniel Clow of Port Byron summed up the frustrations of many when he wrote to the *Midnight Cry*, "We feel as if we have been very much neglected by our friends who are lecturing upon the Advent, and passing and repassing us, to and from the west,— we have had no opportunity of hearing the subject ably discussed, for some time—most sadly were we disappointed when it was announced that brother Miller had returned to the east. We expected that he would tarry a while in Auburn, and give us a course of lectures, which, we have flattered ourselves, would be the means of opening the eyes of the blind, and moving a multitude of souls from the yawnings of an eternal

[27] The dispute between Marsh and the Connexion's publishing Board can be found in Marsh's letter to the *Midnight Cry*, November 16, 1843, and in Sarah Marsh to Miller, February 4, 1842. The Connexion presented its side of the story in the *Palladium*, July 5, 1843. A copy of the single Albany issue of the *Glad Tidings* is located in the Jenks Adventual Collection.

[28] Himes, *Midnight Cry*, July 20, 1843; Nichol, 106–11.

hell."[29] Exasperated souls in by-passed towns sensed lecturers' desires for large numbers of converts and tried to entice speakers by emphasizing their village's strategic location. Syracuse was "central" and therefore "well situated for scattering light, to the populous districts around;" Warsaw was "the County Seat and quite a central place;" from tiny Perry an influence "might be thrown over a wide territory."[30]

Fortunately for these frustrated souls, the movement in central and western New York did not have to depend solely on the labor of eastern volunteers. Native recruits took up much of the slack. Delivering courses of advent lectures based on Miller's book, on the lectures of other Millerites, or on whatever knowledge they could glean from tracts and pamphlets, amateur preachers took up a new calling to sound the alarm. After perusing the *Midnight Cry* and studying the Bible, W. D. Cook of Sodus Point began to lecture "according to the ability which God had given me" at a schoolhouse near his home. Although poor weather forced him to desist, he planned to resume "as soon as the traveling will permit." Edward Canfield lectured in and around Clyde, and one eastern itinerant spoke of "several ministers and lay brethren who have commenced lecturing" throughout the upstate area. Some, like O. R. Fassett, a Seneca Falls physician, George W. Peavey, and Henry H. Gross itinerated all over the state, but most natives restricted their travels. Samuel W. Rhodes lectured almost exclusively in Oswego County, Asahel Chapin in Chautauqua County, E. R. Pinney in the northern Finger Lakes region, Edward Canfield in Wayne and Seneca Counties, and J. Adrian along the west shore of Lake Champlain. An even larger number of native volunteers preached only in their own churches—S. B. Yarrington in Hamilton, W. D. Cook in Sodus Point, L. P. Judson in Warsaw. Many were settled pastors and would have agreed with Judson's statement, "I have not left my own people on the sabbath to give the cry 'to others.' I have more calls for lectures than I can possibly answer and retain my charge."[31]

In 1843 western New York Millerites gained their most important local leader when Elon Galusha, Baptist pastor in Lockport, began to preach the Second Coming of Christ. Son of a governor of Vermont, Galusha had by 1843 earned a reputation as "one of the most famous men in the State" because of his abilities as a preacher, missionary, and abolitionist. After ordination in 1814 Galusha had filled pulpits in Utica,

[29] Hugh Hancock, *Midnight Cry*, February 8, 1844; Daniel Clow, ibid., February 15, 1844.

[30] Hugh Bremner, *Midnight Cry*, December 21, 1843; I. C. Bronson to Miller, January 11, 1843; Josiah Andrews to David Bernard, December 24, 1843.

[31] W. D. Cook, *Midnight Cry*, December 21, 1843; Edward Canfield, ibid., August 3, 1843; L. C. Collins, ibid., April 13, 1843; C. R. Griggs, ibid., June 13, 1844; L. P. Judson, ibid., May 11, 1843.

Buffalo, and Rochester. The first New York Baptist missionary sent to the Michigan Territory in 1822, he had subsequently served for many years as chairman of the New York Baptist Missionary Convention. As an abolitionist leader he had chaired the Monroe County Antislavery Society. He reportedly possessed "a rich imagination, glowing enthusiasm, and, when his sympathies were thoroughly enlisted, pure eloquence. Few men could carry a large congregation with such overwhelming power as Br. Galusha."[32]

Galusha's decision to exert his great influence on behalf of Millerism was gradual and deliberate, the result in part of a concerted Millerite effort to recruit him. He once read Miller's lectures and "deemed them worthy of a critical examination," but in the beginning he did not take them seriously. Early in 1843, though, a "beloved son," perhaps his own son E. C. Galusha, began sending him "letters, papers, and publications" on the Second Advent. The earnestness of the communications to him moved Galusha to examine the work more closely, to compare Miller's exegesis with others, and to decide that Miller's was "the only safe one." Then Nathaniel Whiting, an old friend and an important eastern Millerite lecturer, wrote to Galusha "expressing the convictions of his own mind, the result of a long and patient examination of the subject, in which he sifted the arguments pro and con." Deeply moved by his friend's discussion, Galusha and over sixty members of the Baptist Church sent Miller a petition begging him to lecture to them so they might know "*what* and *wherefore* you affirm." During his western tour, Miller did visit them; indeed, the ten days he spent in Lockport was the longest stop he made on the entire trip. Up to this time Galusha was sufficiently convinced of Miller's predictions that he preached the Second Advent in his pulpit, spoke at Millerite gatherings in Rochester, and helped run the bookroom there, but he still had hesitated to accept the date of Christ's return. Himes and Miller apparently persuaded him, however, for at the end of their December visit with him, Himes wrote triumphantly to the *Midnight Cry* that Galusha had decided to throw "the whole weight of his intellect and influence with the Adventists." Miller wrote too, "Bro. Galusha came out full in the faith of '43. He is a happy man, and a strong man in faith. . . . With him I am well pleased."[33] Galusha fully lived up to Miller's expectations. He employed

---

[32] William Cathcart, *The Baptist Encyclopedia: A Dictionary of the Doctrines, Ordinances, Usages . . . of the Baptist Denomination in all Lands*, I (Philadelphia, 1843), 432; David Benedict, *A General History of the Baptist Denomination in America and Other Parts of the World* (New York, 1840), 561, 571–72; *Rochester Daily Democrat*, August 11, 1843, and July 8, 1838; Elizier Wright, Jr., to Gerritt Smith, July 16, 1836, Gerritt Smith Papers, Syracuse University.

[33] "Address by Elon Galusha," *Midnight Cry*, April 4, 1844; Lockport Baptists to Miller, October 2, 1843; ibid., December 14, 1843, and January 18, 1844.

his preaching experience to awaken sinners, urging audiences to "fly to Jesus; *swiftly fly*; your sins confess; for mercy plea, while He is on the mercy seat." At any moment "the song of revelry . . . will cease; the voice of mirth be heard no more forever; the chilling horror will suddenly seize upon you—the sheltering rocks will not protect you; the falling mountains will not hide you; the fiery stream will not spare you; the wail of anguish will not relieve you—Nor gushing tears; nor mercy's name; nor bleeding Lamb will then avail you!"[34] This was the terrifying message he took to Rochester, Brockport, Seneca Falls, Auburn, Weedsport, Buffalo and East Mendon, stirring audiences and gaining converts to God and to the advent cause.

Another episode also illustrates how prolonged study of Miller's ideas could convert even the best educated. O. R. Fassett was a trained and licensed physician of Seneca Falls. He had lost most of his interest in religion, and when Miller arrived in town to give a series of lectures he attended out of curiosity "at the same time supposing that [he] was one of the worst men that ever lived." But Miller looked respectable, and he supported all of his ideas by quoting the Bible, "the book I believed and always have in some measure to be the word of Jehovah!" So Fassett felt compelled to attend the rest of the lectures. "I thus reasoned if you speak I must hear," he wrote to Miller, "if it be truth it is of the utmost importance that I as an individual know it, if it be error there was no need of embracing it." A particular biblical verse struck him forcefully so that he "became more and more interested. I broke up the fallow ground of my heart, I studied, prayed, wept and confessed my sin—and light broke more and more into my soul." He read the works of other Bible interpreters and compared their ideas with Miller's, talked about adventism with his minister, and finally became convinced that Miller was correct. As with Galusha, conviction led to action, and Fassett became an itinerant adventist lecturer.[35]

The same combination of empirical verification and pietist Biblicism converted and recruited many others. Curiosity and desire for entertainment were enough to draw people initially to Second Advent lectures, and hellfire-and-brimstone sermons could frighten sinners temporarily into a conversion. However, to instill a lasting belief in Miller's views and to evoke commitment to them required patient and constant exhortation. A course of lectures usually ran over sixteen evenings during which the unconvinced and the merely curious withdrew, leaving behind a core of interested or convinced attendants at the end. Then it was up to resident volunteers in the community to form a Bible class to

34 "Address by Elon Galusha."
35 O. R. Fassett, *The Biography of Mrs. L. R. Fassett, a Devoted Christian, a Useful Life* (Boston, 1885), 1–11; O. R. Fassett to Miller, September 2, 1846.

continue the instruction and to keep morale and commitment high. In Castile, for example, following a course of lectures by Augustus Beach, "a number of the members of the Congregational church . . . formed a Bible class to examine the subject." Meeting together and studying the prophecies daily for several weeks produced "the thorough conversion of most of the members of the class."[36]

Visual aids were an important part of the educational process. When lecturing, Samuel W. Rhodes always "let people bring their Bibles, and work out the time on a slate or blackboard." Lecturers and teachers used large chronological charts personifying Daniel's four kingdoms as the "Man of Sin" with a head of gold representing Babylon, a torso of silver for the Persian Empire, brass legs personifying Greece, and feet of clay to illustrate Rome and the Roman Catholic Church. Dates for the rise and fall of each kingdom would appear in the margins in bold typeface, and as one worked down the figure the progress of cosmic history became clear. Until, at the feet, only one date was left—1843. Charles Fitch and others printed a "standard chart" and distributed thousands of copies, but creative Millerites often painted their own. Joseph Marsh's daughter Jane later remembered seeing a particularly impressive specimen. "For the darkening of the sun, there was a woman with a candle, looking up into a tree where what was meant to represent fowls were roosting at what we were told was midday. It was the spectacular display of the falling of the stars from heaven that delighted us most. They were coming down in a brisk shower, children running to pick them up and carry them away by armfuls." Some Millerites made their point even more dramatically by using wooden models of the Man of Sin with detachable parts. Jane sometimes made her own by piling up four books or boxes, and, with the fall of each empire, she dashed them to the floor one at a time till there were none left.[37]

Preachers and lecturers abounded, but others volunteered their mite through the written word. Henry Jones not only assisted Himes with the *Signs of the Times* but also served as editor of a short-lived newspaper in New York City called the *Second Advent Witness*. H. H. Gross of Albany published a journal there called the *Sure Word of Prophecy*, while Orlando Squires printed a similar sheet in Utica called the *Day Star*. E. R. Pinney of Seneca Falls printed at his own expense two thousand copies of a pamphlet he called the *Trump of Jubilee*. All these people took material for their papers from the major advent journals, from Miller's book, or from other adventist publications.

Many other volunteers worked quietly and without fanfare in each

---

[36] *Midnight Cry*, June 15, 1843.

[37] Jane Marsh Parker, "A Little Millerite," *Century Magazine*, XI (November 1866– April 1867), 315.

community to organize Bible classes, conferences, and camp meetings. These local committees would recruit speakers and make necessary arrangements to hold a successful gathering. Guest lecturers usually stayed with a local adventist. In towns where Millerism was popular, or even where the public was tolerant or disinterested, meeting places were easy to find. Millerites in Syracuse had a choice of spots. The Methodists offered them the use of their church, but the Millerites turned it down because it "was not situated sufficiently central; neither did we consider it large enough."[38] In towns where churches were hostile and closed their doors to the adventists, the schoolhouse, courthouse, or a private residence served. Sometimes the guest speaker would find himself or herself delivering lectures in a saloon, a tavern, or a ballroom, the only places available. But at least in such cases the speaker, though terribly embarrassed, had the satisfaction of knowing he had taken the message right into the Devil's own parlor. Where no buildings were available speakers plied their doctrine in the streets. Generally though, well organized Millerite groups had a place of their own for regular Bible classes. Adventists in Rochester used a civic building, Talman Hall; those in Ithaca occupied an unused floor of a factory; in Fowlersville they met in a tavern; in Buffalo a theater served as the frequent meeting place. Energetic Millerites in West Troy and Dansville built their own tabernacles. Rental fees for space sometimes caused a problem. Utica Millerites had to pay five dollars a day for use of the Second Presbyterian Church. To cover expenses they asked for donations from the attendants. Himes sometimes sold tickets for Miller's lectures, a practice that may have been common.[39]

Camp meetings were more difficult to arrange. Local Millerites had to find a suitable plot of land large enough to accommodate hundreds of tents, land with sheltering groves of trees, fresh water springs, and pasturage for the horses. The site needed to be close to more comfortable lodgings for those without tents and close to good transportation between the camp site and neighboring towns. Such locations were hard to find and were likely to require a high rental fee. Frequently a sympathizer would donate a site. As with other kinds of religious gatherings, camp meetings required good publicity to draw big crowds and well-known adventist lecturers; so it was up to the local committee to advertise their meeting well in advance in the Millerite newspapers and to write directly to prominent speakers inviting them to attend. Careful planning produced successful meetings; the mammoth Scottsville camp meeting in 1844 reportedly drew up to five thousand people.[40]

[38] E. Jacobs, *Midnight Cry*, November 6, 1843.
[39] Reports of rental fees appear commonly in Millerite publications and correspondence.
[40] See particularly issues of the *Midnight Cry*, June 15, 22, 1843, and August 1, 8, 1844.

Uncounted and uncountable were the contributions of the poor, the old, and the ill who had few social connections or resources but who did what they could for the cause. One Binghamton woman who was unable "by being Poor" to do "What i Would do if Was other Wise" helped spread the doctrine in her own small way. "i doant Let anny boddey Come in My house and go out again With out telling them of and trying to Make them understand What we Mean," she wrote. An earnest Millerite in Pitcher described himself as "a poor man 73 years old. I am deaf as a stone—have not been able to hear a human voice for many hears." But he lent his copies of the *Midnight Cry* "all over the neighborhood."[41] The part of such zealots is incalculable. By such service the Millerite movement succeeded spectacularly in reaching into every corner of New York State.

The evangelization of western and central New York was explosive.[42] It took Miller eight years to establish his views in eastern New York and Vermont, but only a few months after Himes initiated the western enterprise, L. D. Fleming in Rochester could say, "Few, comparatively, will be able to say at least that they never heard the sound, directly or indirectly."[43]

Exactly how many people became Millerites is impossible to say. Estimates range from 10,000 to 1,000,000 believers across the nation, but all such compilations are purely conjectural. Up to 1843 Millerism was non-sectarian. Millerites remained in their home congregations, although there were special Millerite Bible and prayer classes within some churches. But no membership lists exist, and even when Millerites began to withdraw from the churches, they left behind no records of their separate meetings. Occasionally an entire congregation "went over to Millerism," as was reportedly the case with the Oswego Baptist Church,

---

[41] Mrs. Livingston to Miller, January 14, 1843; letter from H., *Midnight Cry*, May 11, 1843.

[42] We can document this by comparing the rate at which communities in eastern New York were evangelized with the rate at which communities in the western regions of the state were evangelized. If, for purposes of discussion, we accept Whitney Cross's demarcation of "western New York" as New York State west of Rome, then we can chart the shift of attention from the east to the west by noting for each year the number of towns by region introduced to Millerism for the first time:

Year	East of Rome	West of Rome
1831–39	32	16
1840	2	2
1841	9	5
1842	13	4
1843	25	62
1844	17	61

Each year before 1843 eastern New York communities were introduced to Millerism at a rate twice as fast as western New York communities, but in 1843 and 1844 that tendency more than reversed.

[43] *Midnight Cry*, June 29, 1843.

and in some instances names appear in church records of individuals whom the congregation disfellowshipped for "Millerism." Otherwise, the only clues we have from traditional research resources as to numbers or names of Millerites are petitions that church members signed and sent to Miller asking him to preach to them. Even here, we do not know whether these petitioners were Millerites or simply curious evangelicals.

The principal difficulty in identifying Millerites is in defining who *was* a Millerite. Miller's doctrine was so orthodox that it appealed to many people who never "joined" the movement, from the expectant millennialist to those who simply hung on to the crusade just in case Miller was right. Within Millerism there was enormous theological diversity—not all believers believed the same things. Thus it is impossible to define simply by belief who was a Millerite and who was not, even when we can identify the beliefs of particular persons. It is by their action that we best identify committed Millerites, those who publicly stated their support for the crusade, contributed to it, labored for it. This criterion leaves unconsidered many (probably the bulk of the movement) who believed strongly but took no action on behalf of Millerism, but it does at least provide a reliable measure for identifying the leadership. According to this standard, in New York State alone some 400 people were sufficiently committed to sign letters to the leaders and to the editors of adventist journals, to write articles and pamphlets, or to take other public action. Assuming that for each of these were twenty other anonymous believers (of one degree of faith or another), then the number of Millerites in New York alone would have been about 8,000. Regardless of what their specific numbers might have been, Millerites were correct to congratulate themselves on their evangelization by 1843, the year of Jubilee.

So far we have concerned ourselves with how Millerism achieved this wide support, a relatively simple task. More difficult to explain is *why* Millerism caught fire at this particular time. Throughout American history, prophets had arisen from time to time to predict the end of the world or the imminent beginning of the Millennium, and some had even established sizable sects.[44] But none had achieved a mass following like Miller's. The rise of Millerism at this particular time is best explained by identifying its essential characteristics up to 1843; it was revivalistic, millennial, and pietistic.[45] The combination of these forces created the Millerite personality and the social and religious context in which that personality developed.

[44] Again one can profitably refer to Marini's work.

[45] The word *evangelical* is consciously omitted here. Social scientists frequently misinterpret that word, suggesting that it implies a "world view" or mentalité. What they are actually describing is not evangelicalism, which is simply the commitment to spread the "good news" of salvation through Christ, but pietism. My discussion of the role of pietism in shaping Millerism appears in chapter 5.

We have already discovered the essential contribution of revivalism to propagating Miller's message, but before turning in the next two chapters to the effects respectively of millennialism and pietism let us note how revivalism stamped the personality of the Millerite movement. Revivals, occurring among hundreds and thousands of people and involving wholesale conversions of congregations and families, gave to Millerism its bent toward collectivism. A Millerite evangelized among his or her circle of family, church, and profession. Many Millerite itinerants traveled in family groups, teams of husbands and wives, brothers, fathers and daughters. Under the influence of Elon Galusha sixty Baptists in Lockport joined the movement as did twenty-five Baptists in Ithaca and twenty-two in Lewiston. According to the 1850 manuscript census, two Ithaca Millerites were wagonmakers implying a professional association as did the presence of many ordained or licensed ministers in the movement (a full 40 percent of our identified adventists). Group affiliations provided targets for evangelization and, after conversion, a structure for mutual support.

But revivalism also fostered individual religious expressions. Stephen Marini has noted the development of what he called "radical evangelicalism" among the converts in the First Great Awakening and the 1780s refreshing, and this radical temperament resulted in the rise of many new sects including the Free Will Baptists, Universalists, Shakers, and others. The same was true of revivals of the Second Great Awakening, which witnessed the rise not only of Millerism but of the Christian Connexion, Mormons, Anti-Mission Baptists, and Perfectionist groups of many kinds. Revivalism's frenzy helps to account for much of this antinomianism.

But it cannot account for all of it. By 1843 it was apparent that Millerism was developing its own personality, quite distinct from its quality as a revivalist movement, and within this new personality were strains that many adventists found shocking. Their very success in creating a mass movement assured their inability to govern the crusade they had called into existence, for the millennialism and pietism that helped make adventism a mass movement also ensured that it would grow uncontrolled, and uncontrollable.

Chapter 4
A CULTURE OF CATACLYSM

William G. McLoughlin has argued that American history is "best understood as a millenarian movement." He cites the interaction of "individualism, pietism, perfectionism, and millenarian ideology" as part of the "process of reorientation and redefinition of the core of beliefs and values that has enabled us to emerge from each crisis with renewed self-confidence as a people." These values help Americans to "refashion our pattern of life and enculturation to enable rising generations to cope with the unfolding complexities of human redemption."[1]

Insofar as Millerism was a product of a continuing process of intellectual and spiritual regeneration in American Christian life, the movement was conventional. To the extent that Millerites participated in this process of renewal in their own individualistic way, the movement was random, libertarian, and to some extent radical. Millenialism, therefore, helped give Millerism a Janus-like personality, making it orthodox while opening doors to free thought.

Millerites and non-Millerites alike noted the movement's essential orthodoxy. Jenny Marsh Parker said years after the demise of the crusade, "Millerism was the logical outcome of the theological teaching of centuries." Lydia Maria Child, well-known social commentator, wrote similarly that Millerism was not "a singular delusion." Though she never adopted Miller's views and objectively reported some of the movement's sillier qualities, she also noted that Millerism stemmed from ancient Jewish messianism and was related to the beliefs of the early Christian martyrs, medieval theologians, and the modern evangelical denominations. "The people have been told for a series of years that the world would be destroyed by material fire and that the Messiah would come visibly in the heavens, to reign as a king of the earth. It is but one step more, to decide when these events will occur." This orthodoxy attracted many to the movement, one Millerite averring characteristically that for "forty-three years I have been established in the Doctrine of Christ's Coming."[2]

---

[1] William G. McLoughlin, *Revivals, Awakenings, and Reform* (Chicago and London, 1978), xiv-xv.

[2] Jenny (Jane) Marsh Parker, *Rochester, A Story Historical* (Rochester, 1884), 253;

Indeed, the cultural soil of antebellum New York was ready to receive the adventist seed Miller planted. Enriched by decades of popular speculation about Last Things (eschatology) and including a wide seam of cataclysmic imagery, that soil fed adventism and sped its growth. Miller's eschatology was part of an apocalyptic tradition deeply rooted in the human contemplation of two seemingly contradictory themes, cosmic destruction and universal renewal. Its sources lie hidden. Perhaps apocalypticism results from the collective memory of actual global disasters, from the desire for escape from hard realities, from the culturalization of internal psychological tensions and fears, or from divine revelations of events yet to come. Each theory has its champions. Whatever its causes, the universal cultural theme, always present at a subliminal level, erupts periodically in theological eschatology, in messianic or millenarian movements, in literature, in revolutionary movements, or in the religious experience, individual or collective, of spiritual renewal.[3]

In Western Christian culture, apocalypticism has manifested itself in the tradition of the Second Coming of Christ (Parousia), the end of the world and Last Judgment (Apocalypse), the creation of the New Heavens and New Earth, and the inauguration of the Millennium. Its impact on the religious and secular life of America and Europe has been enormous. The Puritans who settled New England were steeped in prophecy, and the Book of Revelation guided their British brethren and sisters in the overthrow of Charles I in the 1640s. Speculation about the Second Coming of Christ was both a product and a generator of the First Great Awakening during the 1740s and 50s and of the Second Great Awakening during the first decades of the 19th century.[4]

Millennialism is enormously complex. Scholars have traditionally sought to impose some order on it by classifying its intellectual structure, thus the dimorphic distinction between postmillennialists and premillennialists (or millenarians). As we have already seen, Millerism achieved a certain distinction as a modified form of premillennialism that, on the basis of a hermeneutic (prophetic interpretation) that saw the prophecies fulfilled through history, anticipated the fulfillment of the Second Coming of Christ and inauguration of the Millennium simultaneously at a

Lydia Maria Child, *Letters From New York* (New York, 1845), 240; Samuel Hough, *Midnight Cry*, February 15, 1844.

[3] As with other general topics, discussion of millennialism as a field of scholarly study appears in the bibliographical essay. However, I can point out here that millennial studies are so numerous and cover so many cultural regions and periods in history that apocalypticism as a cultural theme is revealed as nearly, if not actually, universal.

[4] See particularly James W. Davidson, *The Logic of Millennial Thought* (New Haven and London, 1977), and Ernest Lee Tuveson, *Redeemer Nation: The Idea of America's Millennial Role* (Chicago, 1968).

fairly specific time—sometime in 1843. This structuralist approach helps us place Millerism in a certain intellectual context.

But structuralism has a built-in difficulty, for millennialists do not always adhere to one theory. As James W. Davidson has noted, "Millennialists were not by and large a notably consistent lot when it came to interpreting the prophecies. . . . The equivocation about past and future events found in [their] works reinforces the conclusion that explaining millennial thought in terms of the logic of the external structure can be misleading."[5] He offers interesting examples of this among eighteenth-century exegetes, and we can provide one more from the nineteenth century. Eliphalet Nott, President of Union College in Schenectady in the first decades of the nineteenth century, was a well-known scientist and theologian. In his interpretations of the prophecies, scholarly exegesis combined with terrific impatience to see the prophecies fulfilled. The religious fires of the Second Great Awakening from 1798 to 1806 convinced him that the "kingdom of God is at hand," and he urged Christians to "anticipate its glory; let us fill our minds with ideas of its duration and extent; let us endeavor to hasten its approach; let us invite by our charities and our prayers, the Savior from the skies; let us show that we are willing to receive him on the earth, and, placing on his altar the humble means which we are able to furnish, for advancing his interest, with one general burst of passion, that shall fill the heavens, and reach the place where His glory dwelleth, let us say, 'Come, Lord Jesus, come quickly.'" His expectancy sounds premillennial as though he fully expected the personal appearance of Christ soon, before the inauguration of the Millennium. Yet, he believed that humans must create the Millennium themselves, a traditionally postmillennial position. As a scientist, Nott was convinced that the cosmic catastrophies predicted in Revelation would actually occur. God had implanted "principles of decay" in the universe, and the unfolding of time would see the moon fall from the sky and the light of the sun darkened forever. But if, as he confidently expected in 1806, the Millennium was about to begin and the Apocalypse would take place after that thousand year period of bliss, it seemed to leave little time for natural processes to work the expected effects. "It does not appear," he admitted, "that these heavens and this earth which, after the lapse of six thousand years [according to Archbishop Usher's chronology of the Creation], still display so much magnificence, and shine in so much glory, will, in little more than a thousand years have grown old *as doth a garment*, and become unfit for use."[6] It was a contradiction

---

[5] James W. Davidson, "Searching for the Millennium: Problems for the 1790s and 1970s," *New England Quarterly*, XLV (June, 1972), 254, 257.

[6] Eliphalet Nott, "A Sermon Preached Before the General Assembly of the Presbyterian Church . . . May 16, 1806," in *Miscellaneous Works* (New York, 1910), 157–59, 155–56.

he never reconciled, essentially a contradiction between his millenarian hopes but postmillennial theology. So in this case, as in others, structuralism would not only fail to reveal the complexity of Nott's thinking but would actually obscure it by oversimplifying.

More important for us is tracing millennialism's cultural impact on the rise of the Millerite movement, for it was the liveliness of Miller's imagery as much as the quality of his formal hermeneutic that made his views so real and so believable for thousands of Americans, many of whom would not have understood the niceties of his theology. Certainly, formal apocalyptic was one seam in that culture. Highly structured, traditional, and with a certain intellectual authority, what we might call "apocalypticism from the top down" informed opinion, set the themes of apocalyptic, and established rules for seeking the hidden secrets of Last Things. The inquisitive Christian could study apocalyptic in thousands of tracts published in Britain and the United States alone or backtrack through Greek and Latin texts of Joachim of Fiore, St. Augustine, Origen or hundreds of other church fathers. Contemporaries of Miller could choose from a variety of exegetical treatises. Jonathan Edwards, Timothy Dwight, and a score of other well-known interpreters had made careers by writing biblical commentaries. Moses Stuart, probably America's best-known early nineteenth-century commentator, upheld the postmillennialist position, George Duffield championed premillennialism, and George Bush, leader of the Swedenborgians, preached that Christ had already returned in spiritual form. Beyond these exegetical leaders were hundreds of amateur interpreters who published obscure pamphlets around the country, and any religious journal of the day included commentaries on the prophecies from one theological position or another as part of their regular fare.[7]

Millennialism was not static. Attitudes toward how the Millennium would occur had shifted dramatically over time. In the 1740s, under the powerful effect of the First Great Awakening, premillennialism gave way to postmillennialism. This shift from the teachings of the Puritan divines that God alone could perfect the world to the belief in human agency to bring about the Millennium was largely the result of the Bible commentaries of Jonathan Edwards. He preached that humanity must prepare the world for the Millennium by evangelizing Christianity around the world, converting the Jews to Christianity, and obliterating sin. Evangelicals increased missionary activity and established tract societies to accomplish these objectives. Widespread revivals in the 1740s, 1780s, and late 1790s seemed to prove that God was showering grace on Christians to strengthen them for the task, and the Second Great Awakening offered millennialists

---

[7] For an introduction to the complex subject of hermeneutic in America see Jerry Wayne Brown, *The Rise of Biblical Criticism in America* (Middletown, CT, 1969).

hope that their work was speeding to its glorious conclusion. The editor of the *New York Missionary Magazine* wrote in a characteristically optimistic mood in 1800, "The most respectable interpreters of the prophetic scriptures have generally agreed in assigning the present as an highly interesting and eventful period. Their remarkable coincidence of system in viewing these *perilous times* as introductory to the *latter day glory*, should be treated with respect even by the most credulous. It is no small token for good, in this respect, that so many in the Christian world are so anxiously looking and so earnestly praying for that happy day." Another cited the "revivals of experimental religion" and the "missionary spirit, remarkably poured out" as proof that the Millennium was approaching. Tracts on the prophecies appeared locally, like Benjamin Gorton's obscure *A Scriptural Account of the Millennium* published in Troy in 1802, an amateur's prediction that the glorious era was on its way.[8]

Anyone who wished could read the signs. A Dutchess County physician viewed Deism as one of the false prophets to arise in the Latter Days. Surely this was an indication that the Church "in her militant, or suffering state" was drawing near. He exclaimed, "THY KINGDOM COME." To many Universalism was another false voice guilty of the "perversion of the sacred records" leading to the "injury of Christian morals, and the disgust of its rational, and the terror of its timid friends."[9]

Christian missions created to convert the Jews seemed to be doing well. In 1816 a group of New York City philanthropists and churchmen formed the American Society for the Melioration of the Condition of the Jews whose purpose was to send missionaries to Jewish settlements in Europe and the Holy Land. Although it met with little real success, the society's periodical, *Israel's Advocate*, kept hopes alive with stories of dramatic conversions. The secular press borrowed stories from the *Advocate* and reported the same news to a wider audience. Catching the spirit of the times Mordecai Manuel Noah, a prominent Jew of New York City, tried to establish a Jewish commune appropriately called Ararat on Grand Island in Lake Erie near Buffalo as a new Jewish homeland, and his attempt received laudatory publicity from the secular press. While Christians' expectations were hardly realistic, they gloried in the warmth of the vision of Jewish conversion, one poetaster exclaiming,

> Praise him—ye tribes of Israel! praise
> The king that ransom'd you from woe!

[8] *New York Missionary Magazine*, I (1800), 2–3; "A View of the Millennial Felicity of the Church," *Connecticut Evangelical Magazine*, I (February, 1801), 320.

[9] Robert Scott, *An Antidote for Deism* (Pittsfield, 1816); Aaron B. Frosh, "Lake of Fire," *Connecticut Evangelical Magazine*, I (February, 1801), 320.

Nations! the hymn of triumph raise,
And bid the song of rapture flow.[10]

As time passed, despite accumulating missionary societies and the disseminations of tracts, the Millennium did not commence, and increased conversions failed to bring about the expected regeneration of the world. By 1830 human agency in creating the Millennium seemed to some to be futile, and from among disheartened expectants Millerism gained considerable support. E. E. Paine, a Millerite of DeWitt's Valley, wrote, "I have formerly been a believer in the world's conversion and a temporal millennium, which I now deem a fable, not found in the Bible." Now he believed the Bible taught "the destruction instead of the conversion of the wicked." Asahel Chapin, Baptist Millerite preacher in Jamestown, likewise stated, "I have abandoned my long and dearly cherished belief of the spiritual reign, and the universal triumph of the gospel, previous to the personal coming of Christ." Eliphalet Nott, though not a Millerite, expressed his disappointment in 1833, "If Christianity as it now exists should be propagated over the world, and thus the Millennium be introduced, we should need two or three millenniums before the world would be fit to live in."[11] This kind of disillusionment could turn a postmillennialist into a millenarian when he or she heard Miller speak of the rapidly approaching fulfillment of all prophecies when God would create the Millenium.

The principal difference between a belief in human agency and a belief in divine agency is that the latter implies something quite dreadful. Both promise the arrival of the Millennium, but in the view of the latter to get to the Millennium one must first undergo the terrors of the Apocalypse. To New Yorkers in the 1830s and '40s the theme of cataclysm was every bit as real as the shining vision of the New Jerusalem. Belief in the future destruction of the world and Last Judgment was an essential doctrine of all the evangelical churches. The 1830 covenant of the Chenango Presbytery, which was no different from any other, required belief in "a general resurrection of the body, and its reunion with the soul—that the saints in their glorified state will be clothed with spiritual bodies—that there will be a general Judgment: that the Lord Jesus Christ will judge the world in righteousness, and that from the Judgment-seat, according to his sentence, the righteous will be received

[10] See A. E. Thompson, *A Century of Jewish Missions* (Chicago, 1902). The publication of *Israel's Advocate* sparked a quick and heated rejoinder from Jews who published an opposing journal called the *Jew* that condemned the Society's work. For a biography of Noah and a history of Ararat see Isaac Goldberg, *Major Noah: American-Jewish Pioneer* (Philadelphia, 1938). The poem is "The Restoration of Israel," *Methodist Magazine*, III (1820), 120.
[11] E. E. Paine, *Midnight Cry*, April 13, 1843; Asahel Chapin, ibid., May 23, 1843; Codman Hislop, *Eliphalet Nott* (Middletown, Conn., 1971), 381–82.

into eternal blessedness in Heaven, and the wicked shall go away into endless misery in Hell." Many Presbyterian preachers believed the threat of the Last Judgment could "deter men from sin," and they exhorted their congregations with descriptions of the terrible scenes when "the judge shall appear in the clouds of heaven, clothed with awful majesty. . . . Then shall the last trumpet sound, & with tremendous blast shall awake the *slumbers* of the *tomb*. Thousands of miserable wretches would wish to lie undisturbed, & never hear the solemn summons. But no!—their wishes are utterly unavailing. . . . The dead in Christ, who at their death, were prepared to meet their God, will be caught up to meet the Lord in the air & so they will be forever with the Lord." Sinners would rise to meet the wrath "of an angry God." They would be consumed, the "heavens will melt with frervent heat; the Earth shall be burned with fire; & the rocks & the mountains will be no more found."[12]

Orthodox Baptists also employed these images. Typical was the warning of the Calvinistic New Hampshire Confession of Faith that "the end of this world is approaching: that at the last day, Christ will descend from heaven, and raise the dead from the grave to a final retribution: that a solemn separation will then take place: that the wicked will be adjudged to endless punishment, and the righteous to endless joy: and that this judgment will fix forever the final state of man in heaven or hell, on principles of righteousness." In their hymns the Methodists used the same imagery. "Let this earth dissolve, and blend/In death the wicked and the just;/ Let those pond'rous orbs descend,/ and grind us into dust." How terrible will be that day when "Nature, in wild amaze,/ Her dissolution mourns,/ Blushes of blood the moon deface;/ The sun to darkness turns."[13]

Natural imagery bridged the gap between formal apocalypticism of the theologians "from the top down" and vernacular apocalypticism "from the bottom up." Those who could not read or understand tomes on the prophecies could read the signs of the times in eclipses, thunder storms, and comets. The prophecies in Revelation identified God as an anthropomorphic deity of wrath, the Lord of Nature "who holds the lightning in his hands, and directs them where to strike." He was "Heaven's awful sovereign, whose almighty hand/Holds his dread sceptre o'er the subject land";[14] who would use the forces of nature as weapons to melt the world and destroy sinners. So while the Bible and formal

---

[12] *The Constitution of the Presbyterian Church in the United States of America* (Philadelphia, 1834), 135; Samuel Boorman Fisher, "Prepare to Meet Thy God," manuscript sermon, Samuel Boorman Fisher Papers, Cornell University.

[13] W. J. McGloughlin, *Baptist Confessions of Faith* (Philadelphia, 1911), 307; Methodist Episcopal Church, *A Collection of Hymns for the Use of the Methodist Episcopal Church* (New York, 1829), 498, 505.

[14] *Advocate for the People* (Auburn), September 17, 1817; "Description of a Storm," *Hudson Balance and Columbian Repository*, III (1804), 154.

apocalyptic pointed out the events to take place on the Last Day, nature provided evidence of God's ability and willingness to destroy the world.

In the rhetoric of popular apocalyptic thunder storms were omens of God's intent. One poetaster who found himself caught in a violent storm described the awesome power of the wind and lightning which had come, he felt, directly at the bidding of the Lord. "[F]ar as the keenest eye/ Can dart its vision, forests prostrate lie;/ The smiling trees with various fruitage crown'd/ And golden honors, prostrate strew the ground;/ Aghast and pale the aw'd spectators stand,/ And view the wonders of th' almighty hand." A second discomfited traveler published his poetic conclusion that the storm that lashed him was "but a preface to the day,/ An herald to proclaim abroad,/ That Christ the judge is on his way." To the Reverend Benjamin Russell, an upstate Presbyterian preacher of the 1830s, a heavy storm should be a reminder "of that day when the Deluge of Gods wrath will utterly abolish this mighty fabrick on which we stand." Soon will come the day "that shall burn as an oven, and all the proud, yea and all that do wickedly, shall [be] Stubble, and that day that cometh shall burn them up saith the Lord of Hosts." Stories abounded in the secular as well as religious press of the fateful, and fatal, significance of lightning. The *Rochester Telegraph* told of "a daughter of Mr. Barnett Peters, in Palmyra, [who] was summoned in a moment to the world of the spirits. . . . She was lying in bed with three of her younger sisters . . . when the fatal bolt, commissioned for her destruction, singled her out with such infinite precision that the three sisters around her were not injured. The ways of God are truly mysterious, and past finding out."[15]

Eclipses often evoked the Revelation prophecy that on the Last Day God would extinguish the light of the sun and shatter the moon. One writer described the fearful reaction of "unwarned swains" who thought a solar eclipse was a portent of the end of the world. "Plain honest kinds, who do not know the cause/ Nor know of orbs, their motion and their laws,/ Will from the half plow'd furrow homeward bend,/ in dire confusion, judging that the end/ Of time approacheth; thus possest with fear,/ They'll think the general conflagration near." Popular reaction in Albany to the total solar eclipse of June 16, 1808, proved the point. Eliphalet Nott witnessed the event and noted the reactions of a crowd of spectators among whom several "broke forth in supplications, some fainted and some were flung into convulsions." A scientist, Nott was

---

15 "Description of a Storm"; "Thoughts on a Thunder Storm," *Connecticut Evangelical Magazine*, II (1801), 4; Benjamin Russell, Diary and Autobiography, 1810–1896 (June 16, 1843), unpublished manuscript, Benjamin Russell Papers, Local and Regional History Collection, Cornell University; *Rochester Telegraph*, August 11, 1818.

anything but an unwarned swain, but even he could not repress a "tottering emotion" as the light of the sun seemed to be "extinguished and was to be rekindled no more. . . . It appeared as if the moon rode unsteadily in her orbit, and the earth seemed to tremble on its axis." Similarly, eclipses became reminders of the darkening of the earth at Christ's crucifixion, an "admonition to man—an omen of the destruction of Jerusalem and the dissolution of the world, and of the final judgment." During a very dark day in February of 1808, people participating in a court trial panicked "as there was every appearance of a sudden termination of earthly affairs, and that they, as well as others, would soon appear before a higher tribunal."[16]

The northern lights aroused similar fears. "Aurora Borealis, let others call/ This fearful display of Ominpotence—/ I acknowledge it to be the ensign/ Of the mighty God display'd on high to/ Warn a guilty world. The day's at hand, when/ From heav'n, drest in all glorious flames our God/ Shall come attended by his num'rous guards,/ To judge a guilty world, and a period,/ Put, to all things here on earth below." Heber Kimball, an early Mormon, remembered witnessing in September of 1827 an unusually spectacular display of northern lights in western New York. He saw in the dancing lights "the muskets, bayonets, and knapsacks of the men" marching for the Lord to the Battle of Armageddon. As the "front rank approached the western horizen," Kimball heard "the clanking and jingling of their instruments of war" and the "report of the arms and the rush" as God's forces closed with the ranked brigades of Satan in the sky. "No man could judge my feelings when I beheld the army of men as plainly as I ever saw armied men in the flesh. . . . [I]t seemed as though every hair of my head was alive."[17]

Secular trends in the arts contributed to the mood of impending disaster during the early nineteenth century. Farther removed from the life of the common people, high literature and painting exhibited much the same concern with cataclysm as did popular religion and theology, illustrating how deep the seam went. A preoccupation with themes of destruction, degeneration, and decay marked the romantic temper of the times. For Thomas Cole, painter of the Hudson River School, the inevitability of the Apocalypse was but the cosmic symbol of civilization's cyclical development. In his series of landscapes called "The Course of Empire" Cole portrayed society's development from simple pastoralism through republican and imperial stages, culminating in the general collapse of the nation in

---

[16] "The Solar Eclipse," *Hudson Balance*, V (1806), 224; Hislop, 111; "On the Crucifixion of Jesus Christ," *Connecticut Evangelical Magazine*, VIII (September 1806), 100; *Panoplist*, III (February 1808), 424.

[17] *Western New York Baptist Magazine*, I (June 1815), 238; Stanley P. Hirschson, *The Lion of the Lord: A Biography of Brigham Young* (New York, 1969), 8–9.

"Destruction." The fall of the Roman Empire provided a graphic model of this cycle. Particularly symbolic of the ultimate decay of man's works was the destruction of Pompeii described in graphic detail by Sumner Lincoln Fairfield and Bulwer Lytton.[18]

Evidence of nature's destructive power clearly convinced many that Miller's predictions were correct. Miller and others reminded their audiences that God had promised "signs in the sun and moon and stars" as portents of the approaching end of the world, and they invoked the long-held images of God as the Lord of Nature who would bring "voices, thunders, lightnings, a great earthquake" to the destruction of proud Babylon. Said Miller, "The natural world, fire, earth, air and water, are the instruments of death to man. The animal world, from the mastodon to the gnat, may be, and have been, the means of natural death. The mineral contains its poison, and produces death in all living. The vegetable, from the cedar to the hyssop are but so many weapons in the hands of the king of terrors, to bring men to the dust, and all living to their mother earth." So a "tempest of thunder and lightning, wind and rain" that inundated a Millerite camp meeting became a reminder of the "importance of *humbling* ourselves and not waiting for God to *humble us.*" Soon, the "foundations of the mighty globe shall tremble to their centre! The continents shall disappear, 'the elements shall melt with fervent heat,' and all the wicked upon the face of the whole earth shall become ashes!" This, wrote one Millerite, was "no fussy sketch. . . . The startling feature in the whole of this is that it is NEAR! IT DRAWETH NIGH!"[19]

Natural proof of this contention abounded. Millerites harkened back to the Dark Day of 1780, the Shower of Stars of 1833, and other peculiar astronomical phenomena to support their beliefs. Several adventists reported seeing the letters G-O-D appear in the sky "from a long narrow (or serpentine) silvery colored belt." Others saw peculiar lights surrounding Venus and Jupiter, and Henry Jones published a pamphlet about an unusual shower of "meat and blood" that fell on Jersey City in 1844. A cross on the moon became a promise that "Our Best Friend will come and will not tarry," and others cited "signs in the heavens" as evidence of the approaching Apocalypse. In 1843 a comet appeared in the night skies and produced great excitement among Millerites and non-Millerites alike. The effect of such phenomena is illustrated by an incident in Skaneateles. A Millerite preaching in the streets there met with a cold reception from the good people of the town who pummeled him with

18 Curtis Dahl, "The American School of Catastrophe," *American Quarterly*, XI (Fall 1959), 380–90.
19 *Circular Address of the General Conference . . . Held at Low Hampton, New York, November 2–5, 1841*, 67–68; Calvin French, *Signs of the Times*, August 24, 1842.

snowballs and dumped pails of water on his head. Scorn turned to apprehension, however, when they saw the comet "streaming halfway across
the sky," followed by a display of northern lights which "deployed in
line, and turned blood red." Afterwards, when the Millerite preached his
warnings of a "swift destruction to the earth and the inhabitants
thereof," the villagers paid closer attention. One witness to this later
preaching remembered it as a "scene to make a deep and thrilling
impression."[20]

Not everyone reacted to natural phenomena with fear. Rationalists
constantly decried against "superstitiousness" and lambasted the naiveté
it exhibited. Interestingly, so did many leading Millerites. Himes and
other newspaper editors, increasingly embarrassed by "mystical" elements in the movement, spoke out against reliance on peculiar events for
their faith. Regarding the appearance of the comet, the *Signs of the
Times* said, adventists "care little about such things. They believe that
the lord is coming, and that right speedily, and whether He sends this as
the messenger of His fury is immaterial." The *Midnight Cry* wrote in a
similar vein, "Our faith rests on the word of God, and such things are
not needed to confirm it."[21] Editors early adopted a policy of keeping
embarrassing material out of their papers. Henry Jones's letters and
articles appeared frequently until he published his pamphlet about the
shower of meat and blood on Jersey City, but after that his name never
appeared in major adventist journals again. Charles Fitch warned followers about placing too much reliance on astronomical evidence. "The
darkening of the light of sun, moon, and stars," he wrote, "must have a
figurative fulfillment, because there is to be no sign of our Savior's coming, that will open the eyes of an unbelieving world, until he shall come
upon them as a thief in the night." Because astronomical phenomena are
visible to everyone—not just to the Elect—they could not be portents.
Himes too publicly castigated those who cited "evidence wholly independent of the prophetic periods," and he added sarcastically, "Thus the
Lord is giving us premonitions of his coming suited to minds of every
class."[22] But though they might take steps to dissociate themselves from
such attitudes, they could not obliterate them. Secular newspapers gleefully published adventists' interpretations of natural events though the
Millerite papers did not. Here was an early sign of the leaders' inability
to control their mass movement in the last years of the crusade's life.

Another such indication was the ease with which impressionable free

[20] Veritas, *Midnight Cry*, March 10, 1843; Henry Jones, *Modern Phenomena of the
Heavens* (New York, 1843); W. M. Beuchamp, "Notes of Other Days in Skaneateles,"
Annual Volume of the Onondaga Historical Association, 1914 (Syracuse, 1914), 76–77.
[21] *Signs of the Times*, March 29, 1843; *Midnight Cry*, April 13, 1843.
[22] Charles Fitch, *Midnight Cry*, December 23, 1842; Himes, ibid.

thinkers attached themselves to Millerism to publicize their own peculiar prophecies. Messianism is another form of popular apocalypticism with which adventists had to live, like it or not. Throughout history world redeemers, reborn Christs, and modern-day Eliases, male and female, have proclaimed themselves to the startled masses, sometimes gaining adherents, almost always meeting with imprisonment and harassment, often finding their careers terminated on the gibbet or at the stake. Such cases became more numerous, and more significant, during times of political unrest such as the Puritan Revolution of the 1640s and '50s, the Reformation, the French Revolution of 1789. In reality such prophets are always around us with their dire warnings and reminding us that earthly comforts are transitory. Whether they see salvation coming in God's fiery chariot or in flying saucers, these prophets belong to the same tradition of messianism.[23]

During the 1830s and '40s, Millerism was but one expression of the period's millenarian expectancy, and Miller but one of its proponents. Compared with some he was very conventional. Other leaders also attracted wide followings and succeeded in establishing sects. The Shakers, for example, had existed since the 1770s, but in the 1840s they achieved probably the height of their support. According to their beliefs, Mother Ann Lee, the sect's founder, was the female personification of Jesus Christ. When God imbued her with the Holy Ghost, prophecies of the Second Coming of Christ were fulfilled, and thus the Shakers believed they were actually living in the Millennium. Therefore they were peculiarly premillennial.

But while the Millerites looked forward to the Parousia, the Shakers believed it had already taken place. Despite this theological distinction, to Miller's horror an affinity did exist between Shaker and Millerite millenarianism. Predictions of the impending return of Christ coincided with Shaker dreams of the immediate reunification with the male/female Godhead and the end of terrestrial history. Also, the Shakers themselves inaugurated a new mysticism in the early 1840s. Always highly spiritual, they believed that they enjoyed a direct connection with the next world, and their rites included visions, speaking in tongues, and receiving messages and spiritual gifts from the departed. In 1843 and 1844 many family communities created special "Holy Mount Zions" in secret locations on hills or in woods close by their settlements. Here occurred very special spiritual feasts and ceremonies the meaning of which is not exactly clear. Perhaps in these holy locations the Shakers felt closest to God. At any rate, the premillennial significance of this phenomenon, coming as it did at the height of the Millerite movement,

---

[23] An excellent cross-cultural study of prophets is Mircea Eliade, *Shamanism: Archaic Techniques of Ecstasy* (New York, 1964).

is clear. Both emphasized Zion as the home of the Christian, and although the Millerites foresaw its physical descent in 1843 and the Shakers spiritualized its meaning, both groups looked forward to living soon on its slopes.[24]

Not surprisingly, therefore, we find an occasional Shaker trumpeting predictions about the end of the world under the aegis of Millerism. The most colorful was Michael H. Barton, who often lectured with other Millerite itinerants. In his public discourses he displayed such Shaker gifts as speaking in tongues, prophesying the future, spiritual healing—and claimed these gifts as proof that the Lord was on his way. In a long letter to Miller, Barton described a particularly clear vision in which God had told him "by dream, and by two open visions that a pure church must be developed to the world" before the Last Judgment. God then took him on a spiritual journey around the world to show him that this was actually happening. "I left my body and found myself flying thru the air. At length I found myself in heaven, and heard a voice saying 'I am Christ.' But the Being who said I am Christ left heaven with us and drawed me after him to the earth, as a nickel would be drawn by a powerful load stone." Barton then watched as God showered blessings on the Millerites. Here was proof that God was preparing the world for the Second Coming of Christ. He said, "Things are moving just as I saw in my trance."[25] The rationalistic Miller must have cringed as he read this letter.

Another important millennial sect of this period was the Church of Jesus Christ of the Latter Day Saints, or Mormon Church, founded in Manchester, New York, by Joseph Smith in 1831, the same year Miller began preaching. Like Millerites, the Mormons believed the Second Coming of Christ was yet to take place, but they believed Smith's rediscovery and publication of the Book of Mormon inaugurated the Latter Days preparatory to the arrival of the Millennium. There is little direct evidence of Mormon participation in the Millerite movement, although Miller once noted with shock that the Mormons were among those drawn to his views. But the influence of Millerism on Mormons may have been the reason Joseph Smith published among the last of his revelations God's assurance to him that "the Lord will not come to reign over the righteous in this world in 1843, nor until everything for the bridegroom is ready."[26]

[24] For Shaker theology see Edward Deming Andrews, *The People Called Shakers* (New York, 1953), and a contemporary elucidation by the Shakers themselves, *A Concise Statement of the Principles of the Only True Church* (Bennington, VT, 1790).
[25] Michael H. Barton to Miller, April 19, 1844; for a description of his public lecturing see the *Baptist Advocate*, April 16, 1844. A marvelous source book on all mid-nineteenth century sects is John Winebrenner, publisher, *History of the Religious Denominations of the United States* (Harrisburg, 1848). Leaders of each sect wrote articles about their particular group for this book. For the Shakers see pages 567–69.
[26] See in Winebrenner, "Latter-day Saints, or Mormons," 244–349.

The early nineteenth-century doctrine of Perfectionism, sometimes referred to as Perfect Sanctification or the Higher Life, was closely akin to millennialism. Proponents believed that once an individual devoted full faith to Christ, the Lord could restrain the believer from falling into further sin, that he or she could actually achieve perfect sanctification in this world. Thus, humans had the power to create the Millennium by converting everyone and thus destroying evil. The doctrine flowed quite logically from Finney's New School Theology, and it was a principal theological position of Oberlin College. Charles Fitch, an Oberlin graduate and leading Millerite itinerant, was a Perfectonist disciple. Others included E. B. Crandall, Butler Morley, and David Plumb of Utica. Wrote one anonymous adventist, "God does 'permit' many of his dear children here to 'go on unto perfection,' attain 'the full assurance of hope,' and 'lay hold upon it as an anchor of the soul, both SURE and STEADFAST.'"[27]

Though never responsible for the creation of a particular sect, the doctrine of Perfectionism was responsible for many cultic expressions (under the leadership of a strong charismatic spokesperson), including the Oneida Community founded by John Humphrey Noyes in Oneida, New York. A Finney convert, he preached that Christ had already returned the second time and that the world now exists in a probationary period in which individuals may achieve perfect sanctification. Oneida was essentially a community of Saints striving for perfection. Its most famous characteristic was its program of scientific matching of sexual partners, called stirpiculture. Oneida's reputation for peculiarity in this regard was but one instance of Perfectionism's unwholesomeness, at least so far as the general public was concerned. Rumors flew that Perfectionist groups practiced feet washing, free love, spiritual wifery, naked dancing, and the like. Because of the nature of the doctrine, some of these stories may be well-founded. With Perfectionists in the Millerite movement, much of this reputation and some of these rites worked their way into the crusade. For instance, a Perfectionist commune in Hannibal, New York, reportedly kept a dead child in the parlor and attempted by constant prayer to raise it from the dead. A similar incident took place among Millerites in Jamaica, Vermont, and it was reported in the Millerite press. Ira Young, an early Millerite of the 1830s, had founded a sizable adventist group there. On October 15, 1844, Young's wife died, and because this occurred so close to the final predicted date for the Apocalypse, "most of the brethren and sisters were strong in the faith that she would be raised, and remain with them till the Lord should appear." Accordingly they laid the body in a bedroom and prayed over it around the clock. Rigor mortis set in and then departed, after which

27 Butler Morley, *Midnight Cry*, December 21, 1843.

"her body for the most part resumed nearly its usual warmth [and] a sweet smile remained upon her countenance." A posse of townspeople who had heard about these strange proceedings arrived at the house and demanded an inquest, obviously supposing that someone, perhaps the entire Millerite band, had murdered her. This intervention had disastrous effects, for in the excitement the group stopped praying over her. "She not only lost her warmth, but so great was the change, she would scarcely have been recognized as the same person." It was all the fault of the mob, reported the adventists. "There are no doubts in the minds of the brethren and sisters then present, that had the rabble remained away, she would have been raised to life again."[28]

Thus Shakerism, Mormonism, and Perfectionism contributed to the apocalyptic and millennial expectation of the 1830s and '40s. They and Millerism interacted, not always to the liking of the adventist leaders. Other prophets of the day who never achieved wide followings took advantage of the millenarian excitement to publish their own tracts and preach their own messianic messages. An interesting example is John T. Matthews who in 1842 published a tract he called *A Key to the Old and New Testaments, Exhibited by the Initials of the White Stone*. He claimed that in 1812 while serving in the war against Britain he found a small white stone that had mysteriously materialized in his pocket. On the stone were two letters—either S and M or W and S, depending on which way one held it. Matthews believed they meant either "Secret of Masonry" or "World's Savior." God had promised to give a secret stone to "him that overcometh" as a sign of power, wrote Matthews, and this white stone must be the very one, proof that God had chosen him to be "the promised comforter." Through the stone's special powers of discernment, Matthews had discovered that God would return to earth in 1848 and give him "power over all nations of this earth." Everyone must "yield to my commands," he warned. Those who would not, he would "break in pieces like the vessels of a potter."[29]

There seems to have been no relation between this man and Robert Matthews, the notorious Matthias. This Matthews was from Washington County, near Miller's farm. Like Miller and John Matthews, his prophetic career began shortly after the War of 1812. He gained a local

---

[28] Perry, *Midnight Cry*, December 12, 1844; the story is also recounted in David M. Ludlum, *Social Ferment in Vermont, 1771–1850* (New York, 1939), 257–58; on the Hannibal incident see the *Gospel Advocate* (January 3, 1840), 1. One must bear in mind that the *Advocate* was a Universalist journal and loved to publicize stories that discredited the orthodox sects. However, there is no evidence this story was concocted; indeed, in Oswego today there is a home on a public square said to have housed a family that also tried to resurrect a dead child. Possibly these two stories are of the same incident, the location having become confused.

[29] John T. Matthews, *A Key to the Old and New Testament* (New York, 1842).

reputation for zealousness, and in 1830 he began to predict disasters around the world. He went to New York and teamed up with a Mr. Pierson, who called himself "Elijah the Tishbite." Matthews changed his name to Matthias, proclaimed himself to be a Jew, and kept a kosher kitchen. He preached in the streets of the city, carrying a large ruler with which, he claimed, he would measure all men at the Last Judgment. He, Pierson, and a small band of followers established a residence in the village of Sing Sing and hired to keep house a black woman who later took the name Sojourner Truth. The commune ended violently when Pierson was murdered and authorities charged Matthias with the crime. Though exonerated, he fled the state and went west.[30]

Neither of these self-proclaimed messiahs was a Millerite, though Matthias's proximity to Miller's home and the strong adventist support in Washington County suggests he might have received ideas from his neighbor. Still, so far as the general public was concerned, all prophets were equally fanatical, and adventists suffered from the adverse publicity they caused.

Both formal and popular apocalyptic shaped the culture out of which Millerism arose, the most dramatic and widespread but not the only millenarian movement of the 1830s and '40s. Contemporary millennial rhetoric provides evidence of the prevalence of these beliefs and also illustrates Millerism's essential orthodoxy. In perusing early nineteenth-century archival resources, one often has difficulty deciding whether or not a particular writer was a Millerite, for Millerism's imagery was common to all evangelicals. Judah L. Richmond was a Baptist preacher in Chautauqua County and brother-in-law of a well-known Millerite itinerant lecturer. He was "not convinced that this world will perish this . . . year," he wrote in his 1843 diary, but he was sure that "the time is not far distant when that momentous event will take place." He expressed many of the adventists' social biases which we will encounter later, and he interpreted current sin and wickedness as signs "of the last times." Without hesitation he prayed, "'Come, Lord Jesus, come quickly.'" But there is no evidence that he crossed the line from conventional millennialism to adventism. Also Lavinia Rose of South Cortland wrote letters to her aunt Elizabeth Abell in the 1830s full of religious and, seemingly adventist imagery. "The night cometh when no man can work," she advised her aunt. "I expect if we live, to visit you before the year closes, but hope not to boast of tomorrow. It seems as if the stream of time runs more swiftly than formerly. I feel the importance of having our work done, our lamps trimmed and burning." Thus could any number of Millerites have written, but again there is no evidence that she was an adventist. Most likely the event she was expecting

---

[30] See William L. Stone, *Matthias and His Impostures* (New York, 1835), and Sojourner Truth, *Narrative of Sojourner Truth* (Chicago, 1970 ed.), 64–73.

was not the Second Coming of Christ but her own death and personal judgment.[31]

Obviously, one quality that set Millerism apart from the millennialism of the age was the set time, Miller's prediction that the Apocalypse and Parousia would occur "sometime in 1843." This prediction seems to militate against the movement's rhetorical and theological orthodoxy, for had not the Bible said regarding these events that "of that day and hour knoweth no man"? Miller honestly responded that he did not predict a specific time. "The day and hour are not revealed, but the *times* are."[32] To some this appeared an evasion of the Bible's intent, to keep the day secret to ensure that Christ would come unawares, like a thief in the night. Though formal and popular apocalyptic could make Miller's themes believable, how could adventists ignore the tradition of secrecy regarding time?

Many adventists did not. A large number never accepted the predicted time; nor did they preach it publicly. But for those who did, the predicted year rested on a firm foundation. Through the centuries, interpreters of the prophecies (eschatologists) have approached chronology in different ways. To many, particularly since the 1870s, the prophecies in Daniel, Revelation, and other books of the Bible foretell events that will occur immediately before the end of time. But historicists, like Miller, believe these prophecies are like a cosmic clock running inexorably from the first second of Creation toward the last moment of time and the fulfillment of all the prophecies (Eschaton). Thus history reveals the world's progress toward this Great Event. Beginning almost immediately after the crucifixion of Christ and continuing to the present day, exegetes trained and untrained in theology have searched the scriptures, compared the "types" (prophecies) with actual historical and astronomical events, and compiled charts and chronologies (some of them finely-tuned hermeneutics, others jumbled speculation) setting forth hundreds of different agendas for the end of the world. Through the years, historicist speculation has focused on particular years—1000, 1689, 1843.[33] Miller's hermeneutic was part of this long tradition, and he was but one of many interpreters who predicted a great event in 1843. That year made sense for empirical reasons. The numbers worked! Computing the year when the Beast would fall and the prophecies come to their

[31] Judah L. Richmond, Diary, 1844, microfilm of the original held by the University of North Carolina; Lavinia Rose to Elizabeth Abell, March 13, 1836, August 2, 1839, August 7, 1842, Abell Family Papers, Local and Regional History Collection, Cornell University.

[32] Miller to Hendryx, October 23, 1834; also see *Signs of the Times*, January 4, 1843; and White, 177.

[33] Froom, particularly vol. III. See also Henry Focillon, *The Year 1000* (New York, 1969), and Peter Toon, *Puritans, The Millennium and the Return of Israel* (Cambridge, MA, 1970).

fulfillment was not a mystical or peculiar feat. Any mathematician could do the same thing and prove the prediction for himself or herself.

And the Millerites did just that. Miller once wrote that he did not rely much on "profane history" to prove his theory, but he recognized its value in swaying audiences. History, he once wrote, "is an argument to convince the men of the world that the Bible is true, for they are always ready to admit profane history. But not the Bible." He and other advent lecturers spent weeks in Bible classes and lectures painstakingly leading their audiences "by slow and easy steps" along the advent chronology. Thus Napoleon's capture of Rome in 1798 terminated the Pope's temporal power, the French Revolution of 1789 fulfilled the opening of the sixth seal, the Greek Revolution of 1820 testified to the waning power of the Moslem heathen and completed the prophecy of the opening of the sixth vial, and so on. People in the audiences worked along with the lecturer for they had their own charts or blackboards. This empirical method was quite effective. One adventist wrote to the *Midnight Cry,* "I do not see how any person acquainted with the rise and fall of the kingdoms of this world, can for one moment doubt that Daniel has given us a brief and faithful outline of the world's history, from the head of gold, down to that fearful and alarming position we are now occupying." Surely the time of the end "is not far distant."[34] Once again, in terms of their exegetical method, the Millerites could argue cogently that they were orthodox, rational, traditional.

As with so many other elements of Millerism, exegesis had a dual effect. Millerites could justify the predicted year on the grounds of empiricism and a long tradition of historicist exegesis, and thus attract a certain rational element into the movement. But advocacy of the set time also rested on an emotional base. Many people believed the predictions because they *wanted* to believe them, because Millerism promised the final realization of the Christian's dream—release from the sin and pain of this world and union with God in love, peace, and joy. Arguments of the mind mattered not so much as the yearnings of the heart, and whereas religious intellect might be susceptible to authority and conformity, religious sentiment would not. For Millerism promised more than just the fulfillment of prophecy. It comprehended the pietist core of Christians' religious life and became the vehicle by which hundreds reshaped their lives in the light of New Jerusalem's warming glow.

[34] Miller to Hendryx, November 28, 1834; Horace S. Burchard, *Midnight Cry*, February 8, 1844. For a full exposition of Miller's historicist exegesis see *Views of the Prophetic Chronology* (Boston, 1842).

Chapter 5
PRISONERS OF HOPE

Pietism was as significant a force as revivalism and millennialism in shaping the Millerite movement's personality, but to understand the reason for Millerism's rise and popularity, one must consider the combined effect of all three. Revivalism, essentially a method for inculcating commitment to God, provided the vehicle for evangelizing Christianity and Millerism in the world. Millennialism, a fairly structured theological doctrine, set the intellectual framework for the movement and the culture from which it emerged. Pietism's contribution was to define the individual's relationship to God, a relationship that simultaneously defined his or her position in this world. Whereas revivalism supplied the method and millennialism the idea, pietism established the temperament for the Millerite crusade. Let us now investigate what pietism was, how it affected the religious culture of New Yorkers in the 1830s and 1840s, and how it shaped Millerism's view of and response to the world.

All people yearn for release from earthly troubles, for a life of peace and joy in which all requirements are met, for union with Divinity, and for an eternity of love. To Christians this Millennial dream unites the dual images of the Edenic garden of simplicity, innocence, and beauty and the apostolic church with its collective purity and grace and projects them into the future, the New Jerusalem, where all will be restored under God's direct rule. As one New York State preacher put it, "In times of darkness and calamity, Christians ought not to despond. These things are a sure pledge of the certain accomplishment of all the good things which God has promised to his Church." Indeed, to Eliphalet Nott, the children of God were "prisoners of hope." Caught in a worldly cage of pain and wickedness, their only guarantee of release in this life was the establishment of the Millennium and the final victory of righteousness over sin.[1] Other Americans defined this perfectionist vision in secular terms—manifest destiny, communitarian socialism, moral reform—but whatever contemporary Americans called it, the vision was similar for all. America was destined to be the spiritual, moral, and economic model for the rest of the world.

[1] Fisher, "Revelation 11:3.6," unpaginated, manuscript sermon, Fisher Papers; Nott, *A Discourse Delivered in the North Dutch Church in the City of Albany . . . July 29, 1804* (Albany, 1804), 32.

Pietism is the process by which this dream inspires behavior in this world. William G. McLoughlin has defined pietism as an imperative to moral action, "the belief that every individual is responsible for deciding the rightness or wrongness of every issue (large or small) in terms of a higher moral law; that he must make this decision the moment he is confronted with any question in order to prevent any complicity with evil; and having made his decision, he must commit himself to act upon it at once, taking every opportunity and utilizing every possible method to implement his decision not only for himself and in his own home or community, but throughout the nation and the world."[2] This process implies specific qualities. First, pietism is *individualistic*—each person is responsible for making moral decisions. Second, it is *comprehensive*, calling for the eradication of worldwide sin. Pietism thus may express itself in evangelism, a word from the Greek *evangelos* meaning "to bear good news."[3] Some pietists, though, are not evangelical, but feel it sufficient to protect themselves from participating in sin by removing themselves from the world and creating a fortress against evil (the Amish, for instance). Third, it tends to be *immediatist*, though we will soon encounter one form of pietism that is more immediatist than a second. But this essentially humanist definition omits two specifically Christian qualities. Pietism is also, fourth, *Biblist*, for it is only in the revealed word of God that the believer can find the necessary information on which to base moral decisions and action. Also, pietists believe that all Christians can understand the Bible on their own, that the revealed word of God is absolutely clear to those who truly seek its meaning. Finally, fifth, pietism is *Christological*—it is only through the suffering, death, and resurrection of Christ that the individual can participate freely in the moral universe.

A subtle relationship exists between pietism, revivalism, and millennialism. Revivals and the conversion experience are the process by which the individual commits himself or herself to make moral decisions. Millennialism gives specific shape to pietists' dream by envisioning the New Jerusalem and providing the cosmic timetable for its construction and completion. Pietism, then, guides the convert's life in this world in preparation for living with God in the Heavenly City.

But here we encounter the pietist's dilemma. *How* should they live? What are the specific obligations and rules that must guide them? If the

---

[2] William G. McLoughlin, "Pietism and the American Character," *American Quarterly*, XVII (Summer 1965):173.

[3] Social scientists have tried to portray an evangelical sociology that led in the nineteenth century to moral reform. I would argue that they are confusing evangelicalism with pietism, the former being principally a method for fulfilling the pietistic dream worldwide closely associated with revivals. Much of what they would describe as evangelicalism is here elucidated as pietism.

individual is personally responsible for destroying sin, what methods should one use? Or is it enough simply to protect one's own sanctity, to gather the Elect together in the visible Church and shut out the wicked world? In other words, what is the proper behavior of a pietist? The Bible contains the answer, of course, and it is the pietist's obligation to find the answer by studying the Bible in the light of God's grace. But then how does one know whether the answer he or she receives comes from God? Is direct revelation legitimate, and if so how does one verify it? Who should have the authority to verify revelation or Biblical interpretation? The process of trying to reconcile these dilemmas creates what we might call the pietistic dynamic.

Traditionally pietists have answered these questions in one of two ways. One group, the formal pietists, emphasizes the word—the law, authority, and structure as revealed in the Bible and incorporated in Christian institutions. Churches, tract societies, Sunday schools, all have the quadruple functions of interpreting scripture, evangelizing the world, converting sinners to righteousness, and enforcing obedience to the rule of divine law. Institutions assume authority to specify behavior by elucidating law and then persuading others to live by those laws. We have already encountered a similar temperament in postmillennialism which looks to human agencies to perfect the world in preparation for the inauguration of the Millennium. This attitude is also present in orthodox Calvinism of the Old School. The second group, the antiformal pietists, emphasizes the spirit over the word. They believe individuals must be absolutely free to interpret the Bible in the special light God gives them, implying a more direct relationship with God. Antiformalists believe human agencies are inadequate to reform sin—only God has the power to do that by working directly on sinners. Human authority inevitably absorbs human depravity and holds the potential for setting itself up in opposition to God's authority. Those who believe this are closely akin to premillennialists and Perfectionists.

Both formalism and antiformalism are necessary to the pietistic dynamic. All pietists recognize the need for *both* the word and the spirit, authority and inspiration, collectivism and individualism. In trying to balance these conflicting needs the pietistic dynamic manifests itself. Long ago Ernst Troeltsch and H. Richard Niebuhr described this process in terms of the social development of sects. According to their theory, a sect arises as part of a spiritual rebellion against calcified denominational authority. As churches lose the spirit of Christianity, they come to emphasize law and structure. Those who seek to revivify the spirit rebel against the church and its clergy, separate from the churches, and then over time establish their own polity, which then eventually emphasizes

authority once more until a new rebellion takes place, the process beginning once again.[4] Thus we witness the struggle between formalism and
antiformalism. An excellent example of how the process works is the rise
of the antinomian sects in New England in the 1770s and 1780s—the
Free Will Baptists, Universalists, and the Shakers—that Stephen Marini
has described. Nor need we limit our search for the dynamic to American pietism. British Puritanism, German Protestantism, and a number of
sects in Medieval and Renaissance Europe were products of it, as was the
short-lived Jewish messianic cult centering on Sabbatai Zevi. Indeed, we
can consider the rise of Christianity itself an attempt to recreate the
spirit of rabbinical Judaism in the face of stultified Pharisaic authority.[5]

In this light we can best understand how Millerism became a mass
movement in the 1830s and 1840s. Essentially, the Millerite movement was
an antiformalist rebellion against the formalization of the evangelical
pietistic denominations. Millerism was only one, albeit the most dramatic,
expression of this rebellion. Others were the Christian Unionists, Perfectionists, Mormons, the new brand of Shaker spiritualism of the 1840s, and
other smaller groups. All expressed the pietist's denigration of materialism
and worldliness which they shared with formalists, but also they condemned corruption in the pietistic churches which, they felt, were selling
out to "the world." They all sought the victory of the spirit over human
institutions secular and religious, in the revelation of Christ's united and
restored Church of the Elect—a primitive church that would live according to the spirit and polity of the apostles and early martyrs. Though they
shared this vision with formalists, the antiformalists of the 1830s and 1840s
denied the capacity of existing churches to create the Restored Church,
and they provided their own alternative methods for building that Church.
In formulating its specific alternative to the sects each group exhibited its
exclusivity—each felt it had found the correct answer and rejected all
other alternatives. The Millerites believed Christ would create the
Restored Church when He comes again, and increasingly this belief
became an article of faith for them, a process that eventually drove them to
sectarianism. Their differences with other antiformalists, however, reveal

[4] This theory is presented in Ernst Troeltsch, *The Social Teaching of the Christian
Churches* (New York, 1949–1950), and H. Richard Niebuhr, *Social Sources of Denominationalism* (New York, 1929).

[5] In contrast with Marini, I ascribe rebellious antinomianism in this period to a particular quality of pietism rather than to evangelicalism. Also, I wonder how "radical" these
groups were; has Marini accepted a label their opponents placed on them? If so, we
should seek a more objective term to describe them. Finally, in discovering common
denominators among these groups, an essential task for any comparativist, perhaps Marini
has neglected qualities of each group that made them exclusivist. Why did antinomian
groups condemn each other as much as they fought orthodoxy? For a review of the birth
of European denominational pietism see F. Ernest Stoeffler, *The Rise of Evangelical
Pietism* (Leiden, 1971).

the distinguishing quality of Millerism and the reason for its mass appeal. Let us then examine Millerism within the context of antiformal rebellion first by establishing Millerism's pietist credentials and searching for the roots of adventist pietism in the evangelical churches from which the Millerites principally came; second by discussing anti-formalists' critique of the evangelical churches and the rise of restorationist sects;[6] and third by elucidating Millerism's particular antagonism toward the churches and the process by which that antagonism drove them to separatism.

Since the settlement of Plymouth Plantation, pietism has been a dominant quality of American Protestantism. Puritanism itself represented a Calvinist pietistic rebellion against the authoritarianism and "deadness" of the Anglican Church. German Reformed sects in Pennsylvania and the Transmontane region and the Dutch Reformed Church in New York were likewise pietistic products of the Reformation. From 1740 to 1800 there was a decided shift in America toward antiformalism and against the spiritual "incompetence" of the formalist churches—Presbyterians, Congregationalists, and Anglicans particularly. Two forces account for this. First, revivalism militated in favor of emotion and the spirit and against doctrinalism. Although Jonathan Edwards and others tried to intellectualize Calvinism, revivals affected the converts' hearts as much as their brains.

The second force was physical mobility. Settlement of the Connecticut Valley and central New York in the last decades of the eighteenth century made antiformalism inevitable. With few preachers on the frontier, with clerical authority far removed, and with emotion in religion high, the door was open for individual initiative, for reliance on the Bible and on direct personal revelation rather than on doctrine, and for volunteerism in the calling of churches and pastors rather than formal ordination. Stephen Rensselaer Smith, a pioneer Universalist preacher in early nineteenth-century New York, noticed that many "who had thought little of the importance of public worship [in their former homes], when it might be attended without inconvenience, now felt the absence of the privilege as among the greatest of their many privations." This was particularly true of parents who feared that "their children might *possibly* grow up unaccustomed to the quiet devotion, the humanizing and elevating influences of the public Sunday worship." The result was improvised interdenominational and non-creedal meetings and revivals where theological differences among the attendants drowned in emotional fervor. Frequently, continued Smith, "it was less a matter of

6 The term *restorationist* has a specific theological meaning. Restorationists believe the souls of the dead will be remade in righteousness and joined with Christ on the Last Day. Here I use the word to suggest the attempt to restore the primitive church of the early apostles and martyrs.

consideration of who would preach, or to what denomination he belonged, than that it furnished an opportunity of attending church."[7]

The combined effect of revivalism and physical mobility created an environment in which antiformalism could exhibit itself in the triumph of the Methodist and Baptist Churches and in the rise of new sects. The Baptists' polity, emphasizing the independence of each congregation and the calling of an untrained lay clergy, and the Methodists' circuit riders met the frontier's needs for preaching, and the Baptists (being less structured than the Methodists) met its desires for lay control of the church. Several smaller sects also arose that were dedicated to antiformal pietism. By 1800 a sizable number of Methodists in North Carolina and Virginia, Baptists in Vermont and New Hampshire, and Presbyterians and Baptists in Pennsylvania, Kentucky, and Tennessee rebelled against creeds in their churches and established independent Christian congregations. Eventually throughout the South most of these congregations merged with the Campbellites to form the Disciples of Christ, but in the North the Christianites maintained their independence and formed a loose confederation, the Christian Connexion. As we know, it was from the Connexion and from the Baptist Church that most New York Millerites came. Their pietism shaped Millerism's view of the world.

As Nott suggested, the pietist while living in this world constantly yearns for the next. E. E. Paine, a Millerite in New York's Southern Tier, wrote in a characteristic way, "The subject of the 'new heavens and earth, wherein dwelleth righteousness,' is a glorious thing for contemplation; and the hope that I have of being an inhabitant of that country—of which new Jerusalem is the capital, God its everlasting king, 'where the righteous bear rule, and the people rejoice,' where the 'wicked cease from troubling, and the weary are at rest,' where there will be no more oppression, intemperance, licentiousness, profanity, sabbath breaking, etc., of which our land and world is full—fills me with joy and gladness."[8] Thus Millerites anticipated the final fulfillment of the pietist's dream, but the dream itself was not specifically Millerite. Pietists of all stamps in every age have yearned for the same thing. The New Jerusalem beckons to them like a great lamp that illuminates not only the glories of the age to come but also the depravity of the world as it is. This bright vision provides both the pietist's goal and the basis of a scathing social critique.

In the 1830s and '40s pietists felt besieged. They felt that social and political change focused the individual's attention on worldly power and wealth and distracted the pious Christian from his or her true responsibility, living a Godly life and preparing for union with God in the next

[7] Stephen Rensselaer Smith, *Historical Sketches and Incidents Illustrative of the Establishment and Progress of Universalism in the State of New York* (Buffalo, 1843), 244–45.

[8] E. E. Paine, *Midnight Cry*, April 30, 1840.

world. When we peruse the minutes of Baptist association meetings and the writings of Christianites, we see the source of Millerite condemnation of the world.

Pietists were hostile to professional politics. Jacksonian Democracy had released the libertarianism implicit in the basically deferential political system of the Jeffersonians and had opened the suffrage and offices to more men than ever before. In proclaiming this popular democracy the Jacksonians (and the Whigs who assumed the Democrats' rhetoric after 1836) stole Christians' attention away from religion and focused it instead on worldly ambition. Pietists condemned the ballyhoo of political barbeques and rallies particularly during the presidential elections of 1840 and 1844. Averred one Baptist association, "Many professing godliness seem to be more solicitous touching the success and ultimate triumph of the political party to which they belong, than the cause of God or the salvation of perishing sinners." Wrote another, the "political excitement, ceremonies and measures" of the day truly produced "degenerate times." Millerites said much the same thing. "Politics has been the all engrossing theme for some time," wrote Himes, and E. B. Crandall was angry that religion in Troy was "at a low ebb—politics on the top notch." He deprecated the fact that from Maine to Georgia "the cry of Log Cabin, Reform—Harrison and Old Tip forever is the song as they go up and down—to and fro."[9] The adventists' objections went further than those of other pietists. Their reason for concern was that politics diverted attention and interest from their own more important campaign.

Materialism was another serious distraction from religion. Americans in the period were preoccupied with acquiring riches, and to pietists the price of progress seemed too high. In their "eager pursuit of wealth," wrote the Harmony Baptist Association, speculators often overreached "the bounds of honesty," cheating not only worldly men (which was bad enough) but brethren in the church as well. "The sinfulness and pernicious influence of such a course are readily discovered," and no person of integrity "can fail to look upon it with merited contempt." The Millerites described materialism as one of the predicted signs of the Last Days when people would show great "desire for riches and laying up of worldly treasures." They condemned "our rich men laying up their gold, silver, and treasures in abundance. . . . Go to, ye rich men, weep and holler, for your miseries are come upon you." Christians "should retrench from the consumption of the Lord's goods for their own enjoyment." They should not "expend one particle of the Lord's goods, for their

9 *Minutes of the Oswego Baptist Association, 1844,* 12–13; *Monroe Baptist Association, 1844,* 11; Himes to Miller, November 12, 1840, Himes Papers; E. B. Crandall to Miller and William S. Miller, both letters dated September 24, 1840.

present enjoyment, except to preserve human life, and health." Again, adventists went further than other pietists in condemning the hoarding of wealth. What if Christ were to come and find that a believer had held onto money "which might have done much good to the poor and needy, and assisted in spreading knowledge on this subject [the Second Coming of Christ]." As one conference report bluntly put it, "It is the *duty of all who say they believe* that Christ will come in 1843, or that he is near, to make such disposal of their earthly possessions, in the distribution of publications on this subject, and in sustaining those who have given themselves wholly to the work of proclaiming, 'Behold the Bridegroom cometh, go ye out to meet him,' as will give them joy when they see 'God in glory and the world on fire.'"[10]

Necessarily new institutions such as banks, insurance companies, and corporations that arose to accumulate and manage wealth met with pietist disapproval. The people generally blamed the panic of 1837 on banks, and the Millerites reflected a significant segment of public opinion when they condemned as signs of the times the many "companies and monopolies" that the rich used to "heap treasures together." When in the history of the world, asked the *Signs of the Times*, "can there be shown so many banking institutions as now? When so much insurance capital as is heaped together at this day? Are not our rich men perfectly infatuated with stocks of all kinds? Monopoly is the order of the day; to grind down the poor, and heap treasures together for the last days. Can any man, who has knowledge of these things, deny that this sign of the last days is now evidently accomplished?"[11]

And where were wealth, banks, and sin of all sorts located? In the growing cities. Wrote the Washington Union Baptist Association, "Our cities and villages, of every class, present scenes of awfully blackened depravity. It walks at noon day—it is dressed in the richest attire—it assumes the more refined culture—it sits in the most fashionable circles—and, it is to be feared, meddles, too unceremoniously, with the holy things of our religious institutions." Miller lectured in New York City in 1842, and what he saw there both awed and horrified him. "Nature is almost driven out of the city," he wrote. "[N]othing appears natural, all is artificial, the earth is changed." Everywhere was nothing "but the works of man." He felt it would be horrible to have to live in New York City. "I would choose the state prison as soon as I would this city for a place of residence, were it not for the name." Here were all

---

[10] *Harmony Baptist Association, 1841*, 13; *Signs of the Times*, March 20, 1840; Calvin French, ibid., March 20, 1840; Calvin Fench, ibid., July 20, 1842; resolutions of the Black River Congregational Association dated August 1836, reprinted in the *Signs of the Times*, January 11, 1844; C. Morley, *Signs of the Times*, September 28, 1842; Calvin French, report on the Burnt Hills Conference, ibid., June 24, 1842.

[11] *Signs of the Times*, March 20, 1840.

the purveyors of sin, "sellers of rum" whose sign ought to be "death's head and cross bones," banks and brokerage houses which he called "shaving shops," the homes of the wealthy "known by their closed doors, to shut out the cries of widows and orphan children," and stores selling baubles and other vanities. Here indeed was mighty Babylon of which John the Revelator prophesied, "Alas! alas! thou great city, thou mighty city Babylon! In one hour has thy judgment come." For Millerites the Millennium would be pastoral, a *land* flowing with milk and honey, a naturalist's utopia. Apparently the irony of their condemning cities while envisioning the Millennium as the New Jerusalem escaped them. Certain that the wrath of God would descend most heavily on populous areas, one adventist warned Christians to "abandon the Cities and large villages and flee into the open country as Lot did," else they might "lose their lives and *probably* their souls." Soon will come the day when every "city, town, and village on the face of the earth, will, in a short time, together with all their ungodly inhabitants, be utterly destroyed."[12]

Millerite antagonism extended to governments that licensed corporations and municipalities and encouraged the growth of materialism. As a Christianite Himes once condemned President Van Buren for attending the theater. "Instead of giving his countenance to an institution that depends upon the vulgar and licentious for its support, and of receiving with apparent pleasure the *'deafening applause'* of the vulgar rabble in attendance, he should set upon it the seal of his reprobation, as one of the greatest evils of the Republic." How could a Christian government license *"grog shops*, theaters, and kindred establishments of a viscious tendency"? Joseph Marsh, also a Christianite, felt that all governments "are corrupt in the fundamental principles upon which they are established. Sins of a high and aggravated character are not only countenanced, but in many respects supported by the arm of civil authority. To oppose these, and all evils, and to purify our world from sin, should be the chief concern of the minister of Christ, and of the Christian."[13] Antagonism toward government was so great that some Millerites refused to vote in the presidential election of 1844.

Conventionally pietistic too was the Millerite view of Catholics, Universalists, and sectarians of the day. A Catholic of Rome, New York, wrote correctly that hatred for Catholics in America "is not accidental—it is inculcated—it is carefully instilled, and as carefully kept alive from the cradle to the grave as though it formed an essential part of Christian instruction." To pietists Catholicism was the epitome of authoritarianism

---

[12] *Washington Union Baptist Association, 1836*; William Miller to William S. Miller, April 25, 1842; N. N. Whiting to Miller, October 24, 1844; "Uticanian," *Midnight Cry*, August 24, 1842.

[13] *Christian Palladium*, VIII (September 2, 1839), 140–41, 136–37.

and creedal tyranny, of human authority setting itself up in opposition to Divine authority. Most Protestants would have agreed with adventists' designation of the pope as the Antichrist, "the one that sitteth in the temple of God, showing himself that he is God." During the 1840s the Catholic Church in America grew in size and influence. In New York City Catholics successfully petitioned the Board of Aldermen for a fair share of available funds for education, funds which the Aldermen had already given to Protestant schools. The Baptists noted with consternation the "footing the Catholics are getting in our country," and Himes said to Miller of the New York City school issue, "It makes the people *feel*—it opens the eyes of many to see and feel your views are correct." Other adventists were certain that Catholics were seeking to "bring this country to subjection to the Pope of Rome," and Charles Fitch equated Catholicism with slavery. The adventist press copied secular newspaper reports of Catholics in Mexico and Chazy, New York, burning Protestant Bibles.[14]

To pietists Universalists were nearly as bad, for they soothed peoples' minds with spurious hopes of salvation for all. They were the false prophets of whom the Bible spoke, who in the Last Days would preach "peace and safety when sudden destruction cometh." Rapid growth of Universalism after 1800 contributed to pietists' siege mentality. Not only did Universalists preach error, but worse, they were successful at it! Because Universalism was pietism's principal competitor in the frontier regions of New England and New York, pietists focused their anger on them. Miller debated long and hard in the 1830s with a brother-in-law who was considering joining the Universalists, and Miller implored him to reconsider before he lost his soul to the deceptive promise of Arminianism.[15]

Finally, adventists and pietists generally condemned the many new sects of the day—Mormons, food fadists, social communitarians and others—calling them false prophets. "Seducing spirits are evidently at work," the Millerites warned. "Hypocrites are multiplying among us; Roman Catholics, Shakers, Fanny Wright, Owen, and others forbid marriage. Roman Catholics and many others among us are teaching to abstain from meats and drinks, which God hath created to be received with thanksgiving of one which believes and knows the truth."[16] This sounds surprising when we consider that in the public mind Millerism itself was a radical sect. But at least up to 1843 the adventists did not

[14] John Blakeney to Miller, May 13, 1838; *Midnight Cry*, June 15, 1843; *Union Baptist Association, 1842*, 14; *Baptist Register*, November 8, 1844.

[15] *Signs of the Times*, March 20, 1840; Miller to Joseph Atwood, May 31, 1831, September 16, 1833, February 28, 1835.

[16] *Signs of the Times*, March 20, 1840.

consider themselves to be sectarians. By including these fringe groups and "isms" under the heading of enemies of Christianity, the Millerites were expressing their traditional pietism and confirming their orthodox credentials. Thus they hoped to create a moderate public image and avoid being smeared with the brush of sectarianism themselves.

Though adventists chose to interpret contemporary wickedness in apocalyptic terms, their rhetoric would not have sounded foreign to Baptists, Methodists, or any other pietist denomination. Likewise, the Millerites absorbed traditional pietist Biblicism. To pietists of all stamps the Bible was, as Miller described it, "given by God to man, as a rule for our practice, and a guide to our faith—that it is a revelation of God to man." He told Hendryx that the best way to convince audiences of the truth of the imminent advent was to "preach *Bible*, you must prove all things by *Bible*, you must talk *Bible*. you must exhort *Bible*, you must pray *Bible* and love *Bible*, and do all in your power to make others love *Bible*, too." He had developed his adventist hermeneutic specifically to prove that the Bible was the divine revelation of God's plan for the universe, and he hoped that by inciting others to study the Bible, too, "some minds may be led to believe in the word of God." Many who took up his challenge found the Bible to be virtually a new book. "Never has the Bible appeared to me such a harmonious system of truth as it does now," said one adventist. "It seems indeed that the time has fully come when God's word is no longer a sealed book to those who search for truth as for hidden treasures." Said another, "Never before has the scriptures seemed so full of sublimity, beauty, and harmony—so full of promise and hope and encouragement to those who would labor for him in the world." The logical pietistic corollary was that each person had the capacity to find Truth by studying the Bible on his or her own. Said Miller, "Nothing revealed in the Scripture can or will be hid from those who ask in faith, not wavering." His own hermeneutic was proof of this. "I know my own weakness," he wrote to his son, "and I do know that I have neither power of body or mind to do what the Lord is doing by me as an instrument." He never claimed special revelation, but he became "more and more convinced that God is speaking through me."[17]

These statements indicate that Millerite pietism went beyond the pietism of the evangelical sects, for within them is an unstated complaint. The fact that for these adventists it took a special hermeneutic to reveal the hidden secrets of Last Things implies a failure of the churches to provide the truth. Isaac Fuller, for one, recognized this failure and also knew the reason why. "It is perfectly astonishing that our Ministers

[17] Miller to Hendryx, March 26, 1832; Miller, *Evidence*, 10; S. W. Paine, *Midnight Cry*, April 27, 1843; anonymous to Miller, December 12, 1843; Bliss, 69–70; Miller to his son (otherwise unidentified), November 19, 1838.

are so ignorant, and many of them so willingly on a subject of such vast importance. . . . And you very well know the worldling and the scoughfer will despise a system and him that declares it that will so soon blast all his expectations and worldly prospects."[18] What differentiated the Millerites from their evangelical pietistic brethren and sisters was that the adventists saw the denominations as obstacles to the realization of the pietist's dream. For the Millerites were antiformalists but the Baptists were becoming increasingly formal, and it is here we see how the pietistic dynamic set the Millerites and other anti-formal groups apart from the pietism of their day.

The effects of the pietistic dynamic are most visible among the Baptists. Whether we trace the Baptist Church's roots to English rebellion against Anglicanism, to Roger Williams's revolt against Puritan authority in Boston, or to mid-eighteenth-century theologians' rejection of infant pedobaptism in favor of adult immersion in New England, those roots rest firmly in antiformalism. Baptists scorned presbyterian polity. They called instead for a lay clergy and for independent congregations devoid of superceding authority, basing these demands on strict Biblical precedent. Fiercely independent, Baptism was one of the most powerful forces that produced the separation of church and state in America. As elsewhere, the revivalism and social mobility in upstate New York from 1780 to 1830 militated in their favor. In 1795 there were only five Baptist churches in the state and only one north of New York City. Thanks to the Second Great Awakening there were over 300 by 1815 and 800 by 1830 with a total membership that year of over 60,000, making it probably the third largest church in New York after the Presbyterians and Congregationalists.[19]

But the church's libertarianism created a dilemma for it. Theological disputes forced the Baptists constantly to reassess the limits of their antinomianism. During the 1770s for instance, the Free Will Baptists, Universalists, and Shakers, all of whom espoused tenets in opposition to orthodox Calvinism, either withdrew or were expelled from the Baptist Church. The very informality of life in developing regions which made success for the church possible also assured schism. For when a group relies on individuals' study of the Bible for instruction about the Christian life the result will be diversity. Without an overriding Baptist authority to enforce conformity, a charismatic Baptist could lead a congregation into all kinds of errors. In 1795 Elder John Peck undertook a tour of the Baptist churches in eastern New York and found there a doctrinal fluidity that was most unsettling. "The infant churches being unsuspicious, hospitable, and eager to hear the gospel preached were often subjected to imposition from artful

---

[18] Isaac Fuller to Miller, September 7, 1834.
[19] Benedict, *Baptist Denomination*, 540.

and designing men, claiming to be Baptist ministers, who, dangerous in principle and corrupt in practice, had already obtruded themselves upon the new settlements, and shamefully abused their confidence." He recommended that order be imposed "for preventing a repetition of such impositions, and [to] preserve the churches from further contamination." Therefore, a ministerial conference in eastern New York appointed Elder Joseph Cornell to "examine the churches and ministers concerning their faith and practice." The result of the investigation was a recommendation that a Baptist association of member churches be formed to maintain discipline. Accordingly, in 1795 the Otsego Baptist Association was established, and subsequently Baptists organized new associations across the state as soon as a sufficient number of churches in a locality had arisen.[20]

Formalization of Baptist authority proceeded apace. One sign was the growing trend toward an educated, ordained clergy. In 1817 there were only three college-educated Baptist ministers west of the Hudson River. Preachers were called from within the congregation on the basis of their preaching ability and piety, and they did not expect to make a living at their calling. They received a license to preach from their home congregation, and in order to support their families, they held traditional jobs. But in 1817 a new Baptist Education Society of the State of New York called for the "improvement of the ministry," and in 1820 it established a Baptist seminary at Hamilton, forerunner of Colgate University. Here students learned Greek and Latin, read the classics, and partook of rhetoric and logic as well as theology. By 1836, 150 students had completed the entire course of training, another 200 had studied there without finishing the course, and 170 more were currently enrolled. Along with improving formal education went more frequent ordination rather than licensing of preachers.[21]

The increasingly educated and ordained clergy now expected to make their living in their profession rather than from worldly jobs. Throughout the 1830s and '40s ministers attending annual associational meetings complained about low pay and delays in receiving their salaries from their congregations. "Because [a preacher] cannot live on the air," reported the Lake George Association, "God will not perform a miracle to sustain him. He needs meat, drink, and clothing as well as other persons; and ought to have such as to fit him to enter any society; receive any that should call on or visit him; and thus have an advantage in every way, and in every sphere,

[20] John Peck and John Lawton, *An Historical Sketch of the Baptist Missionary Convention of the State of New York* (Utica, 1837), 16–17.
[21] Ibid., 55f. According to their figures, by 1836, 81 percent of the Baptist clergy was ordained while only 19 percent was licensed. A valuable work to consult is Donald M. Scott, *From Office to Profession: The New England Ministry, 1750–1850* (Philadelphia, 1978).

to exert a beneficial influence." The ministry had no desire to be "pampered by luxury," and it certainly would not ape the "conditions of the reverends, right reverends, double right reverends, and other wine-imbibing, fox-hunting dignitaries of national churches." Nevertheless, preachers "ought to be so situated as to be comparative strangers to pecuniary embarrassments." The Genesee River Association also claimed that a lack of "punctuality in pecuniary matters had probably caused more removals among ministers than all other causes put together."[22]

Clerical removal was a second complaint of the clergy, who desired a stable pastorate. Social mobility was one principal cause for frequent removals. A central New York religious journal explained, "This portion of our State has been for many years, the half-way house of the Eastern States on their way to the far West, and many who pitched here for a season, have resumed their line of travel at the call of imperious occasions, and hasted away to their ulterior destinations." This "half-formed state of society" was responsible for the "decrease of numbers [in the churches] and the divided state of religion" which, in turn, produced "churches in our connection without ministers, and ministers without churches." This "instability in the pastoral relation" was a sore point among the Baptist associations. The Cayuga Association reported in 1843 that "all of the churches of this association have changed their pastors twice; eight have changed three times, three have changed four times; and two have changed five times," all in one year! Such a habit was "attended with disastrous consequences to the church." The Ontario Association also noted that frequent removals produced irregularity of instruction, abridgement of discipline, and disunity in the churches, and it denied ministers the settled condition necessary for the development of high spirituality. Preachers bore some responsibility for the situation, however. "Hardly is the pastor settled before he begins to look for another home. If he finds in the church, obstacles to its prosperity instead of taking hold of them, he reflects that the church is not his permanent home, and when his 'year is out,' he will find another place." The Madison Association ascribed the fault of frequent removals to preachers' "inadequacy for their work: to their ability to edify or to instruct a congregation longer than a few months at a time; or to that indolence which hates the study; that restlessness and desire of change, which can never be long satisfied in one place; or that ambition which is ever grasping after something higher."[23]

[22] *Lake George Baptist Association, 1840*, 12–16; *Genesee River Baptist Association, 1842*, 13; *Genesee Baptist Association, 1844*, 14; *Union Baptist Association, 1842*, 18; *Saratoga Baptist Association, 1841*, 19–24.

[23] *Religious Recorder of Central and Western New York*, June 19, 1844; *Oneida Baptist Association, 1842*, 10; *Cayuga Baptist Association, 1843*, 10–11; *Ontario Baptist Association, 1843*, 8–16; *Madison Baptist Association, 1845*, 7–8. On the situation in the Cayuga

That is only one side of the story. The other cause of pastoral instability was a general loss of deference by the laity toward their preachers. The Madison Association continued, "No one can doubt, that within a few years past, those views of the sacredness of the pastoral relation, which were held by the fathers of our churches, have been in a great measure abandoned. The time was when the pastoral relation in the Baptist churches in England and America, was looked upon as possessing something of the divine character of a marriage covenant. . . . NOW it is not uncommon to hear churches talk of *hiring* a man to preach to them for six months or a year, as though the engagement was just about as solemn and important as that of a farmer who hires a laborer to assist him in weeding potatoes, or of a gentleman who hires a man-servant to curry his horses or to drive his carriage." Instead of working out problems with their pastor, congregations were too quick to remove him and look for someone else. "If the church sees some faults in their minister—sees that he is 'a man of like passions to other men,' instead of making these known to him in Christian kindness, they whisper among themselves that his '*year will soon be out*' when they *presume* he will call for his dismission."[24]

The most common cause of lay dissatisfaction with their preacher was his inability to foment and sustain revivals. By the 1830s enthusiasm had become the standard of success in many Baptist churches and the measure of the preacher's ability. Itinerants challenged resident ministers to match their enthusiastic preaching style. Many could not. As Whitney Cross says, "The protracted meeting . . . played up the itinerant to the disadvantage of the settled minister, for it helped to establish the notion that special efforts under a person of particular talents would create a keener spirituality than the ordinary course of events could achieve." The Cayuga Association charged that a church's demands for a special revivalist implied that "the pastor is not the man for a revival." Consequently, his "influence is diminished in that community. . . . Ere the meeting has closed, it is whispered in the church, 'If we only had such a pastor, our revival would always continue.' Application is made to the revival preacher, that, in case they should be destitute he might be obtained. It is often exceedingly difficult for the revivalist to satisfy these wishes of the churches; and though he reject their application, and urges them to retain their pastor, the dissatisfacton is there; and some of the revivalists have insinuated their wish, as they have passed from church to church, to settle with them if they become destitute. These insinuations have driven many pastors from the churches."[25]

Association see also A. Russell Belden, *History of the Cayuga Baptist Association* (Auburn, 1851), 72–78.

[24] *Cayuga Baptist Association*, op cit; *Madison Baptist Association*, op cit.

[25] Cross, 183; *Cayuga Association, 1843*, 11.

Social issues, too, often divided pastors and laity. We have already seen that the Anti-Masonic Movement disrupted Miller's own Washington Baptist Association and caused him personal problems in the Hampton church. Isaac Fuller, preaching in Chautauqua County in the early 1830s, found there a "wicked, ungodly, unreasonable, Anti-Spirit." Anti-Masons told him that he "must take sides," but he carefully maintained neutrality so that "both sides come to hear me preach." Thomas S. Sheardown, Baptist preacher in central New York and a Mason, once faced a mob of Anti-Masonic Baptists who did not wish him to preach. But Sheardown said he would speak, and he did. Violence did not take place, but it threatened.[26]

Tension between the clergy and laity frequently resulted in the church's indictment and trial of their preacher and class leaders. The Pittsford Baptist Church, for example, voted one Sunday in 1844 to suspend the celebration of communion for that day. The pastor, Elder Shute, censured the church for the action and vowed that "he would administer the ordinance tomorrow if their was not more than three to sit down to partake of it." The congregation responded by resolving that "While Elder Shute persist in his assumtion of authority he is hereby suspended from Ministerial labours here." A council of churches met to conciliate the argument. The Pittsford Baptists argued that Shute had "assumed authority which does not belong to a Baptist minister and cast contempt on the authority of the Church." The council agreed, for though it criticized the church for suspending Shute, it recognized that he had "on two or three occasions exceeded the limits of his official authority—especially in refusing to put the Resolution offered for the Brethren and declaring a Meeting dismissed against the voice of the majority of the brethren." They recommended that Shute find another church in which to preach. In 1841 a member of the Old Seneca Baptist Church charged that his class leader "lusted for power and imposed the gag law." The Pompey church undertook an intensive investigation into the character of its pastor the following year. William Miller himself presided as moderator over the trial of Robert Brisbin, deacon of the Keeseville Baptist Church, in 1834, at which the associational council found him guilty of "a constant habit of misrepresentations and false statements" and excluded him.[27]

The fact that associational tribunals decided these cases points to another sign of Baptist formalization, increasing associational authority.

[26] Miller to Hendryx, April 10, 1833; Thomas S. Sheardown, *Half a Century's Labors in the Gospel* (Philadelphia, 1866), 118–19.

[27] Pittsford Baptist Church Records, June 1, 1844–August 6, 1844, American Baptist Historical Society; Records of the Old Seneca Baptist Church, May 22, 1841, Methodist Collection, Syracuse University; Keeseville Baptist Church Records, June 26–November 21, 1834, American Baptist Historical Society; Robert C. Brisbin to Miller, June 4, 1834.

Associations were initially intended to enforce conformity among Baptist churches, but over time the range of their activities increased. The annual associational meeting examined candidates for the ministry and ordained them, recognized new churches, and settled disputes within the churches and among them. Some Baptists felt that regular meetings and special councils were subverting congregational independence and assuming too much authority. In 1840 the Pomfret church, Chautauqua County, underwent a serious dispute over "church discipline on *conduct*." Exactly what the issue was is unclear, but the church required a "mutual council" of neighboring churches to arbitrate. This council proposed a solution, but whereas the winners accepted its decision, the losers treated it "as counsel merely." When their opponents refused to be bound by the council's decision, the first group seceded from the congregation and asked the association to recognize it as *the* Chautauqua Church. When the association concurred, the second group seceded from the association and formed what it called the Reorganized Chautauqua Association. This new body sent a circulating letter to local churches justifying its secession as a rebellion against excessive power of church councils. "The church's duties to its members cannot be done by proxy, in any case whatever." Christ had given each congregation authority over its affairs, and "it cannot lawfully be transferred to any other tribunal." Councils were to be "merely advisory, as advice from friend to friend," but could not justifiably exercise power over member churches.[28] Eventually, the two sides reconciled, but the episode illuminates resentment against Baptist collectivized authority.

This issue caused schism among Baptists in New Hampshire and Vermont in the early nineteenth century and the formation of independent Christianite churches. Though this development had no single leader, Abner Jones of Hartland, Vermont, and Elias Smith of Portsmouth, New Hampshire, both Baptist preachers, encouraged the separation. The extent of Christianite growth is unclear, but by 1836 it was loosely embodied in the Christian Connexion that established a headquarters in Albany and was publishing the *Christian Palladium*. Their theology was very similar to that of the Baptist Church, but in one respect they diverged from it. Christianites rejected all human authority in determining belief and ceremony, and they preached the absolute independence of each church. Excessive authoritarianism in all the churches had divided the Saints. They looked forward to the restoration

---

[28] *Chautauqua Baptist Association, 1840*, circular letter; *Chautauqua Baptist Association, Reorganized, 1845*. See also a history of the Pomfret church in *Erie Baptist Association, 1872*, 18, and in S. S. Crissey, *Centennial History of the Fredonia Baptist Church, 1808–1908* (Buffalo, n.d.). The dispute may have been over Millerism. The movement was long-entrenched in Chautauqua County, and the disciplinary action may have been against Millerites in the Pomfret church.

of the primitive church "when *ferocity and blood thirstiness* shall be
changed into *harmlessness, innocence, and love*; when harmony, peace,
plenty and happiness shall reign triumphant among all the sons and
daughters of Adam, of every nation, kindred, tongue and people, and
nought shall annoy or disturb the exquisite relish and enjoyment of the
heavenly boon!" But the denominations, preoccupied with their "dark
mysteries of the conflicting dogmas," could never accomplish this state.
"The government of the 'mother church,' down to her youngest daughter, is aristocratical. The right of suffrage is taken from the people. The
supreme control of all things pertaining to faith and conscience, and the
government of the church, is vested in a few aspiring ecclesiastics. The
great mass of laymen of the different sects, are ignorant of their
bondage, and strangers to the principles of equal, Christian rights, and
the right of free suffrage guaranteed to them in the gospel. They are
mere vassals to their rulers." The only answer was to return to sole
reliance on "the language of the sacred oracles" in determining Truth. If
all Christians would subscribe to this principle, union and sanctity would
be assured, "a union in that truth which makes men free, a Union which
experimental religion inspires, a spiritual, a gospel union."[29]

Although these comments illustrate deep-seated antiformalism among
Christianites, signs indicate that the pietistic dynamic was working among
them as well as among Baptists, and by the mid- to late 1830s there are
indications of internal dispute. Joseph Badger, Joseph Marsh's predecessor
as editor of the *Christian Palladium*, was quite formal in his pietism,
stressing human agency in bringing about the restoration of the primitive
church. Marsh was clearly antiformal, ascribing to God alone competence
for achieving union and sanctity for the Church. The Connexion itself
tended to formalization in the 1830s, as indicated by occasional complaints
about "conferences" developing within the Connexion on regional levels,
very much like those of the Methodists. The debate among Christianites of
New York of whether or not to amalgamate with the Campbellites and
thus join the Disciples of Christ is essentially a debate between formalization and congregational independence. Thus when Christianites joined the
Millerite movement they may have done so in reaction against formalization in their own sect.

Antiformalism made Christianites natural compatriots of other restorationist groups. Many joined the Millerite movement, but many others

---

[29] For a brief contemporary discussion of the Connexion see Winebrenner, 164–69; *Chris-
tian Palladium*, October 8, 1838; "Christian Union," ibid., September 15, 1838; and issues of
September 2, 1839, August 22, 1844, September 15, 1836, and January 2, 1837. See also
Margaret Badger, "Joseph Badger, Circuit Rider," unpublished typescript, Cornell
University.

participated in the Christian Union movement. Like our own ecumenical movement today, Christian Unionism was interdenominational. It sought the restoration of Christian unity based on sole reference to the Bible, to the example of Christ, and to early Christian founders. Unionists held several conferences in New York in the 1830s, and the *Palladium* always printed their conference reports. Silas Hawley, Secretary for the Syracuse Union Convention of 1838, summarized their philosophy: sectarianism "is a sin of the first magnitude." It was the Christian's duty to collect the Church's "disjointed and scattered fragments" and form them "into a body of perfect symmetry, unsullied beauty and undivided strength." The plan of union was simple: Christians had but to follow "the example of our living Head" and make the Bible the "supreme authority."[30] These commonly held sentiments caused close cooperation between Unionists and Christianites and also propelled many Unionists into the Millerite movement. By 1843, for instance, Silas Hawley was one of upstate New York's most active adventist speakers.

A third element of Baptist formalization also sparked schism. During the early decades of the nineteenth century, the Church established mission and tract societies to evangelize developing areas of the country. The first of them, the Hamilton Baptist Missionary Society, appeared in 1807. Its fortunes ebbed and flowed until 1820 when Elder John Peck traveled across the state on a promotional campaign to solicit members and contributions and to form women's auxiliaries and youth leagues. His labors were well blessed; 28 chapters sprang up across New York, 491 members paid $1 each in annual dues, and cash contributions amounted to $1,571. The Society grew so rapidly that by 1825 the infant and struggling New York State Baptist Missionary Convention merged with it. The organization, which retained the Convention's name, now hired agents to sell subscriptions to its newspapers and tracts, prodding agents and missionaries "to exert themselves in obtaining subscribers . . . and also to receive moneys due." Each Baptist association and church received from the Convention a quota of money it was expected to raise during that year, and preachers who met their quotas received loud praise at the Convention's annual meeting and in its published minutes. The result was that a large sum of money accumulated in the treasury. Most of it was spent to support missionaries, Indian schools, and the Convention's publications. By 1836, Peck, looking about the state, could exult in good formalist fashion over the institutional and social progress of New York and the Baptist Church. He noted "the widely extended fields—the populous towns, villages, and cities—the turnpikes, canals, and railroads—the churches and houses for worship—the Bible, tract

---

[30] *Christian Palladium*, October 1, 1838.

and missionary societies, domestic schools and Bible classes—the extensive revivals of religion—and the literary and theological seminaries."[31]

What he took to be cause for pride, others saw as vanity. Baptist
benevolence precipitated a boisterous Anti-Mission schism in eastern
New York that resulted in the 1830s in the formation of two Old School
Baptist Associations. They founded their own journal whose title, the
Signs of the Times, reveals its millenarian bent and whose pages condemned formalism in typical antiformal pietistic rhetoric. They rejected
"humanly devised institutions, with the corruption in doctrine, which
they fostered, the spirit of the world which they brought into the
churches, the confusion and contentions, which they occasioned in the
associations." What need had they of human authority and institutions
when "the scriptures [are] *'the only and a perfect rule of faith and practice',*" when Christ was "the Foundation, the Head, and the life of the
church, the only source and medium of salvation"? Why form benevolent societies "when there is sufficient virtue in the Religion of Jesus
Christ, and a sufficient code in the law of Zion, and a sufficient obligation in a profession of religion; to restrain the Saints, and to exclude the
offenders"? Benevolent organizations were "picking the pockets of the
ignorant and unsuspecting, and at the same time by their speculations on
the best of all Books, becoming a wealthy and powerful body." They
"profess to be the Lord's Treasury, and would make men believe that all
that is given to them is given to the Lord, and that the Lord has authorized them to beg money in his name, for their own use." The paper
lampooned the quota system by annotating the Convention's own published report. It was intended to "'aid in rendering their (the people's)
sacrifices, (alias money) regular (i.e. inform the people when, how much,
and to whom their sacrifices must be made) and effectual, (as all the lib-
erality of the saints will be null and ineffectual unless it pass through
their priestly hands, as is the unhallowed loaf, until it receives the blessing of the Pope.)" They found the root of the evil in the worldliness and
ambitions of the clergy, a clergy grown soft with education. A seminary
was the "workshop of the Devil, and the hotbed of all kinds of
delusions. . . . It is there [Satan] keeps his Library, or Tool-chest, and
there he Manufactures his Magicians." Ambition for education led to lust
for power, to "the advancement of Priest-craft, and Clerical power
amongst the Baptists of the present day." Damned for corruption, the
Baptist Church received from the Old School Baptists the worst of all
possible epithets—it was the Anti-Christ.[32]

Anti-Mission Baptists expressed widespread antagonism to formalization of the Baptist Church as evidenced by the professionalization of the

[31] Peck and Lawton, op cit..
[32] (Anti-Mission) *Signs of the Times*, February 13, 1833, and September 25, 1833.

clergy, accretion of associational power, and formation of benevolent organizations. But the Old School schismatics did not become the standard bearers of the antiformal revolt. They retained a strict Calvinism that was decidedly out of step with the more liberal theology emanating from the Finney revivals. Indeed, they probably failed to participate widely in the Millerite movement, despite their obvious similarities in tone and rhetoric, because of Millerism's public association with the New School. Despite Miller's personal orthodoxy, his movement did have the proper revivalist credentials; thus it was the adventist crusade that inherited the antiformal brigades. The fact that the adventists had not tried to create a new sect up to 1843 meant that their movement could claim to be a legitimate alternative to Baptist worldliness; they preached reform, not rebellion; they sought regeneration, not power. Furthermore, though Miller's solution to church corruption was dramatic (the physical return of Christ and His personal restoration of the primitive church), it rested on traditional millennial beliefs and evoked traditional pietistic visions.

Sectarianism was not limited to Baptists and Christianites; other evangelical denominations also were splitting apart. Methodists' efforts in the 1820s to impose conformity of belief and ritual in their conferences may have contributed to the rise of the Wesleyan Methodist Church in New York and elsewhere dedicated to greater representation of the laity in church affairs and to abolition of slavery.[33] Presbyterians and Congregationalists were being torn apart regionally by the issue of slavery and would soon dissolve into Northern and Southern churches. As Millerism already enjoyed an interdenominational audience, it could provide a logical home for pious Protestants of all kinds—Baptists, Christianites, Methodists, Presbyterians, Congregationalists—who were dismayed by the divisiveness and worldliness of their churches. So, armed with zeal, the adventists led antiformalists into battle.

Millerism's indictment of the churches was no different from that of the other antiformalists. The churches' duty was to create the united Church of the Elect, but instead they were the chief obstacles to its revelation. "Has not the discord among the disciples of Jesus rendered the host of God's elect weak and imbecile, in their onward march, to the conquest of an entire world, to the reign of King Jesus?" went the adventist plaint. "Presbyteries—Synods—Associations—and Consociations—are reeking and rocking as if drunk with the spirit of contention and division. Whole organizations are splitting in pieces, and new ones are forming. Jealousies, strifes of words, heresy-hunting and the like seem to characterize many of the meetings of ecclesiastical bodies in the region,

---

[33] For complaints of loose ritual and practice among Methodists and the necessity for standardizing, see reports of the Oneida Methodist Conference, Methodist Collection, Syracuse Universtiy.

while the heart of humble piety is compelled to weep and bleed in secret places." Sectarianism was proof that the church "is corrupt—is not the *house of God*, while thus divided against itself—and is not the *body of Christ* which cannot be divided." To Miller schism was a sign of the Last Days, for "before Christ comes in his glory all sectarian principles will be shaken, and the votaries of the several sects scattered to the four winds; and that none will be able to stand but those who are built on the word of God."[34]

Authoritarianism caused this divisiveness. "How many difficulties do you think we have in our Churches," asked Miller, "where the spirit of Christ is manifest through the whole trial: or where it began with 'father forgive them for they know not what they do?' . . . Oh, how much iniquity is done, in church discipline. The hypocrite uses it as a tool to make others think he is verry pious—the envious use it as a weapon to bring down those whom they imagine are getting above. The bigot to bring others to his faith; the sectarian to his creed." The churches' lust for earthly power prevented them from fulfilling their responsibilities. "Instead of prayers, exhortations, and sermons in our publick meetings as formerly we have reports, resolutions, and speeches. Instead of union, division. Instead of being separate from the world we amalgamate. Instead of religion, money—instead of humiliation, pride. In the room of persecution we have flattery, and popularity in the room of shame and contempt."[35]

How worldliness has corrupted the clergy. "What a great change in our ministry within 30 years. The present are no more like the past than a dandy is like a farmer in a striped shirt and woolen frock." Take a good look at a modern preacher. "What do we see? A modern dandy dressed 'cap a pie.' A 50 dollar cloak. A 30$ cap. A 20$ vest. 15$ boots and a safety chain worth 75$ or 100$. This is a modern Baptist classical Priest. O God! is it come to this, in my day, am I to experience the time, when the dear Baptist sheep and lambs of Christ, have got to depend, on fops for food, on blind for light." Preachers are a "lazy set of dogs" and preaching "no more than a trade" peopled by the "great, the learned, the eloquent, the popular, the man pleasing." Hamilton graduates, instead of relying on their Bible, take "some novel *Idea* from some of their 'standard writers' as they call their *Rev. Masters*" and then dress it up "with a host of classical phrases, spotted over with a little *Hebrew, Greek, & Latin*, all obtained with a few months study of old Pagan Philosophers, obscure writers, and classical blockheads."[36]

---

[34] *Niagara Baptist Association, 1844*, 8; L. P. Judson, *Midnight Cry*, May 11, 1843; George W. Burnham, *Voice of Truth*, July 27, 1844; Manuscript Sheriff's Book, op cit.
[35] Miller to Hendryx, April 10, 1833, and July 27, 1838.
[36] Ibid., October 26, 1837.

Millerites, like the other antiformalists of their day, condemned the world in a typical pietistic fashion, but they included in their indictment the formal and formalizing denominations. The indictment compiled by O. R. L. Crozier condemned "the exalted popularity, ease, wealth, and pride of the nominal church, the form of Godliness, but practical denial of the power, the great and constant 'learning' [of the clergy] without ability 'to come to the knowledge of the truth,' their corruptness of mind and reprobacy concerning the truth; . . . the nonendurance of sound doctrine; the leaping of teachers 'after their own lusts' to please their 'itching ears' with flattery and scholastic eloquence; and mockers walking after their own ungodly lusts; . . . the heaping of treasures; the defrauding and oppression of the laborers; living in pleasure, wantonness and luxury." The Millerites' *Signs of the Times* created similar lists of worldly sin, secular and ecclesiastical, that claimed to describe perfectly "private characters, domestic circles and public societies of our own times."[37]

If condemnation of the churches set antiformalists apart from formal pietists in the 1830s and '40s, the adventists' rejection of human agency tended to separate them from other antiformalists. The millenarian quality of their doctrine coincided with antiformalists' condemnation of human authority, but Christianites, Unionists, and Anti-Mission Baptists still believed in reform through human reliance on the Bible. Nevertheless, the distinctiveness of adventism attracted other antiformalists. It may seem paradoxical that so many reformers could exist in a movement so antagonistic to human agency until one considers that for adventists the Apocalypse was the ultimate reform, the sudden and total obliteration of evil. Joseph Bates, an active Millerite lecturer in New England and New York who had previously been a laborer in moral reform movements, explained, "In embracing the doctrine of the second coming of the Saviour, I found enough to engage my whole time in getting ready for such an event, and aiding others to do the same, and that all who embraced this doctrine would and must necessarily be advocates of temperance and the abolition of slavery; and those who opposed the doctrine of the second advent could not be very effective laborers in moral reform."

Miller, himself an abolitionist, once gave shelter to a runaway slave. (Indeed, Hampton was on one of the main routes of the Underground Railroad, and his farm may have been a regular station.) But when in 1840 he attended a meeting of the Antislavery Society in New York City, what he saw convinced him that human agencies for reform were totally inadequate. "They are in trouble, divided, split in two, scattered,

---

[37] O. R. L. Crozier, *Midnight Cry*, May 16, 1844; Silas Guilford to Miller, January 2, 1843; *Signs of the Times*, March 20, 1840.

and weakened by their uneasy designing and master spirits." Squabbles between immediatists and gradualists in the antislavery movement hurt most those whom the abolitionists wished to rescue. "The poor slave, has but little chance to be liberated by these two parties. . . . The slave-holder may call in his picquets, he may need no additional guards, his citadel is safe. While the pretended friends of the slave, are expending all their ammunition on each other the release of the captive will be little thought of." He believed that Blacks had only one real hope. "So the year of Jubilee to the poor Slave is not near if man is the cause. But God can & will release the captive. And to him alone we must look for redress."[38]

Corrupt humanity could not reform corruption; progress was an illusion; formalists and postmillennialists, according to the adventist perspective, preached reform in vain. "They tell you that the world is growing better and better, while the truth is as it was in the days of Noah, waxing worse and worse. They tell you that all sects will be one, and will see eye to eye; but the facts in the case are, that the old sects are dividing, and new ones are rising to an alarming extent. And they must acknowledge that, to all appearance, their temporal millennium is receding rather than advancing; confusion and anarchy are now in the ranks of all sects, and disunion and division have broken the bonds and removed the most ancient landmarks among them." So yearning pietists had only one hope left—the Second Coming of Christ, the sudden and total eradication of evil, and the Divine restoration of the primitive church. How compelling the message, how real the vision, how enticing the hope. What joy it creates, wrote one adventist, "and especially the hope that the present is the last year, month, or perhaps day, that we shall be obliged to stay on this earth before it is cleansed, inspires my soul with new courage to toil on yet a little longer, and do all the good I can before Christ does exchange his mediatorial seat for his great white

[38] Joseph Bates, *The Autobiography of Elder Joseph Bates* (Battle Creek, 1868), 250; Miller to William S. Miller, May 16, 1840. On November 8, 1844, Philander Barbour of South Granville, N. Y., wrote to Miller, "The bearer [of this letter] is a fugitive from the iron hand of slavery & as appears from letters in his possession & his own statements of some considerable consequence to his claimant. His master with United States Officers are in hot persuit of him. Not being acquainted with anyone in your section that would be more ready to feed the hungry & direct a stranger fleeing to a city of refuge than yourself I have directed him to you. I think it is best for him to keep on through Vermont as far as Vergennes or Burlington, at least, before he strikes the Lake [Champlain]. You will probably be able to refer him to some Abolitionist on his way North. Should you think of any other course more safe you will advise him." Nichol believed Miller was an anti-abolitionist, basing this interpretation on a letter Miller wrote to Hendryx on February 25, 1834, in which he seemed to castigate radical abolitionists. However, a careful reading of this letter shows that Miller was writing sarcastically and was actually condemning slavery and its supporters.

throne, and comes in the clouds of heaven in the glory of his Father."[39]

Pietism gave the Millerites their vision, revivalism their vehicle, and millennialism their specific beliefs. The union of the three produced widespread belief in Miller's prediction and even wider suspicion among pietists that he might be correct. More important, pietism evoked a yearning for his views to be right, for the final fulfillment of all the pious Christian's hopes, for release from this world, from time itself, to be united with God in joy forever.

Anticipation inspired action, a part of the pietistic dynamic which in turn creates sects. Millerism and other antiformal rebellions of the day were products not only of belief and yearning but also of positive commitment to act on those beliefs, as one earnest adventist pietist suggested, to "do all the good I can." The problem is that once antiformalists get inspired to act, the principle of liberty obviates control of their actions. In other words, antiformalism suffers from the effects of its own philosophy. If one person can rebel, why not all? If no church has authority to dictate belief and practice, then how can the antiformalist groups require coherence? The Millerites would discover that the centrifugal forces that pushed them into rebellion against the evangelical churches would require a countervailing centripetal force to keep adventists on the right road rather than spinning off into error. That force was sectarianism—the creation of a specifically Adventist identity. Up to 1843 Millerism was not sectarian; for the most part adventists stayed in their churches and sought no earthly identity as a group. Indeed, to have done so would have seemed blasphemous, a sign that they were seeking security in a world that they knew was speeding toward destruction. By 1843, however, that group identity was already gestating, and in the months surrounding the predicted end of the world, it would be born.

[39] Miller, *Circular Address of the General Conference of Believers in the Advent Near . . . Held at Low Hampton* in Second Advent Library, volume III; E. E. Paine, *Midnight Cry*, April 13, 1843.

Chapter 6
FLIGHT FROM BABYLON

Though gestation had been slow up to 1843, the Adventist identity was born suddenly and painfully when thousands of Millerites established meetings independent of the churches. Separation was a natural product of Millerite theology. Pietism injected a natural sense of alienation, a belief that the Christian's true home is not Earth but Heaven. Furthermore, the antiformalists' rejection of human agency and then consequent sense of the degenerating moral condition of the world added to Millerite feelings of separateness. So, to be sure, many adventists willingly withdrew from the world.

But many others were expelled from it. Millerism generated enormous opposition, religious and secular. The movement's success in publicizing the doctrine of Last Things evoked wide public discussion of millennialism, religious "radicalism"[1] and reform that sometimes assessed Millerism objectively but more often focused on the movement's peculiar beliefs and effects, real and imagined. The result was a critique of Miller and his followers that was as comprehensive and scatological as adventists' condemnation of the world. Opponents not only used many of the same techniques as Millerites to spread their views, but they also turned to violence and to church trials to restrain Millerism's growth and to excise the "cancer" when it appeared in their midst. If those hostile to Millerism hoped to destroy the crusade, the effect was the opposite. Opponent's actions tended to confirm adventists' interpretation of them as anti-Christian, to instill in Millerites the soul-satisfying experience of martyrdom, and to strengthen rather than diminish their fervor. So armed, Zion and the world went to battle.

It is difficult to separate religious from secular life of Americans in

---

[1] Scholars still apply this word to sectarians of the nineteenth century, including the Millerites, but its use is hazardous. It implies nontraditional belief and action, and while this is true of some Millerites we have already noted the movement's essential orthodoxy. The word *radical* also implies a spectrum of belief with sectarians occupying a position on the fringe, probably on the left. What that spectrum was is not clear, even if one existed at all, and the Millerites, being restorationists, were not only conservative but even reactionary. Finally, simply in terms of behavior the Millerites and other religious innovators were no more radical than the mobs that harassed, beat, and occasionally even murdered them.

the 1830s and '40s. While many journals, for instance, were specifically religious or denominational in content they frequently commented on secular events and issues, and likewise supposedly secular newspapers frequently discussed religion and ethics. The rhetoric of religion permeated secular life. Even people who were not actively religious absorbed and expressed religious culture in their daily lives. Nevertheless, for our purposes it is helpful to separate specifically religious (theological, ecclesiastical) arguments against Millerism from more secular concerns of the nonadventist world.

Because Millerism was essentially a religious response to perceived spiritual and social decay, the most sophisticated criticism of the movement came from theologians and millennialists. Indeed, adventism sparked intense discussion about the Millennium. In 1841 the *Princeton Review*, in commenting on a millennial tract, said, "The second advent of the Lord Jesus Christ begins to attract more attention in the American churches; and there are probably ten times as many students of the prophecies concerning this event, as there were ten years ago." Bible commentators took advantage of the interest Miller had sparked to publish their own tracts, most of which took issue with him. They all had axes to grind. Moses Stuart, who interpreted Biblical apocalyptic as allegorical history rather than prophecy of future events, rejected Millerism out of hand. New York State's *Baptist Register* sided with Stuart claiming that his views "were the understanding of Baptists particularly, and indeed of all other evangelical denominations." This was hardly true, but the journal probably said so in order to place distance between themselves and the Millerites, so many of whom were Baptists. The Universalists got into the fray. They, too, allegorized apocalyptic, but because they were competing with the evangelical churches for members, juxtaposing their more humane doctrine of universal salvation against Calvinists' doctrine of limited atonement, it was in their interest to associate Millerites closely with evangelicals and thus discredit both. So their New York State journal, the *Gospel Advocate*, was closer to the mark but still exaggerated when it said, "All the orthodox sects, have always, since their origins, entertained precisely the same views that Mr. Miller holds."[2]

To some commentators, Miller was too literal. The idea was ridiculous "that the Messiah is again literally to make his appearance on earth, and reign a thousand years . . . that a literal bodily resurrection of the saints will take place at the commencement of the Millennium." Another antiliteralist averred that there would be no actual Final Judgment,

[2] *Princeton Review*, III (January 1841), 150; Moses Stuart, *Hints on the Interpretation of Prophecy* (second edition, Andover, 1842); *Baptist Register*, April 12, 1844; *Gospel Advocate*, XV (November 1, 1844), 350.

rather the "day of death is to each one *the day of judgment*." Others denigrated adventists' "superstitious" interpretations of natural phenomena. "Knowing nothing of science, and supposing science and revelation in conflict," said one, "they have been driven to the alternative of denying scientific truth, or of asserting that God established one kind of truth in the natural and another and different and even contradictory kind of truth in the moral world." There simply was not sufficient time for the sun, moon, and stars to wear out with age, as the Bible actually predicted. "365,000 millenia might be expected before that event." Dramatic phenomena, wrote the *Gospel Advocate*, "always impress the mind, as they should do, with ideas of the greatness and power of God," but Millerites inexcusably and purposely perverted the meaning of natural events to gain converts. "We can easily excuse the weakness that converts the common occurrence into a prodigy, or exalts an eclipse into a sign of the coming of the Son of Man; but we can not . . . so easily excuse ministers of the Gospel, who on so grave a subject, either recklessly or ignorantly publish to the world that which is untrue."[3] Adventists were not just wrong, they were culpably wrong.

Others criticized Miller for not being literal enough. To them, his interpretation was "spiritualist," too figurative. Moses Stuart, who treated prophecy as an allegorical history of the fall of Jerusalem to the Romans, was ironically in the proliteralist camp, too. These critics focused specifically on Miller's predicted time of the Parousia. Stuart reminded his readers of the "many predictions of the like nature which have already been wrecked." A correct interpretation of scripture would instruct Christians that "IT IS NOT FOR YOU TO KNOW THE TIMES OR THE SEASON, WHICH THE FATHER HAS PUT IN HIS OWN POWER." The *Baptist Register* also condemned "any human being fixing the time of the Savior's second advent with definiteness, not only without warrant, but actually in the face of scriptures." For if the Millerites' prediction was wrong, not only they but Christianity and religion generally would be discredited. Their error would "tend to dissipate the seriousness, in setting the people to speculating about things foreign to the interests of their soul, and thus grieve away the Divine Spirit." Would not people then say "and with reason, too, 'Where is the promise of his coming?'" Secular newspapers also commented on the predicted time. Why would not adventists "leave the event with Him who has said 'of that day and hour knoweth no man?'" No one could "set bounds to a period, which even the great Head of the Christian faith, was unable to

[3] A. L. Crandall, *A Brief Explanation of the Book of Revelations in Alphabetical Order* (Troy, 1841); James G. Hamner, "The Suddenness of Christ's Coming," *National Preacher*, XVI (February 1842), 41; *Angelica Reporter*, November 20, 1844; *Gospel Advocate*, XIV (April 21, 1843), 124–25.

define." Besides, was it not better always to be ready for Judgment than to prepare for a specific date? "What matters it to me whether the world is destroyed in 1844, or in 18,044?" asked Lydia Maria Child. "Even if I thought the end of all things was so very near, I could see no better way of preparing for it, than by purity of life and conversation, a heart at peace with all men, and diligent efforts to do all in my power to save and bless. And if the earth is to revolve on its axis for millions of years, still in that direction only lies the spirit's ascending path."[4]

Millerism's most outspoken proliteralist critics were millenarians. Adventism put them in a terrible position. Because they seemed so similar intellectually and temperamentally, the public might blame them as well as Millerites for the failure of the date. Scoffers already lumped the two together. Said the *American Millenarian and Prophetic Review*, "Attempts have been made to make the impression that Millerism and Millenarianism are identical. . . . It is their ignorance only that saves them from the charge of gross and shameful, malicious falsehood."[5] In fact, there were clear distinctions between the two groups. Millenarians interpreted prophecy quite literally and fully expected the decay of the physical universe, the conversion of the Jews, the restoration of Israel, and the rise and defeat of the Anti-Christ before the Second Coming of Christ. All this would take time, much more time than Miller's predictions allowed. Why, asked George Duffield, Jr., America's leading millenarian, do Millerites not see this contradiction?

Indeed, there was an inconsistency in Miller's method of interpreting scripture. On the one hand he preached the literal, personal, physical, Second Coming of Christ, the actual destruction of the globe, and the real creation of the New Jerusalem. With this millenarians could agree. But on the other hand his chronology resulted from figurative interpretations of apocalyptic. Prophecies "always have a figurative meaning," Miller wrote, "and are used much in prophecy to represent future things, themes, and events—such as mountains, meaning governments; . . . beasts meaning year, &c." So when he encountered the prophecy that the Jews must convert to Christianity and return to Israel before the Second Advent, he was able to provide an interpretation that complemented his predicted year. When the prophets used the word *Jew*, they were actually talking about Christians, since "the putting on of Christ constitut[es] them Abraham's seed, and heirs according to the promise." All who accepted Christ, then, could be considered converted "Jews," and all the Saints together at the Last Day would constitute the kingdom

---

[4] Stuart, 21–23; *Baptist Register*, April 12, 1844; *Vermont Telegraph*, November 14, 1837; *Tompkins Volunteer*, January 17, 1843; Child, 238.

[5] *American Millenarian*, 106; see also George Duffield, *Dissertations on the Prophecies* (New York, 1842), 157–58.

of Israel. When Christ comes and gives them the New Jerusalem, He will fulfill predictions of the restoration of Israel.[6]

To Duffield this was rubbish. The adventists, who were unable to reconcile literal prophecy with their predicted date, "allegorize the whole, and say they will have their accomplishment in the resurrection of the dead, the renovation of the globe, and the eternal state of things to be introduced immediately at Christ's coming." Such an "occult sense" was inexcusable and unacceptable, and it made Miller "the most ultra spiritualist of the day." For both practical and theological reasons millenarians became Millerism's strongest and most telling critics. Wrote Himes, "Our brethren, who look for the *premillennial Advent near*, in common with us, are as much opposed to us, as those who look for the spiritual Millennium. . . . [Their] influence is greater, and more against us than any other opposition we meet with!"[7]

Postmillennialists defended human agency and competence in the face of Millerite pessimism. Christ would come only when "his dominion shall reach from sea to sea, and from the river to the ends of the earth; til every house shall have become a house of prayer, and every heart a temple for Jesus Christ to dwell in." Stuart believed the Millennium would begin only "when all Christians, or at least the great body of them, come up to the standard of duty, or come very near to this standard, in their efforts to diffuse among the nations of the earth the knowledge of salvation." It was not bad enough that Millerism denied inevitable progress, they actually impeded it by diverting attention, labor, and money from benevolence. Wrote one critic, "The moment a man thoroughly drinks into the spirit of Millerism, whatever may have been his piety, or zeal, or devotedness, in promoting the Kingdom of Christ, previously, that moment he ceases to take an active interest in Home Missions, or Foreign Missions, or in the Bible Cause. . . . I am not conscious of ever having received a dollar for the Bible cause, except in two instances, from any one who has been completely inducted into Millerism."[8]

Formalist church members were shocked at the interdenominational character of Millerite meetings, especially when presiding preachers allowed nonchurch members or members of other denominations to take communion. Baptists in Utica complained, for example, "because the Advent believers of that church join with the Methodist Advent brethren in prayer meetings, and the same with the Methodists for joining with the Baptists." This formalist concern with church order got Elon Galusha into trouble with the anti-Millerite majority in his church in Lockport.

---

[6] Bliss, 71.

[7] *American Millenarian*, 11–17; Himes to Miller, April 27, 1842.

[8] T. Wrightson, *Midnight Cry*, November 9, 1843; Stuart, 186; *Baptist Register*, March 22, 1844.

When they brought him to trial, charges against him included the fact that he "administered the ordinance of baptism to those who desire it, without any regard to their union with the people of God in Church relation." Furthermore, he "administered the Lord's Supper to a company composed of divers denominations, some unbaptized, and many *excluded* from the churches."[9]

The corollary of this charge was that Millerism disrupted church unity by setting laity against preachers and causing deep ruptures within the congregation. How adventists must have blanched! To the public they were guilty of the same sectarianism for which they condemned the churches, and these critics were right. For instance, the Dutch Reformed Church in Schenectady wished to hear Miller preach. The pastor was opposed, but, said one congregant, "he won't stand in the way." Baptists in Troy apparently met some reluctance from their preacher to invite Miller, but the congregation "so urged" him "on the subject" that a vote was taken and the invitation extended. Often churches divided between pro-Millerites and anti-Millerites, and resultant disputes sometimes shattered the church. This was the case in Miller's own Hampton congregation where a small but vocal anti-Millerite minority opposed the preaching of the Second Advent. The church found itself simply unable to function as a united body, and from 1835 to 1839 it failed to send a representative to the annual associational meeting. In 1839 a short-lived reconciliation took place, but by 1844 relations had deteriorated to such a point that the church requested assistance from the association, which advised the regulars to call on sister churches "after due notice to the majority" and allow this council to arbitrate. Accordingly, the Millerites and regulars met that year with preachers from neighboring churches and mutually agreed to separate.[10]

More often Millerites were in the minority. The most serious division occurred in Galusha's church. When he became an adventist after having served as pastor for less than a year, the congregation disfellowshipped him for refusing to refrain from preaching the Second Coming of Christ. He was a "disorderly walker," they said, "by claiming to be a Baptist, and yet laboring to *establish* and sustain an interest among a few excluded members within our bounds—detrimental to the interests of the church here." Of course, once excluded he had no alternative but to do just that. He and sixty sympathizers, most of whom had already been disfellowshipped, set up a new meeting in Perry devoted to the

[9] C. Morley, *Midnight Cry*, February 29, 1844; *A Correspondence Between the Baptist Church and the Advent Brethren of Lockport, and Elders Webster and Galusha and the Baptist Church in Perry* (Lockport, 1845), 16; Nathaniel I. Barber, *Midnight Cry*, November 8, 1844.

[10] Charles Cole to William S. Miller, January 7, 1843, and S. Baldwin and J. Kelly to Miller, January 19, 1843; *Washington Union Baptist Association, 1835–45*.

Second Advent. Similar schisms occurred across the state. J. H. Greene reported of divisions in northern New York as early as 1837. "In Massena the church is divided, and I am fearful it never will be united. Br. Orvis and probably the whole party connected with him (perhaps the most spiritual part of the church) I think will eventually be excluded, if not they will absent themselves from the Church. Elder Pratt's church is divided. Elder Palmer has removed to Canada." He had also asked to be dismissed from his pulpit because of opposition to his adventism. In central New York the "Methodist Church was very much torn and divided."[11]

The most widespread and enduring charge against Millerism, appearing in the secular and religious press, was its supposed fanaticism. The presence of Perfectionists and mystics in the movement seemed to substantiate this. The churches were "all going over to the erroneous doctrine of sanctification," went the complaint, "and the next step beyond that was Millerism." One excluded preacher was convinced the cause of his removal was his "belief in the doctrine of sanctification," and Michael Barton's mystical Shaker gifts, which he casually displayed in public lectures, seemed to provide proof of the union of "Perfectionism and Millerism." A Rochester paper reported that a group of adventists there tried to resurrect a boy who had committed suicide, and in view of the incident in Jamaica, Vermont, this story may well have been true. Miller supposedly granted an interview to the *Baptist Register* in which he told of a female acquaintance who, while hypnotized, "'visited the moon,' and told the wonders she saw; she also visited the New Jerusalem, and sung three anthems such as they were singing there." He would willingly give up "house, lands, everything, for one brief trip to the new Jerusalem." Miller regretted that he was not "impressible," but his daughter, who had been hypnotized, had "been to the moon."[12] Miller never denied giving such an interview, but it certainly seems out of character. Whether true or concocted, however, this was the kind of

[11] *Correspondence*, 16; Joel H. Greene to Miller, September 7, 1847; *Religious Recorder of Central and Western New York*, June 19, 1844. There are conflicting accounts of events. Lyman Spaulding wrote in his diary on January 6, 1844, "Second Advent preaching disturbed the internal harmony of the Baptist Church and Elder Galusha asked to be released which was granted" (Lyman Spaulding Journal, Syracuse University). Galusha charged that the anti-Millerites brought in two preachers to work against him, and he further stated that this was against the wishes of the majority of the church. In fact, the church excluded only twenty-seven people in 1844 (*Niagara Baptist Association, 1844*), but many more voluntarily withdrew so that by the end of that year at least sixty individuals had left the Lockport Baptist Church and joined Galusha's new pro-Millerite congregation in Perry.
[12] Nathaniel A. Barber, *Midnight Cry*, November 8, 1844; L. Delos Mansfield, ibid., March 25, 1844; *Baptist Register*, April 16, 1844; *Rochester Daily Advertiser*, October 7, 1845; *Baptist Register*, May 10, 1844.

information on which the bulk of the nonadventist public based its opinion of Millerism.

Of all stories of Millerite fanaticism, none has been more widely repeated than the rumor that they made and donned white ascension robes
"supposing they should ascend in fiery chariots to the realms of the
blessed." No conclusive evidence exists one way or the other. Jane Marsh
Parker said that "if the Millerites had ascension robes, how is it I never
saw one?" The adventist press never mentioned them, but they hotly
disowned a published woodcut showing Millerites rising in the air to
meet Jesus perhaps because they were all wearing white robes. A rare
comment on the subject appears in a letter from Mary A. Seymour, a
well-known lecturer. "We all have them," she wrote, "not by our own
merits; but they are freely given us by our Father, who kindly bestows
all things necessary for the ascension. We can not, do not, lay them aside
for worldly policy, or for any other selfish scheme; but we do mean to
wear them daily, keeping them clean and white; for they are linen,
which is the righteousness of the saints. If laid aside, moths would soon
devour them. In these robes we shall be caught up to meet our coming
king—in these will our hopes be consummated—in these shall we sit
down at the Marriage supper of the Lamb, when the Groom shall come
and the bride has made herself ready." Was she talking about material
or spiritual robes? Clara Endicott Sears, who interviewed surviving
Millerites in the early 1920s, found a woman who had made a white
robe to present to Jesus. With the strong restorationist impulse in the
movement, some adventists may well have done what the prophet
Matthias did—gone totally over to orthodox Judaism—supposing that
this was the way the apostles lived. In such a case, they might well have
worn robes in imitation of ancient Jewish dress.[13] But if Millerites did
occasionally use them, there is no evidence of widespread habit as the
press suggests. Nevertheless, the public came to identify ascension robes
so closely with the Millerites that the story persists to the present.

Another commonly held belief about adventism was the assumption
that it produced insanity. One newspaper labeled all adventists monomaniacs, a charge early leveled against Miller, and one preacher cited
eleven patients incarcerated at New York City's asylum, Blackwell
Island, as "the fruits of Millerism." Pliny Earle, a pioneer in the science
of psychiatry, reported in the Utica *Journal of Insanity* that thirty-five
patients "whose insanity was attributed to *Millerism*" had been admitted
into northern asylums. The adventists, he said, "are monomaniacs, and
the more their attention is directed to the subject of their delusions by

[13] *Tompkins Democrat*, October 31, 1844; Parker, "Little Millerite," 316; Mary A. Seymour, *Voice of Truth*, January 29, 1845; Clara Endicott Sears, *Days of Delusion: A
Strange Bit of History* (Boston, 1924), 193.

reasoning with them, the more is their diseased faith increased." So prevalent was the notion that when Elzira Fassett learned that her husband had become a Millerite, she feared he had entered a "partial state of insanity, or religious mania." Under the influence of Millerism, according to popular theory, people often committed suicide and perpetrated horrible murders. A typical story appeared in the *Rochester Daily Advertiser*. A shoemaker in Newark "who has been for some time laboring under the Miller delusion" was distracted "to such an extent as to require being watched incessantly to prevent his laying violent hands upon himself or some of his family." In spite of this supervision he obtained a knife and cut his own throat "to such an extent as almost to sever his head from his body." According to another story the wife of a "respectable mechanic" became a "maniac owing to the Miller excitement" and "administered a dose of arsenic first to her two youngest children, one aged three years and the other one year, and then took a quantity herself, which caused the death of the children about 12 and the unfortunate female about 6 o'clock."[14]

Some of this evidence can be viewed skeptically. For one thing, people were sometimes incarcerated for Millerism even when they were not necessarily deranged. Lydia Maria Child told of a shoe vendor who, under the impression that he should divest himself of his property before Christ comes, tried to give away his entire stock of merchandise. But his son intervened and caused "him to be sent to an insane asylum, till the excitement of his mind abated." In this case, the man's illness seems to have been nothing more than an advanced case of altruism. One must wonder if his son's principal concern was his father's well-being or saving his stock of goods. Also, despite his apparently negative attitude toward Millerism, Earle never claimed that it naturally led to insanity. He was well aware that any kind of "religious excitement" could produce distraction. He told of a female patient who attended a nonadventist protracted meeting, became engrossed "in religious exercises," feared for her soul, went for many nights without sleep, and finally tried to kill herself. "The error is not so much in the doctrine preached," said Earle, "as in the too frequent or too long continued and untimely attendance of excitable and nervous persons upon such meetings." Finally, it may well be that "Millerism" became a generic label for any mental disorder that exhibited itself in religious depression. That Millerism itself caused an upsurge in insanity is doubtful. Indeed, the total number of patients

14 *Tompkins Democrat*, October 31, 1844; *Midnight Cry*, April 20, 1843; *Journal of Insanity*, II (January 1845), 251; Fassett, 10–11; *Rochester Daily Advertiser*, December 18, 1844, and October 22, 1844; *Skaneateles Columbian*, March 9, 1843. Millerism may have been partly responsible for increased interest in the subject of "religious mania" in the mid-1840s. The *Princeton Review* reviewed four books in July of 1844 on the subject of religion and insanity.

enrolled in the Bloomingdale Asylum from 1840 to 1845 at the height of the adventist movement decreased markedly from previous years.[15]

Nevertheless a belief in the imminent Judgment could cause enormous emotional and psychological pressure, and some people did crack under the strain. Stephen Marsh wrote to Miller of his intense spiritual agony. Sixteen years ago, he said, he had felt great "anxiety about my souls welfare" and had finally surrendered himself to God in conversion. But he had slid back into sin. Now, "for one year past have been in a state of (not conviction) but great sorrow and remorse of conscience, and many times have attempted to destroy my own life. I often think that I have committed the unpardonable sin. Again I imagine that I am given over to hardness of heart and blindness of mind to believe a lie that I may be damned. . . . and o ye servant of God (Mr. Miller) will ye pray pray pray for me." Silas Guilford, Miller's nephew, expressed similar if less intense feelings: "Shall I in the course of this year and perhaps in a few months, weeks or Days in the General conflagration of everything Earthly be forever—separated from my savior . . . or shall I unworthy as I am—be changed from Mortal to Immortal as in the twinkling of an eye be caught up to Christ—in the air—be divested of everything selfish. . . . Resolve this dout in my mind and grant me that faith in the Savior—that I may be one of those who are watching for and longing for his Appearing." A third adventist confessed his "greatest fears are, that I am not worthy to be numbered" with the saints. Hiram Munger, a Millerite itinerant lecturer, encountered a woman in Erie County who confessed that after becoming convinced of Miller's theory "she had concluded to commit suicide, and once opened the door to throw her girl into the river, and then jump in herself." Only the pleading of her daughter had stayed her from completing the crime.[16]

One should not conclude from these isolated instances that insanity and emotional excess predominated among Millerites. Millerites themselves pointed out correctly that opponents of revivals had for decades charged that camp meetings drove people to distraction. A revivalist in the 1830s was so tired of these stories that he published a sermon contending that "sinners, not believers, are deranged." The *Midnight Cry* printed a story of a lad who attempted to poison his entire family "to escape their importunities for him to join the church—an extensive revival having taken place in the neighborhood, and with the whole family but himself having been converted." This example, claimed the paper, "illustrates the dreadful effects of revivals, quite as directly as the

[15] Child, 236; *State Lunatic Asylum, 1844*, 32; Pliny Earle, *History, Description and Statistics of the Bloomingdale Asylum for the Insane* (New York, 1848), 15, 85.
[16] Stephen Marsh to Miller, n. d.; Silas Guilford to Miller, January 2, 1843; Jonathan Cole, *Midnight Cry*, September 19, 1844; Munger, 110–11.

various stories about Millerism prove its pernicious tendencies."[17]
Because of Millerism's reputation for peculiarity, the public associated Millerites with other religious rebels of the day. To the *Angelica Reporter* Millerism was no different than "any other ism in religion by which imposters gain wealth or power, and believers are reduced into slavery or insanity." (Many people today would feel the same way about our modern cults.) Unfavorable comparisons with the Mormons were particularly numerous. True, both prophets were from upstate New York, transplanted New Englanders, and both were millenialists, though in quite different ways. But neither Mormons nor Millerites approved of the comparison. Adventists were shocked when they heard people claim "our doctrin is as bad as Jo Smiths" and that the people should "put them down immediately, as it might be more easily done now than when it was deeper rooted." Smith's revelation that Christ would not return in 1843 was almost certainly his attempt to dissociate himself from the Millerites, and the Millerites tried equally hard to distance themselves from him. "One day the world represents Mormonism and Millerism as twin brothers. The next, they hear that 'Joe Smith' has wiped all the stain from his pure skirts which a belief in Christ's near coming would attach to him, and they seem disposed to fondle their favorite pet."[18]
Many people believed Miller concocted his entire doctrine to make money, especially from the sale of his book. "Please inform the public how much you have made by your speculation," demanded one skeptic. From all over the state Miller heard of rumors that he "Want Sell books a Nuff to make a fortune," that Millerism "is a money making business," that he had charged thirty-five dollars as an honorarium for a series of lectures. Inevitably, there were some crooks in the movement. The *Voice of Truth* warned readers about a so-called adventist who was guilty of "collecting the subscriptions on your paper, and using it himself, and by so doing defrauding his brethren." The *Midnight Cry* similarly told of an Englishman "professing to be an Advent lecturer" who had been acting "a very dishonorable part . . . has proved himself a villain, and absconded." W. S. Burnham of Montpelier, Vermont, had a stock of Miller's book to sell but had left them in the care of a friend while on a trip. When he returned, he said, "I found that he had sold and lent some what not far from 50 book for which I have not rec'd one dollar. He was and is now a *poor man* in every sence of the world." In these cases, adventists seem to have been victims rather than perpetrators of fraud. But if one considers the adventists' frequent requests for contributions to

[17] Edward R. Hooker, "The Sinner and Not the Believer, Deranged," *National Preacher*, V (April 1831), 168); "Horrid Fruits of Revivals," *Midnight Cry*, March 10, 1843.
[18] *Angelica Reporter*, November 19, 1843; Mrs. Livingston to Miller, January 14, 1843; S. C. Chandler, *Midnight Cry*, July 27, 1843; *Midnight Cry*, March 13, 1843.

carry on the campaign, Himes's frenzy over losing investments in Millerite publications, and the way lecturers judged the success of a meeting by the number of books sold, skepticism seems to be warranted. Some adventists did charge admission fees or sell tickets for lectures in order to defray costs of renting space, lodging for speakers, etc. And on at least one occasion Himes offered to pay Miller for speaking. In 1840 he suggested that Miller spend a few months lecturing in Boston. Because he would have to "leave home, and all its enjoyments," Himes offered to pay Miller $100 a month in remuneration. Himes was quick to point out that he did not make the proposition "with any view of a mercenary character," and just to make sure the offer did not cause unfavorable publicity he requested the offer be "a profound secret between us."[19] There is no evidence Miller accepted the offer, but the tone of Himes's comments suggests adventists' defensiveness.

Some Millerites were financially well off. Though positive identification of Millerites is difficult and information even about these is scarce and not conclusive,[20] what information we have suggests they were above average in wealth. In two communities, Ithaca and Lockport, committed adventists signed petitions to Miller asking him to visit them, twenty-five in Ithaca and sixty-three in Lockport, many names obviously representing family groups. Twenty-three of the Lockport signers and ten from Ithaca appear in the 1850 census which provides information about their financial worth and occupation. That year, our Ithaca petitioners averaged $200 more in financial holdings than the average of a sample of Ithacans, and the same held true for Lockport signers. This evidence is not conclusive. Possibly in the five years since the demise of Millerism, poorer adventists had left their homes and moved elsewhere, whereas those better established in the community were able to weather the derision the Great Disappointment caused and remained. Still, while some adventists described themselves as "poor in the things of this world," several were quite well off. Miller left an estate of about $45,000 when he died in 1849; Clark Flint, a Millerite merchant in Attica, had property and holdings worth over $17,000 in 1850; and Elon Galusha placed his personal worth that year at $12,800. Some social scientists have interpreted millenarianism to be a movement of the poor and

[19] R. D. to Miller, n. d.; Livingston to Miller, January 14, 1843; Erastus Higley to Miller, December 15, 1842; W. S. Burnham to Miller, April 14, 1843; Himes to Miller, October 21, 1840.

[20] Because adventism peaked between the 1840 and the 1850 federal censuses and the 1845 New York State census has practically disappeared, any census we use is five years removed from the period of Millerism's greatest activity. Even when we identify committed adventists it is not always possible to locate their residence. Many were itinerants, others moved, died, or otherwise disappeared. So our sample is so small as to be inconclusive.

dispossessed. In monetary terms, at least, this was untrue of the bulk of Millerites, though as pietists they did feel dispossessed of the object of their greatest desire, Heaven.

However, far from achieving comfort at the expense of a gullible public, many had been well established before joining the movement. In fact, their contributions to Millerism are what made the expensive crusade possible. Miller claimed to have contributed "more than two thousand dollars of my own property in twelve years," and Himes spent over $2,000 during a tour of Ohio. "I did not get half enough to pay actual expenses," he said. "Some speculation this!" Nor did anyone get rich by selling Miller's book. The second edition sold for little more than the printing costs, and Millerites gave away as many copies, if not more, as they sold.[21]

Of course, whether charges of profiteering were true was less important than whether the public believed them. Millerite opponents encouraged these misconceptions, successfully mobilizing the popular secular and religious media against Millerism to dissuade the public from becoming ensnared in delusion. While adventist publications circulated only among those who were already committed or curious, the popular press circulated among a much broader audience. Among these readers, the media created a Millerite image so negative that it endures to this very day. Part of that image was well founded, but much of it was scurrilous.

The religious press united against adventism, though the tone of their comments varied from journal to journal. The Baptist *Christian Review* proclaimed the Millerites heretics, saying the movement was full of "error and fanaticism," and both New York State Baptist journals agreed. The *Methodist Magazine* denigrated chiliasm, though not mentioning Millerism specifically, and pointedly endorsed Moses Stuart's allegorical interpretation of prophecy. The *Oberlin Evangelist* criticized Miller's hermeneutic, but it assumed a tone of Christian charity, particularly when it scolded Charles Fitch, an Oberlin graduate, for his leading role in the movement. Marsh's old journal, the *Christian Palladium*, lashed out at its former editor, and Alexander Campbell's *Millennial Harbinger* tenderly offered its opposition to premillennialism and advocated the cause of temporal church reform. Across New York preachers and laymen delivered sermons and lectures against the movement, some, like George Bush, becoming anti-Millerite itinerants and charging admission fees. Exegetes published their own commentaries on the prophecies, thereby taking advantage of a ready market. Stuart, for instance, published a new edition of his popular *Hints on the Interpretation of*

---

[21] White, 183; Himes to Miller, November 24, 1843. H. B. Skinner wrote from Buffalo, "[We] sell but little, yet we can give away to almost any extent." *Midnight Cry*, October 26, 1843.

Prophecy in 1841. While in most cases their critique of adventism was heated, these opponents sought to dissuade participation in Millerism by appealing to reasoned argument.[22]

The principal weapon of the secular press was ridicule. Generally unacquainted with the content of Miller's message or with Miller's essential orthodoxy, editors used filler material from derogatory reports about adventists in New York City and Boston newspapers. The *Steuben Democrat* copied a typical story from the *Knickerbocker.* A New England farmer's wife became a "thorough going destructionist" thanks to the preaching of Miller, "a cunning old humbug." One stormy night this man's "possessed rib" woke him with cries of "'Husband did you hear that noise? It's Gabriel a coming! It's the sound of his chariot wheels.'" The sleepy and disgruntled farmer cried out, "'Oh pshaw, you fool. Do you s'pose Gabriel is such an ass as to come on wheels in such good sleighing as this?" The Norwich *Chenango Telegraph* told its readers of an English apocalyptic group that predicted the end of the world only to have its prediction proved untrue. "Brothers, when questioned on the *inexpediency* of getting up such a humbug, modestly replied that *but for their intercession with the Almighty for the non-fulfillment of his prophecy, the world would certainly* have been destroyed!"[23]

Local pranksters often made the lives of Millerites unbearable. A. P. Weaver in Sackets Harbor, who had long advocated adventism, received a letter from "Mr. Miller." Since Weaver was the "only man that believed in the 'Second Coming of Christ' in this place," wrote the writer, "I would inform you that the 'World' has commenced burning in Main in the North East corner. It does not burn verry fast, so I had time to write you a few lines before I got ready." The writer asked Weaver to "spread the news as fast as possible. . . . We shall soon meet in another world I hope where parting Shall be no more." A notation on the back indicates the real writer's name, obviously a neighbor out to have some fun. Probably of the same genre were dozens of rumors about Miller that circulated widely and caused confusion among adventists. Many wrote to Miller asking if it was true that he announced a 100-year error in his chronology, and Charles Cole wrote anxiously to find out whether Miller had actually died and on his deathbed renounced his "views on the Prophecies and pronounced them false!"[24]

---

[22] A representative assortment of articles can be found in the *Christian Review*, IX (December 1844), 497–509; *Methodist Magazine*, XXIV (July 1842), 352–77, and XXV (January 1843), 83–110; *Methodist Review*, XXIV (1841), 479; *Oberlin Evangelist*, V (January 18, 1842), 15, and (December 6, 1843), 199; *Christian Palladium*, XIII (October 16, November 13, and December 11, 1844): *Millennial Harbinger*, a series of articles entitled "The Coming of the Lord," in issues from June 1840 through February 1843.

[23] *Steuben Democrat*, January 3, 1841; *Chenango Telegraph*, April 3, 1844.

[24] "Mr. Miller" to Weaver, March 17, 1844, Pickering-Beach Historical Museum, Sackets

Despite its opponents' reasoned persuasion and ridicule, adventism found a home in villages and churches throughout the state. Opponents then tried to ostracize Millerites. Congregations judged and expelled adventists widely, though it is impossible to say how many exclusions in the 1840s were caused by adventism. The number of excommunications generally was high, but the causes were numerous, and church records do not always list the reason for disciplinary action. No doubt Millerism accounted for many of them. An interesting example of the process appears in records of the Immanuel Baptist Church. In 1844 the congregation appointed a committee to "labor with the Millerites" among them, and the committee reported the adventsts had "changed their belief in regard to many points of Baptist Creed. They Beleaved that they ought to Commune with All Christians & had Communed by themselves & in vited Any to commune that would & that they did not beleave in But very little of the present Faith & practis of the ch. Neither Did they Beleave in ordaining Ministers but that any member of the chh. had a wright to Baptize & Break Bread, Preach or any thing else that they thaught the Lord called them to Done, & on the Report of the com. the chh. voted to withdraw the hand of fellowship from them." (Here we also get a clear view of these Millerites' antiformalism.) Thomas Taylor of Half Moon said that in the Baptist Church there "it became an old story with the minister and his followers. There was about 15 or 20 of us that held on to the doctrine called Millerism. The church soon got sick of hearing us talk about the Lord's coming so soon so they cast us all out of the synagogue."[25]

Opponents also ostracized Millerites by refusing them use of facilities for meetings and lectures. A lecturer in Delhi spoke "in the basement of the Methodist Chapel which was then closed—the court house was then procured. Our meetings were full; but the nobility and rulers in Zion shut us out of that also." The Baptist adventist pastor in Covert was presented with a resolution by the anti-Millerite majority that opposed "our meeting house being used for any other purpose than for religious exercises, or such meetings as in the opinion of the trustees are designed for the glory of God."[26]

Finally, when persuasion, ridicule, and ostracism failed, opponents both threatened and used violence. Storrs claimed to have received a threatening note charging him with "'letting [Calvin] French into Grand St. Church'" and saying that unless Storrs "'turn him from your house

Harbor; Isaac Fuller to Miller, January 31, 1840, and William S. Miller to Miller, January 24, 1838.
[25] Records of the Immanuel Baptist Church, I, March 24, 1844, 134–37, American Baptist Historical Society; Thomas Taylor to Miller, November 19, 1845.
[26] *Midnight Cry*, March 10, 1843. See also letters of Samuel Hopkins, ibid., January 11, 1844; Marsh to Miller, August 17, 1843; Halsey, 97–98.

and shut the door from him and his followers, you may expect damage done to your person and property for years to come, at such times as can be done in secret. If fair means wont do, foul will.'" Himes received similar notes during his sojourn in Albany with the Great Tent from a man who blamed him for driving a friend insane. A mob attacked Samuel Rhodes in Ellisburgh. "Boys and beings in the shape of men," including a "professed minister of the gospel and other baser sorts of sinners, and the vilest of the vile" surrounded the house in which he was speaking "and sometime in the night (it is supposed) as the doors were unlocked, entered the house, and poured great quantities of tar upon the seats, pulpit post, doors, etc." Other lecturers had similar experiences.[27]

Attacks on meetings prompted Himes to hire Hiram Munger as a bouncer. When two rowdies tried to disrupt a meeting Munger informed them that "this was a 'time meeting' and it was *time* for them to be going." This led to a small scuffle and the arrest of the troublemakers. Another time, three men arrived at a camp meeting "on purpose to fight with me." Munger challenged one of them to a wrestling match. The group went off into the woods where Munger forced the man to holler "'fairly done' a number of times." Said Munger, "I kept him moving until he was satisfied he was much better off then he would have been to have fought, as he first proposed."[28]

The degree of success of all these opponents' tactics depended on local circumstances. Millerites admitted they could only proselytize where "the ministers of the different churches have co-operated, or indeed where they have not opposed." Elsewhere, as in Erie and Clinton Counties, a united ministry standing against adventism "produced a reaction against Millerism." As one Millerite put it, "It is hard to remain surrounded by ice, and not be chilled by its influence." Although adverse publicity and a negative public image were hurdles, they were not insurmountable. Edward Canfield encountered great skepticism when he introduced Millerism to Waterloo for the first time in 1843, "the doctrine supposed to be an idle theory or fancy, a 'humbug' adapted to scare people and make them crazy." But after his delivering six lectures "the public mind was disabused. They saw that instead of idle fancy, it was substantial Scripture truth and historical evidence."[29] The explosion of support for Millerism in 1843 and 1844 in the face of enormous antagonisms illustrates the movement's powers of persuasion.

[27] *Signs of the Times*, August 3 and 26, 1842; *Midnight Cry*, September 19, March 28, 1844; S. C. Chandler to Miller, April 18, 1844.
[28] Munger, 51–52.
[29] C. S. Loomis, *Midnight Cry*, February 8, 1844; L. Delos Mansfield, ibid., April 20, 1843; A. N. Bentley, ibid., February 8, 1844; Edward Canfield, ibid., April 20, 1843.

Indeed, the very virulence of the opposition diminished its effectiveness. For instance, the wide, albeit unflattering, publicity which the Millerites received aroused public curiosity about them. Also, violent opposition stirred sympathy in many who could not accept adventists' views but who believed them to be "sincere and well meaning" and undeserving of abuse. Furthermore, their doctrine regarding the end of the world and Final Judgment was so orthodox and so awesome that it commanded respect. "The sneers, the laughs, the triflings, the sad indifference of the people to the subject," wrote one nonadventist, "proves no more against the truth of it, than it did against the predictions of Noah, to the old world." One correspondent to the *Baptist Register* criticized the editor's scorn for the Millerites. "Thought too solemn for a religious paper to trifle with, or any other!" And one man cancelled his subscription to the *Baptist Advocate* for its treatment of the Millerites. Non-Millerites who were engaged in other reform movements protested against "closing the doors of a Church against such sentiments as [Miller] advances" just as they would decry "closing them against the principles of Abolition." Lydia Maria Child said, "I am sorry that the Millerites have attracted the attention of a portion of our population, who delight to molest them, though it is more from mirth than malice. All sincere convictions should be treated respectfully."[30]

Millerite criticisms of society struck a chord among people who could not accept their religious views, for social disenchantment was widespread. All Americans, not just Millerites and other pietists, had to adjust in the 1830s and '40s to a new national economy, mass party politics, growing social stratification, industrialization, and religious formalization, and many bemoaned the loss of traditional values.

In an article called "The End of the World, a Vision," James K. Paulding spoofed contemporary society, including the Millerites. He took an imaginary walk among his neighbors on the Last Day as the heat slowly rose to burning temperatures. He encountered one "shriveled, cadaverous, spectre, hugging a bag of gold, and lamenting the hardship of being called away just the day before the interest became payable on his bank stocks." A moneylender was "lamenting that he was not aware of what was coming, as he would certainly have borrowed a good round sum, and thus escaped paying the interest." One who had scoffed at the Millerites regretted now having been "so busy in proving it to be all

[30] *Baptist Advocate*, April 12, 1844; *Rochester Daily Democrat*, October 18, 1844; *Bath Constitutionalist*, November 19, 1841; *Tompkins Volunteer*, January 17, 1843, and January 31, 1843; *Baptist Register*, May 17, 1844. Robert Dickson was the man who cancelled his subscription to the *Baptist Advocate* because he was "disgusted with the course pursued" by that paper, even though he was not himself a Millerite. Nathan Chapman to Nathan Randall Chapman, July 11, 1845, Nathan Chapman Correspondence, Chapman Family Papers, Syracuse University; Child, 239.

humbug, that I . . . am altogether unprepared." Miller was there, too, as disreputable as the others. He had been so busy proclaiming the end of the world he had forgotten to prepare himself for Judgment. "Bless my soul," he said in surprise. "I had no idea it would be so hot!"[31]

Millerism's radical vision of reform attracted Orestes Brownson, mercurial Transcendentalist and former Unitarian, whose personal quest for moral order would eventually propel him into the Catholic Church. Brownson contrasted conservative reform with what he called "come-outerism," his definitions conforming closely with our contrast of formalism *versus* antiformalism. The conservative method of reform was to "accept the existing order, and through it, by such modes of action as it tolerates or authorizes, to seek the correction of abuses, and a more perfect development." Come-outerism sought to "resist the existing order, to abjure its laws, and to attempt to introduce an entirely new order." Brownson found much to criticize and much to applaud in both, but he recognized that come-outers—Millerites, Socialists, Mormons, and others—were part of a long tradition and were very products of the libertarian philosophy on which America was founded. They were "the Jacobins of the eighteenth century, the Independents and Fifth Monarchy Men of the seventeenth, and the Protestants of the sixteenth." Radical reform was nothing less than "the common faith of the country pushed to its last consequences. . . . Assuming individualism in religion, and no government without the assent of the governed, and the right of revolution in politics, we defy any man, who can reason logically, to escape the conclusions of our Come-outers. We may say there is no occasion for the extremes to which they carry matters, we may dispute about this or that practical point, but we cannot object to their doctrines. They are consistent; we who oppose them are inconsistent. They have the courage to be true to their principles. We cowardly shrink from the consequences of our own faith." Considering America's tradition of volunteerism and liberty, what wonder "that men engaged in what they believe a good cause should, on finding themselves resisted or not aided by Church or State, assume the right to set Church or State aside, and to proclaim the absolute freedom of the individual in regard to either?"[32]

Millerites were in that libertarian tradition. If violence against them was meant to intimidate them into silence or inactivity, the effect was the opposite. Opposition strengthened their fervor and directed it into separatism. "Reasoning with those thus affected [by adventism] is of no use," noted Pliny Earle. "In fact, we were assured by one of the believers

31 James K. Paulding, "The End of the World, a Vision," *Graham's Magazine*, XXII (March 1843), 145–49.

32 "Come-outerism; or the Radical Tendency of the Day," *Brownson's Quarterly Review*, I (1844), 370–79.

in the late delusion, that according to his observation, it but tended to confirm him." Several Millerites, facing "contumely and misrepresentation of scoffers," confirmed they had "never been more grounded in the faith of the coming of the Lord."

Their opponents provided Millerites with a negative reference group; they were what their enemies were not. Scoffers were rich and materialistic, but adventists came from among "the common people." The ridiculing churches were split and divided. The fact that in adventist meetings "so great a number from so diverse denominations were gathering on common ground, and Christian love" proved they were succeeding where the denominations had failed. Millerites were responsible for widespread revivalism because advent preaching "embodying as it does the higher elements of moral power" was awakening sinners where "ordinary preaching . . . does no good." Others might take credit for revivals, but the real heroes were "those faithful laborers who have been sounding the midnight cry among us, and have been instrumental, under God, of the glorious revivals of religion which we have witnessed."[33]

All of these signs, the Millerites' assumed commonness, humility, and unity, convinced many that they had actually restored the primitive Church. "Who can look at the bands of believers in the Lord's speedy return," wrote L. Delos Mansfield, "scattered through the land, and not be reminded of the days when no man said that anything was his own, but they had all things in common? Love was the bond of union then, and blessed be the name of the Lord, he is a people now, organized under the very same creed."[34] The Millerite character was distinct, opposite to the evil world, separate from it.

Ridicule affirmed adventists' belief that they were akin to the ancient apostles by providing them with a feeling of martyrdom. Adventists defined themselves as Israelites fleeing from Egypt with the Lord opening "the Red Sea as fast as we go forward." They were like the "patriarchs, prophets, apostles and glorious company of martyrs, and the saints of all ages," the "despised Nazarene" ascending "up the rugged ascent of Calvary." Wrote Butler Morley, "We are now in a similar condition to Noah before the flood came—to Lot before the fire kindled upon Sodom—to Gideon and his despised few before the Midianites fled—to Joshua before Jericho's massive walls gave way—to the pious youth, who though despised for his simplicity of faith, triumphed over the mighty giant of Gath, and the unbelief and fears of Israel and to the

[33] *Journal of Insanity*, 251; Bissel, *Midnight Cry*, December 21, 1843; C. Morley, *Signs of the Times*, August 24, 1842; H. M. Allen to Miller, February 6, 1843; E. S. Loomis, *Midnight Cry*, February 6, 1844.
[34] L. Delos Mansfield, *Midnight Cry*, November 10, 1843.

primitive disciples before Jesus arose from the dead."[35]

This biblical imagery defined their opponents too. If the adventists were the Jews fleeing Egypt, their enemies were the Egyptian oppressors. Adventists vented their anger most against scoffing ministers and churches. Wrote Miller, "I am astonished they cannot see their own character so clearly described in the Bible.—They aim to destroy every conviction of the truth which may be fastened on the minds of the impenitent, and soon God will manifest their deception to the world." By rejecting adventism they were endangering the souls of their flocks. "O! what an account these ministers will have to render who have thus deceived souls to their ruin!" How could they laugh and jeer "at those who would warn the people of their approaching danger." The answer was obvious to the faithful. They do not preach the Second Coming of Christ "because they are not willing to have it true." Because that event will "blast all his expectations and worldly prospects." The natural conclusion was that "the churches occupy the same position with regard to the second advent that the Jews did with regard to the first." They were the Anti-Christ.[36]

Antiformal pietism combined with hostility toward scoffing preachers to create among many adventists nearly unrestrained hostility to the churches and desires for revenge. Tired of ridicule and exclusion, adventists looked eagerly for the Second Coming of Christ not just to verify God and the scriptures but also to justify their faith and to wreak havoc. "O what a dreadful day that will be for those professors of religion, 'who come not to the help of the Lord against the mighty!'" Surely God had purposely deluded opponents "that they should believe a lie, that they all might be damned." Understandably, Miller yearned most strongly for vindication. No one had suffered more than he and his scorned family. He wrote his son, "I have often felt how deep must be the wounds your young, and tender and unexperienced hearts must feel when you see the thousand and one falsehoods which a proud and haughty priesthood have invented, and an hireling press has circulated." Remember that such people are "engaged in the work of their master the devil." But soon "no lying editor will ever have a part in polluting the character or misrepresenting the views of your aged Parrent." The day is coming when "no scoffing Priest will ever mantle your cheek with a blush for what your father endures at the unholy remarks." Then, "the world, the scoffer, and I shall be in another world, to render our account before a righteous tribunal. I will therefore appeal to the Supreme Court of the Universe for the redress of grievances, and the rendering of judgment in my favor, by the revocation of the judgment in the court below. The World and Clergy vs. Miller."[37]

This vengeful spirit was troubling to more cool-headed adventists who warned against "vanity or pride" and a "spirit of commendation, congratulative, almost approaching flattery" that characterized some of those "who are looking for the consolation of Israel." Henry Dana Ward urged patience. "We need not arm in self-defense," he wrote. "We need not throw back the enemies darts, though we *could* with a vengeance; we need not judge any man, we need not speak evil of the church or the ministry, or the Bible Society, or the Temperance Cause; and yet these are all in the hands of frail men, in a cold clime and anyone who is disposed to find fault with them or to scoff at them and their like will find material for his disposition increase on his hands." Ward urged Miller to forget his own bitterness and assert his great influence "in subduing the passions, & restraining the vexed spirits of others, whose feelings are smarting under the undeserved wounds of their friends." Indeed, despite his private rage, Miller publicly advised against "yielding to a spirit of revenge against the churches on account of their injustice toward us and of waging an indiscriminate warfare against *all such organizations.*"[38]

In 1843 such advice came too late. The fact was that hundreds of Millerites were already meeting together separately from their churches, some having withdrawn from their congregations voluntarily, others expelled. The leaders' own words seemed to justify this. "I have advised all men of every sort not to separate from their churches," wrote Miller, but he added the significant caveat, "if they could live among them and enjoy Christian privileges." Obviously, many could not. Himes's attitude was similar. "The Adventists cherish the kindest feelings towards the churches," he said exaggeratedly, "but we are nevertheless firm, and determined to make the Advent cause paramount." The pietistic dynamic was running its course; separation was a fact. It awaited only moral justification, which in 1843 Charles Fitch provided. In a letter to Josiah Litch, subsequently published in pamphlet form, Fitch took Millerite condemnation of the churches to its logical conclusion. Denominations were the Anti-Christ, were prophetic Babylon, and all saints must now "come out of Babylon" lest they partake of the destruction to fall on the wicked. "If you are a Christian, *come out of Babylon.* If you intend to be found a Christian

---

[37] Miller to William S. Miller, April 5, 1844; *Midnight Cry*, December 14, 1843; Miller to Galusha, April 5, 1844 and Miller to Himes, December 7, 1842.
[38] Almond Owen, *Midnight Cry*, June 22, 1843; E. C. Clemons, *Voice of Truth*, July 27, 1844; Ward to Miller, October 29, 1841; *Midnight Cry*, June 13, 1844.

when Christ appears, *come out of Babylon*, and come out *now*. Throw away that miserable medley of ridiculous spiritualizing nonsense, with which multitudes have so long been making the Word of God of none effect, and dare to believe the Bible."[39] The process of alienation was complete. Whoever remained in the churches was not a Christian; only adventists who removed themselves from the churches could hope for salvation; separation was not only desirable but a test of faith.

Soon the cry of "Come out of her my people" could be heard across the state. "It is doubtless as much the *duty* of true Christians to 'come out of Babylon' *now* as it was for Lot to flee from Sodom the morning before its destruction," wrote one. Not only the churches, but governments too constituted Babylon, and one adventist warned in the presidential election year of 1844 against "being connected with the human governments of this world" by voting or holding office. Millerites should "be united to a man in our glorious candidate, the son of God, the true heir to David's throne." And the Millerites fled. In Cooperstown "true and godfearing men are embracing it, leaving their corrupt church and gathering together as 'one in Jesus Christ.'" In Port Byron "the chains of the church discipline and superstition that have hitherto bound us down in darkness and moral delusion, have been burst assunder, and we are no longer the subjects of the vassalating influence of our fashionable religious association." Two Ithaca women asked the Baptist Church "to Exclude them they having embraced the Millerite doctrine." P. P. Ladu of Volney wrote to his Christian Church that although he had resigned from the Methodists and had become a Christianite because he believed in church reform, now he felt that transfer had been "something like Lot fleeing from Sodom into Gomorrah." He therefore resigned from the Christianites and proclaimed, "from this date, I consider myself free from all unscriptural Churches and conferences."[40]

Miller ceased advising against separation, and Himes, who once expressed his determination "to drive the War into the Enemies Camp!!!" accepted separation as sound strategy. Joseph Marsh jumped on the bandwagon immediately. In the very first issue of the *Voice of Truth* in January 1844, he wrote, "We do not hesitate . . . to advise our suffering brethren to come out from such a persecuting church, and hold meetings by themselves." Miller was still advising against separation at the time, and Marsh ridiculed him. He even went so far as to refer to believers in

---

[39] Miller, *Midnight Cry*, November 18, 1842; Himes, ibid., January 18, 1844; Charles Fitch, *Letter to Josiah Litch on the Second Coming of Christ* (Boston, 1841), 2; Fitch, *Come Out of Her My People* (Rochester, 1843).

[40] *Midnight Cry*, March 28, 1844; Mansfield, ibid., March 28, 1844; S. C. Chandler, ibid., May 23, 1844; David Plumb, ibid., March 14, 1844; C. Morley, ibid., March 21, 1844; ibid., February 15, 1844; First Baptist Church of Ithaca, Records, III (October 8, 1844), Cornell University; P. P. Ladu, *Voice of Truth*, November 27, 1844.

the Second Coming of Christ as Adventists, Christians with a special purpose, a special identity.[41]

Public reaction was just as Henry Dana Ward had feared. Come-outerism stamped the Millerites indelibly as radicals and sectarians and thereby destroyed much public sympathy for them. One preacher who believed in the personal Advent, though not a Millerite, had defended the Millerites publicly. But separatism was a personal affront. "The time was when these men were supposed to be honest and sincere, but if a love of party, a desire to build up a new sect, is not becoming prominent, I have greatly mistaken the signs of the times. . . . I confess it does not set very easy on my conscience after having preached this doctrine [the personal return of Christ] for years to be consigned to perdition for not embracing and teaching [Millerism]." The Madison Baptist Association lambasted Millerites for allowing adventism to become the *engrossing* subject of thought and action." Who can deny "that SOME perfectionists and SOME Adventists, and even SOME Abolitionists, for months past, have been COMING OUT from the various christian denominations; that each of these sects have been making its own favorite sentiment, more than any other, the test of fellowship and cooperation." Separation even divided some Millerite groups. In Ithaca the Baptist Church seems to have been largely Millerite, for on July 6, 1844, the congregation approved a resolution affirming that "the Master will soon appear for the relief of our mourning Zion." Their clerk, Henry B. Squires, had long been an adventist and corresponded with the movement's leaders. But in mid-July he adopted come-outerism and resigned from the church. The congregation would not tolerate his secession, and they placed him on trial for "traducing the character of the church pronouncing the Church a complete Babylon." On July 19 the Baptists excluded him, not for being a Millerite but for breaking fellowship.[42]

Adverse public reaction now convinced Miller that separation was a mistake. Privately he suggested, "The enemy has a hand in this, to divert our attention from the true cry, the midnight cry, 'Behold the Bridegroom Cometh.'" Though a true antiformalist, he feared that establishing a new sect would simply corrupt the adventist cause, and a staunch Baptist, he could not reject the concept of fellowship. Because churches are corrupt, he asked, are Christians justified in rejecting them? St. Paul had faced the same question, "and did he say 'come out of *her*,' or did he say cleanse yourselves and put out from among you those incestuous persons? I should be very loth to say to any of Gods people 'Come out of

---

[41] Himes to Miller, October 21, 1844.
[42] *Baptist Register*, November 1, 1844; *Madison Baptist Association, 1844*, 15; Ithaca Baptist Church, Records, July 6, 1844, and July 17, 1844.

his church.'"[43] Yet he would not publicly speak against separation.

He knew it was too late. The pietistic dynamic was in control, rocking the Millerites now just as they had rocked the churches. Babylon and Zion battled against each other. But the Millerite army did not go to battle united. Come-outerism divided Millerites, thus illustrating one last effect of the pietistic dynamic. It precluded the creation of a Millerite consensus. Adventists, whether they stayed in the churches or withdrew from them, still faced the traditional pietist dilemma. How should they act in the light of impending destruction and Judgment? If separatism was one sign of true faith, were there others? Once separate, exactly what was Adventism? More important, who should decide? That these questions now assumed great significance was a sign that Millerism itself was formalizing, seeking a structure of faith and practice. But antiformalism precluded giving this process direction or leadership, for that smacked of authoritarianism. As the time of their Great Event approached, Millerites sought the special meaning of their crusade, but their libertarianism made it impossible for them to agree on what that meaning was. Suddenly there was a Babel in Zion.

[43] Miller to Galusha, April 5, 1844.

Chapter 7
A BABEL IN ZION

Exactly what is Millerism? Many adventists and critics alike had ready answers, but none was sufficient to define the movement. Critics were amazed at the variegation of Miller's following that included "those who were formerly Methodists, Baptists, Congregationalists, Episcopalians, and others who professed no particular creed." Theologically there were "Annihilationists [who believed the souls of the damned would be obliterated rather than suffer eternal punishment] who unite with Universalists in denying that there is any hell for punishment of the wicked; Arians, Socians, etc. etc. and yet united on this one point [Millerism] they are all brethren, hale fellows well met."[1] If combined centrifugal effects of revivalism and antiformalism had thrown diverse people out of many churches, what was the centripetal force that brought them together in the Millerite movement? Sectarianism molded the Millerite body, but what was the specific shape of that body? What were its features?

The *Christian Review* suggested an obvious answer with which most people, adventists and nonadventists, then and now, would have agreed. "We answer, whatever it be, the only feature of it which has given it any degree of currency in the community, is the single article, that the second coming of Christ, to judge the world, was to take place in the year 1843."[2] Yet many adventists did not believe this at all. Many were as uncomfortable as scoffers with the concept of revealed time. Adventists in Busti, Chautaqua County, confessed that "as it respects *time*, we agree that it is 'nigh, even at the door,' but are not all of us satisfied that the *date* is a matter of DEFINITE REVELATION." Albany Millerites stated in 1842 that they "did not expect a *fixed opinion* with regard to the *time*, but that from the light we at present have, we are more inclined to think that 1843 is the time than any other period." Skeptics included some of the movement's most important leaders. Henry Jones refused to count himself among those "who fix the year of the second advent," and Joseph Marsh, in 1842, would preach only that the Second Coming "is near, even at the door." If he had to define the time, "I shall be compelled to say it is 1843," but he was reluctant to commit himself. Henry

---

[1] *Baptist Advocate*, September 14, 1843, and July 4, 1843.
[2] *Christian Review*, IX (December 1844), 599.

Dana Ward, in an address to the Boston Conference in 1841, reminded his audience "with great deference" of the Lord's admonition, "'It is not for you *to know* the times or the seasons, which the Father hath put in his power.'" He went further. To Miller he privately warned, "For the *date* offends many, that, if they first examined the subject *dispassionately* would take no offense at the *date* though they should not be convinced of its correctness. The ammunition of the date also subjects you and those who act with you, to great reproach and obloquy." Even Miller was not dogmatic about time, though he defended it strongly. Ever timorous, he once confessed to Himes, "I wish I could know my adoption as strong, as I believe my calculation is right."[3]

Nor did all adventists accept Miller's figurative interpretation of the promised conversion of the Jews and the restoration of Israel. Levi Hathaway, a Millerite of West Mendon, thought Miller had the correct date but the wrong event. In 1843, he thought, "the proclamation will go forth from the Congress of Sovereigns of the Earth, to the Jews to return to their own land." The issue actually fractured adventism in New York City where a group of "judaizers" who believed that the Jews must return to Palestine before the end of the world seceded from the Millerites' General Conference, established their own meeting, and adopted Jewish customs and clothing. They then set about condemning regular Millerites for their lack of faith. "I am out of patience with these bastard Jews," wrote Miller. "Better be all Jew and have done with it. No getting into them any truth, all fog."[4]

Although the core doctrine of Millerism was the personal, literal, imminent, Second Coming of Christ, the movement's libertarianism encouraged free thinking, not doctrinal unanimity. After all, if Miller, on his own and without theological training, could find secrets in the Bible, why should not others do the same? As Joseph Marsh said to his wife, he was unwilling to "admit *anything* on points which he has not *himself* investigated." Most adventists would have agreed with one crusader's declaration, "I can adopt no man's opinion as my faith any farther than I can see it agreed with scripture and with the Light I have." Furhermore, one person's "light" was another's darkness. If an individual Millerite's light differed substantially from Miller's, the result was confusion in the ranks. Silas Hawley believed and preached that Christ would come in

3 Davis, *Midnight Cry*, February 15, 1844; report of the Albany Conference, *Signs of the Times*, August 3, 1842; Henry Jones, *Midnight Cry*, December 6, 1842; Joseph Marsh to Miller, April 22, 1842; Ward, *Signs of the Times*, January 1, 1842; Ward to Miller, October 29, 1841; Miller to Hendryx, October 23, 1834.

4 Levi Hathaway, *Signs of the Times*, May 15, 1841; Miller to Himes, April 5, 1842. On Millerite interpretations of prophecies relating to the return of the Jews to Palestine, see Ward, "'The Hope of Israel,'" *Methodist Review*, XXIV (1842), 192–220, and David Plumb, *The True Heirs of the Abrahamic Inheritance* (Utica, 1843).

1847, not in 1843. Commented Himes, "He has done nothing to harmo-
nize the *prophetic periods*. Hawley's chronology unsettles *everything*
and *settles* nothing." Determined to put a "double guard upon the *Harmony of the periods, ending in 43*," he decided it would be better to
publish Hawley's views "and refute it, than to *shut him out*." Editors
must be careful to show "that there is no skulking—no backing out—but
we are willing to meet the crisis as honest men and Christians." A group
of adventists in New Hampshire prophesied that "all things here below,
or the end of the world, will happen on the 3d day of April 1843," and
an Albany Millerite's prediction that the world would end on March 12,
1843, received wide notice in the nonadventist press. The public naturally assumed that Miller had authorized these statements, and so did
many Millerites. In order to clarify his position, he published a strong
denial that he had ever predicted "*any other time*" than 1843 and that
he had never "fixed on any month, day or hour."[5]

If the dissident was charismatic, he could actually carry away many
followers from the fold. George Storrs was such a leader. He had been
preaching Millerism in Albany since 1841 and had become an important
regional spokesman for the movement. Before becoming a Millerite, he
had already gained wide notoriety as something of a theological innova-
tor. Storrs was an Annihilationist, an adherent to a doctrine that had
developed in New England during the revivalism of the 1780s. Proponents of Annihilationism, like Universalists, believed God was too kind
to condemn a soul to eternal punishment. Unlike Universalists who
preached that God would restore souls to righteousness at the end of
time, Annihilationists believed the Lord would simply obliterate the souls
of the damned. Storrs not only preached this doctrine, he also published
an Annihilationist journal called the *Bible Examiner*, and he incorporated the doctrine in his lectures on the imminent end of the world. His
view of the "second death" contrasted sharply with Miller's conception
of the "second resurrection, the resurrection unto damnation." Miller,
who grew up during the time when Annihilationism first developed, was
long opposed to its anti-Calvinist tenet, and his disenchantment with
Deism in the early 1800s had resulted in part from a belief that it
"tended to a belief in annihilation." Thus Storrs's doctrine struck a sore
spot with Miller. More important, Storrs, who possessed a "more than
ordinary ability as a speaker and writer," reportedly drew crowds of
"thousands on thousands." His new reputation as an adventist gave him a

[5] Sarah Marsh to Miller, February 24, 1842; Jonathan Cole to Miller, November 26,
1836; Himes to Miller, November 24, 1843, and December 8, 1843, October 23, 1841;
Signs of the Times, August 10, 1842; *New York Herald*, April 3, 1843.

perfect opportunity to disseminate his views, and he republished some of his tracts on Annihilationism.[6]

With Storrs's growing influence among New York adventists already evident, a letter from Charles Fitch which appeared in the *Bible Examiner* in 1844 filled the movement's leaders with consternation. "After much thought, and prayer, and a full conviction of duty to God," wrote Fitch, it was apparent to him that Storrs was correct on "the subject of the state of the dead, and the final doom of the wicked." After this letter appeared, relations between Storrs and the other leaders of the crusade deteriorated rapidly. He failed to attend Miller's lectures in New York City that spring, even though he was in the city at the time, for which Miller wrote him a sharp note. Excusing himself on the ground that his wife was ill, Storrs tried to reassure Miller that "my *heart is with you.*" But it was his words that Miller and others worried about. Sylvester Bliss believed Storrs's views implied the individual had no soul at all. "When men become fully satisfied that *they* have *no* souls, I think we may admit that possibly they may *not* be mistaken respecting *themselves*: but I do protest against their judging of the souls of others by the size of their *own* soul. . . . But I believe we have souls. If it is any satisfaction to others to believe *they* are on a par with the beasts that perish in that respect, I should be loth to take from their satisfaction." And reports suggested Storrs's influence was growing. In Oaksville, a Millerite said, "Bro. G. Storrs opinions on the extent of the kingdom, his Annihilation of the wicked, has raised a controversy amongst the people, yea even amongst the Advent Brethren which I deeply deplore and pray God may be removed."[7]

Leading adventists were indeed determined to remove it. I. E. Jones, Josiah Litch, Nathaniel Whiting, Himes, Bliss, and Apollos Hale agreed on a strategy to discredit Storrs. "As it is now," Jones wrote to Miller, "he virtually wields from our silence virtually the whole, or almost the whole, Advent influence; and from this cause has probably made an hundred converts to that faith [Annihilationism] since he came into these ranks, to where he did one before." Claiming great love for Storrs, they nevertheless agreed they loved truth more. "I fear this has been let alone quite too long; and now the question is, shall we go up to the judgment under these circumstances in silence and not be guilty?" Apparently not, for they had decided to publish a new paper "independent of Advent papers" supporting their views on damnation.[8] Soon the failure of all

[6] Nichol, 192; Wellcome, 281–82; Marini, 55.

[7] Charles Fitch to George Storrs, January 25, 1844, Himes Papers; Storrs to Miller, February 10, 1844; Sylvester Bliss to Miller, September 20, 1844; Jacob Hart to Miller, May 27, 1844.

[8] I. E. Jones, et al., to Miller, April 6, 1844.

apocalyptic predictions settled the problem by discrediting Storrs along with the others.

While the movement's antiformal libertarianism justified differences in belief, the crusade's millenarianism encouraged *active* dissent from Miller's views. For to all active Millerites active faith was as important as correctness of belief in order to win salvation. George Duffield, Jr., described this compulsion to act. "There can be no neutrality here," he said of millenarianism. Those who believe in the personal Second Coming of Christ "to destroy the guilty nations of the Earth by positive acts of retributive violence" had to choose between living for this world or working on behalf of the next. "Indifference and lukewarmness—an attempt to reconcile God and Mammon, Christ and Belial—will only cause him to be spewed out of Christ, and to have his name blotted out of the book of life." Believers must commit themselves to "ever-active effort in bearing testimony to the glory of the Saviour" and to "telling of the doom of a guilty world." The millenarian "enters on the service of Christ, he enlists as a soldier, commences a warfare [and knows] both the service and the war are for life." Millerism was repeatedly described in military terms. "I feel I have put all on board of Zion's ship, and have enlisted for life, be it longer or shorter," wrote one in a characteristic way.[9]

Students of apocalyptic have often assumed that postmillennialism encourages labor on behalf of the Kingdom—missions, distributing tracts, revivals—while premillenialism, essentially pessimistic, encourages a fortress mentality: I will save myself, let others do what they wish. This mentality was certainly characteristic of some adventists, those who withdrew from the churches simply to avoid the punishment that would fall on Babylon. But most Millerites' enormously energetic proselytizing disproves this generality. Adventists as much as postmillennialists felt it a Christian duty to get others to prepare for salvation, and their distinct apocalypticism—anticipating the imminent Last Judgment rather than simply the arrival of the Millennium—added a sense of urgency to their labor the postmillennialist could not have felt. Wrote the *Midnight Cry*, "To conclude that we have nothing to do by way of laboring for the souls of others . . . is to disobey God and bring dishonor on the cause."[10]

Action was also necessary to prove faith. As Miller put it, "If we believe the prophets, shall not our faith be manifest by our works?" Millerites worked for the Lord in many ways—lecturing, forming adventist Bible classes, working with local committees, contributing money, being converted, and making converts. Such action was public and dramatic. But there was a private side, too. Action implied sacrifice. Orlando Squires had to "forsake all and venture all" to commit himself to itinerating, another

[9] Duffield, xii; Samuel W. Rhodes, *Midnight Cry*, March 17, 1843.
[10] *Signs of the Times*, October 12, 1842; *Midnight Cry*, March 17, 1843.

sacrificed his business, a third formal studies and "all the money I had for books," and a fourth a thriving medical practice. Elvira Fassett sacrified the love of her parents. "The family were set against us," wrote her husband, "supposing we had become vagrants or tramps, henceforth to live on public charity till we should be reduced to extreme poverty and wretchedness." Her father even threatened to sue him "for not providing for my family" and to confine their daughter at home. When Elvira persisted in her Millerite activities her father ordered her "'never to write to me, nor visit me again, until you have renounced your faith, and abandoned your present course of life.'" How painful was this separation! "Hers was a martyr's agony, and a martyr's decision."[11]

Itinerants even put their lives on the line. Travel was more than uncomfortable; it was dangerous. On a journey to Albany in 1843 Himes was crossing the Hudson River when his boat capsized forcing him to swim to shore and leaving him "sore and lame." This was "the eighth time since I left home that that had happened," he said. Hard enough on the young and inexperienced, itinerancy sometimes proved fatal to older Millerites. Chauncey E. Dutton of Utica literally worked himself to death. "For several weeks just previous to his death," wrote David Plumb, "he engaged in excessive labors, proclaiming the midnight cry." Finally his "physical nature exhausted," he suffered a stroke and died. Similar labor killed Charles Fitch in 1844 and broke the health of Joseph Marsh. Miller suffered almost constant illness after 1840. Now in his sixties, the tired man found the emotional trials of the campaign almost more than he could bear. Jane Marsh Parker remembered him as "a gentle old man, shaking with palsy." His ill health explains his failure to attend many important meetings and also his nearly paranoid response to criticism. "I find that, as I grow old, I grow more peevish, and cannot bear so much contradiction. Therefore, I am called uncharitable and severe."[12]

Most adventists sacrificed public reputations. S. W. Paine did not mind being called "a crazy man—a fool—a fanatic—a millerite" because he was willing "that God should take care of our reputations." He and many others would have agreed with Calvin French that these sacrifices, "the world and all its desires, character, living, *occupation*, friends, home, comforts, and worldly honors," were worth the price. "I am glad to believe that through the grace of God I shall owe the salvation of my soul to my present views of the glorious appearing of the blessed Saviour."[13]

The effects of action were also private as well as public. To give up

[11] *Midnight Cry*, November 11, 1842; Squires to Miller, November 14, 1844; L. C. Collins, *Midnight Cry*, March 15, 1843; Fassett, 28–30.
[12] Himes to Miller, March 24, 1843; "Death of Brother Chauncey E. Dutton," *Midnight Cry*, April 20, 1843; Parker, "Little Millerite," 314; Miller to Himes, December 7, 1842.
[13] S. W. Paine, *Midnight Cry*, April 27, 1843; French to Miller, August 25, 1842.

this world and devote oneself to working on behalf of the next virtually took the believer out of this world, out of what Mircea Eliade calls profane time, and into sacred (or cosmic) time. It was almost as though believers had been shunted around the terrors of the Last Day and were already living in the New Jerusalem. Having become a Millerite, said O. R. Fassett, "it seemed to me as though in a *moment of time* a *thousand years* rolled into the past and I was standing a *thousand years* nearer the judgment of the great day. . . . Here I was not living in the days of the prophets, nor the martyrs, but in the time to which they looked forward to with the greatest delight living in a day when the church was not to die but be changed—when all alive would see their Lord moving in clouds." By anticipating the removal of time, Millerites almost accomplished it spiritually. Everything was transitory—unimportant. Phrases like "until the Lord come," "while time continues," and "until time ends" were statements of faith that recognized the transitory nature of this world and proved their commitment to the next. When Joseph Marsh moved from New York Mills to Rochester in 1844, he leased a house "until the Lord comes" and filled it only with sufficient furniture "needed for the free hospitality of a 'Pilgrim's hotel.'" When he bought a white muff for his daughter a militant sister in the cause upbraided him for having spent money on such a trifle, "and the *last* winter so nearly over."[14] She was criticizing not just lack of practicality; his lack of zeal also offended her.

Apparently, Millerism's ability to transport the believer from this world to the next could also inspire *in*action. We find commonly reported a tendency of Millerites to refuse to plant or reap crops, clean their houses, go to work. Marsh took his daughter out of school, and she was not sad to leave. "Considering what we had to contend with at school, there was little rebellion on our part." A woman in Owego even stopped eating. A visitor said of her, "This is the *twenty-ninth* day since she has eaten anything, and yet she is apparently in good health, looking well, and the neighbors say that her strength has lately been increasing." How extensive this inactivity was is impossible to say, but it was sufficiently common for the *Midnight Cry* to urge "providing for our temporal wants" and not to "spend our time in idleness."[15]

Action was enormously satisfying. One lay preacher in central New York had, he believed, shaken the region "to its depth and extremities." All "is agitated, houses too small for the hearers, inquiry room more than full, convictions increasing, converts multiplying." He had been "lecturing and

[14] Mircea Eliade, *The Sacred and the Profane* (New York, 1959); Fassett to Miller, September 2, 1846; Parker, "Little Millerite," 314.
[15] Parker, "Little Millerite," 316; William Nicholas, *Midnight Cry*, October 19, 1844; ibid., March 17, 1843.

preaching night and day" and felt "about worn down, 'used up!'" But his crusader's labors brought him great joy; "I am WONDERFULLY sustained."[16] Many people now for the first time found an opportunity, as Millerite volunteers, to be active in religion and actually to become leaders.

Nowhere is this more telling than among women Millerite preachers. The male-dominated society of nineteenth century America circumscribed women's roles in the churches, as in all other institutions. Men assumed women were physically weak, tended naturally to moral depravity, and were fated by God to serve domestic functions alone. The famous Pastoral Letter of the Great Association of Massachusetts asserted these assumptions boldly. "The appropriate duties and influence of women are clearly stated in the New Testament. Those duties and that influence are unobtrusive and private, but the source of mighty power. . . . The power of woman is in her dependence flowing from the consciousness of that weakness which God has given her for her protection, and which keeps her in those departments of life that form the character of individuals and of the nation." Women's function in the churches was to contribute "unostentatious prayers and efforts" to advance "the cause of religion at home and abroad," but they should limit their activities to "such associated effort as becomes the modesty of her sex," in missionary societies and women's auxiliaries.[17] No church and very few people, male or female, would have disagreed with these views.

Since women were ascribed the role of pious private prayer, it is not surprising to find in their diaries and religious testimonies a certain maudlin quality. It would be a mistake to make too much of this, for men's religious sentiments were often saccharin too. But one cannot help wondering whether women's longing for the next world, for "the pearl of great price," had a significance different from that of men. A woman who wrote to Miller, signing her name A. E. C. because she did not want her husband to find out and accuse her of spiritual pride, spoke of adventism's promise of a better world. Miller's sermons had been like "Heavenly bread" satisfying inner hungers. "It had indeed been a spiritual repast when the world's cares had receded from my thoughts and the contemplation of a silent night added sweetness to communion with my Savior." Miller's descriptions of "the Glory of the Father and of his son Jesus Christ" had brought her closer to the Lord, and her soul "filled to overflowing with sensations of holy fellowship that I could not easily suppress." That night she had a dream in which her husband died and went to heaven leaving her alone "to finish my course and suffer and die," and she was so sad she could not "be patient and endure the agonies of death." In the throes of this "excessive desire" for the fellowship of the Saints, and presumably her husband, the sorrowing

---

16 Silas Hawley, *Midnight Cry*, March 13, 1843.
17 Reprinted in the *Republican Monitor* (Cazenovia), August 29, 1837.

woman saw at her side "the glory of the Father surrounding the out-
stretched Savior. My tears ceased. The full and overwhelming billows of
the soul receive the sweet intimation 'peace be still, and there was a great
calm.'"[18] The sexual symbolism is obvious, and perhaps women did find in
religious imagery a socially acceptable rhetoric for expressing sexual
desires. But the metaphor of release is not only sexual. Contemplation of
the joys of the next world, impatience to enter Heaven and be with God,
fear of being alone, all imply dissatisfaction with a woman's circumscribed
life. Millerism offered promise that she would soon realize this dream,
would be reunited with the Saints without even having to suffer the pangs
of death.

Some more courageous women did not wait for eternal fulfillment but
chose to rebel against male dominance here and now. Developing frontiers,
areas with laxity of religious discipline and emphasis on individual competence and action, were ideal settings for women to break out of their bonds.
Upstate New York had long provided opportunities for these modern
Deborahs. Some, like Mother Ann Lee and Jemima Wilkinson, the so-
called Public Universal Friend who founded a commune in western New
York in the 1780s, asserted themselves by organizing their own sects. Others fought for a role for themselves within the churches. In 1814 a Deborah
Pierce published a pamphlet in which she defended the right of women to
preach, and from time to time they were able to do so, especially in the
new sects. The Universalists used women as exhorters, and their journal,
the *Religious Enquirer* published in Cooperstown, defended the right of
women to preach. Though evil had come into the world because of Eve's
folly, as St. Paul and others indicated, "surely the woman (Mary) without
the help of man has, through divine assistance, made up the breach, and
swept up the stain from woman kind, by conceiving and bringing forth
into the world a Savior." The editor stated emphatically, "Women have a
right to preach that Savior." Steven Rensselaer Smith encountered Maria
Cook preaching in Universalist churches in northern New York. Although
she appears to have been a good preacher, said Smith, the Universalist
Association asked her to "seek a more congenial sphere under the protection of a hospitable private family." They claimed her "lack of knowledge"
was the reason, but, claimed Smith, they were really "extremely averse to
her assumption of the ministerial character" and suspected it was a sign of
"mental aberration." She submitted to their demands and left the pulpit to
"avail herself of their protection and kindness," after which her brethren
gave her benevolent regard. Somewhat later in the Second Great Awakening the Finney revivals opened new opportunities for women. For the first
time they prayed in public with men and often served as exhorters for the
major denominations. The Christian Connexion was quietly sympathetic to

[18] A. E. C. to Miller, November 19, 1843.

women preaching, and in New York City Sally Thompson reportedly "drew large congregations" to the Christian Chapel in the 1830s, probably as much for the novelty as for any other reason.[19]

Women often served as preachers and lecturers in the Millerite movement. Female itinerants usually traveled with a male companion (Lucy Maria Hersey was accompanied by her father, and Elvira Fassett and Mary A. Seymour by their husbands), but Miss E. C. Clemons, a fiery Boston Millerite, itinerated alone, a real mark of courage. These women aroused much public curiosity and drew large audiences (Lucy Hersey is said to have attracted "the largest crowd that ever surrounded the 'house of Prayer'" in Albany). They also attracted abuse. A man who heard Olive Maria Rice preach thought that she "would be better discharging her duty and more becoming the dignity of her sex in the private walks of life in the domesticated circle." Her supporters called her an angel, said the skeptic, but he thought "if she once was an angel she has fallen from the first estate. at any rate there was a good many 'fellers' after her and they said that Sam'l Noyes and Holmes flipped a cent to see which should go home with her the last night." Not all comments were derogatory. Lucy Hersey drew admiration from one nonadventist for her "general intellectual endowments" and "subdued tone of kindness and sincerity."[20]

However, so deeply entrenched was opposition to women acting publicly in religion that many Millerites, including women, were disturbed by it. Women preachers themselves had to overcome enormous psychological hurdles before taking the pulpit or lectern. Charles Hersey allowed his daughter to lecture only with extreme reluctance. And Elvira Fassett, too, "was averse to this. She had been taught to believe it immodest and unbecoming a woman to speak in public; and considered it forbidden by Paul." Her husband felt the same way. But friends pressured the two of them, and the fast-approaching end of the world wrought a change of mind. She agreed to say a few words at a camp meeting in their hometown, Seneca Falls, and the reaction to her short speech was favorable. The sight of his wife at the lectern reminded O. R. Fassett of the prophecy that in the Last Days God would pour out divine grace "on my servants and on my handmaidens," and he now feared that further opposition from him would "grieve that Holy Spirit." So he

[19] Deborah Pierce, *A Scriptural Vindication of Female Preaching, Prophesying, or Exhorting (Auburn, 1817); Religious Enquirer* (October 1811), 6–9; Smith, 31–32; I. N. Walter's review of Sally Thompson preaching in New York in the *Christian Palladium* (July 15, 1836), 95.
[20] G. S. Miles, *Midnight Cry*, February 15, 1843; "Perfectionism and Millerism United," *Baptist Register*, April 16, 1844; George Throop, March 23, 1843, George Throop Papers, Cornell University.

removed all obstacles from "the way of her duty," and she became a regular itinerant Millerite preacher.[21]

Less reluctant was Olive Maria Rice. She had no father and no husband to hold her back. From childhood she had been convinced that "god had a great work for me to do," and after a conversion experience in 1837, she begged God to "glorify himself in making me as useful as possible in this world." In 1840 she joined the Methodist Missionary Board and obtained training as a teacher, a role she was fulfilling when she first heard Miller lecture in Palmer, Massachusetts. Convinced his predictions were correct, she now thought it ridiculous "to prepare for future usefulness, when a few months at the longest must close not only my labors in this world, but those of all mankind." With so little time left, she returned to her home in Vermont to awaken her family and friends, and thus began her Millerite career. In 1843 she joined a "second advent company" (perhaps the Hutchinson Family singers) and traveled to New York State. Using a printed advent chart, she delivered lectures in a schoolhouse in Oxford. "Since that time," she wrote to Miller, "there are constantly four or five places calling for my labors at the same time." Conducting powerful revivals with thousands of people (according to her estimate) listening to her lectures, Rice was convinced God "had something more for me to do than to assist in prayer meetings." For the Lord "has made me the instrument of saving more souls within a few weeks past, by sounding the midnight cry, than most missionaries in the east, at least, have had as the fruits of their labors in many years." Though men objected, this was clearly the work of the Lord. "I dare not stop for the only reason that I am a sister. And though men may censure and condemn, I feel justified before God, and expect with joy to render my account for thus warning my fellow beings." In exultation she declared, "I never had such liberty, energy, and the power of the Spirit before."[22]

Not all women Millerite preachers assumed their role out of rebellion, but their careers struck a responsive chord among some other women. Martha Spence, listening to Lucy Hersey preach at the Scottsville camp meeting, said, "Oh what a blessed sight to my eyes, to see a young female, accompanied by her father, preaching Christ and the resurrection." Hersey "is an able and very interesting lecturer, as much so, I think, as any of our brethren in the field." Perhaps it was Hersey's favorable impression on the crowd that moved "sister after sister" to remove "one or more rings, breast pins, strings of gold beads, ear rings, etc." and throw them in the collection basket.[23]

The same forces that compelled Millerites to take action on behalf of

---

21 Fassett, 26–28.
22 Olive Maria Rice, *Midnight Cry*, July 6, 1843.
23 Martha Spence, ibid., August 1, 1844.

faith—desire to save their own souls and the souls of others, the necessity for sacrifice, a search for usefulness, and undoubtedly a more worldly yearning for attention and applause—also moved adventists who disagreed with Miller's views to act on the basis of their particular beliefs. The result was twofold: dissension and schism by Judaizers, Storrsite Annihilationists, and others; and what many adventists themselves considered to be fanatical behavior by Perfectionists, Shakers, and other mystics within the movement. Antiformalism guaranteed individuals fredom of expression and prevented leaders from controlling them. Not that they didn't try. Himes devised a system to deal with disruptive elements. If a rebel was an influential figure, like Storrs or Hawley, he felt compelled to publish their views and refute them publicly. If their views "didn't take much," in other words did not attract a following, he chose to ignore them publicly ("I don't think it of importance to give them notoriety enough to notice them."). As we have seen, there were many rebels, and Miller felt it necessary to warn his followers against "placing any confidence in impressions, and dreams, and private revelations." He strongly criticized those who claimed to possess "the gift of *intuitive discernment of spirits*, the *power to work miracles*, and to believe in the possibility of obtaining what they call *resurrection bodies* here in this mortal state."[24]

Privately though, Himes worked to shut off any opportunities for these antinomians to influence others. Not only did he refuse to give them publicity, he also gave specific instructions in organizing conferences to isolate them. "We do not want a fanatical rabble and an ignorant set of persons to take up the time of debate and conference; and hence something must be done to prevent it—for all these elements will be there." The way to do it was to formulate a tight agenda and stick to it. He and others gave public notice in calling conferences that "in sustaining this union mode of assembling, it should be distinctly understood, that every speaker alone, will consider himself responsible for any peculiar sentiments he may present. In this way no one, either of speakers or hearers, can justly be counted as participants in sentiments not their own."[25]

Other voices, loyal to Millerism's libertarian philosophy, rejected any measures of control. Said Ward, "This is no time for disputing, bickering, challenging of motive, imputing of evil, or slacking in our work." Some adventists "expect the natural Jews to return in this life; others expect the Jews to return in the resurrection of the just; let be, while both expect the Lord will first come. Some look for the end of all things

---

[24] Himes to Miller, September 16, 1844; Miller, *Midnight Cry*, June 13, 1844.
[25] Himes to Miller, undated, but written on the back of a printed flyer dated August 19, 1840; Henry Jones to William S. Miller, October 9, 1841.

within a few months especially; others look for it continually without regard for a particular year. Both sides look for it. If it should occur according to the year, it will also occur according to the continual prayer and hope; and if it should *not* occur according to the year, the continual prayer and hope will yet remain."[26]

Miller's was the strongest voice urging tolerance. "We have no expectation that God's opinion will all see alike," he cautioned, "til they are gathered where they shall see as they are seen, and know as they are known. He who expects any thing different from this must be disappointed. We should beware, therefore, of making any agreement of any subordinate point, a test of Christian character or fellowship." This was a matter of practical consideration. His response to Jones's demands to discredit Storrs is revealing. "As a belief or disbelief of the theory involved may not be essential to salvation—we are satisfied that it would be most safe, and contribute more to our usefulness to leave these questions, if entertained at all, in a position of minor importance." So long as Christ comes when expected, all disputes are meaningless, for He will provide all answers. The only result of bickering would be to divide adventists' strength and leave them open to ridicule from unbelievers. But more important, a fundamental principle was at stake. Inevitably adventists disagree with each other, "for there is no sect or church under the whole heavens, where men enjoy religious freedom or liberty, but there will be various oppinions. . . . We must then either let our brethren have the freedom of thought, oppinion and speech, or we must resort to creeds and formulas, Bishops and Popes, or at least councills convened and governed by the popular will of the corrupted community. I see no other alternative while we are in this state of things." In the strongest language he ever used toward Himes, Miller accused his abbé grise of being authoritarian. "I see in one instance dear Brother you have appealed to one of my rules [of exegesis] as a standard," but he had never intended his rules to "be a standard for others," and he could not consent to being "instrumental of suppressing one particle of religious liberty. We had better suffer the abuse of liberty, than to strengthen the bands of tyranny."[27]

This letter, more than any other document, marks Miller's intellectual power. He grasped what Himes had not, that there can be no compromise between liberty and formalism and that any attempt to impose order was treason against the crusade's essential nature. The very forces that inspired the crusade's rebellion against the world and that spun hundreds out of the churches also guaranteed that there would be no

[26] *Signs of the Times*, January 1, 1842.
[27] "Address to the Boston Conference," *Midnight Cry*, June 13, 1844; ibid., June 13, 1844; Miller to Himes, n.d.

consensus, no matter how obviously belief might define the movement. The one thing that united the Millerites was the bright vision of the New Jerusalem. God's "glorious appearing, and the establishment of his kingdom" would settle all quarrels. "On this heaven-appointed remedy hope may fix her eye with a steady and longing gaze."[28] That it was coming they all agreed, but when, in what manner, and with what consequences they could not say together. So long as the vision shone brightly its glare could cover up dark spots. But let the vision dim, and darkness would surely conquer. All the more reason to cry, "Come quickly, Lord Jesus."

Time weighed heavily on the Millerites. Though many had taken one step into the New Jerusalem, the other foot was firmly planted on earth. Full release depended completely on God keeping a promise. Millerites had kept their part of the bargain—they had sacrificed, worked, and suffered for faith, and now it was the Lord's turn to act. Everything depended on it. The coming Event concentrated the adventist's greatest hopes and evoked enormous fear. What if they were not saved after all; what if they rose to meet the Lord in the air but spouses, children, or parents were left behind? Can you understand, asked Jane Marsh Parker, what it was like to believe "that at any moment, terribly near at the latest, there would come that fearful upheaval of the earth, that fiery rending apart of the heavens, and in the indescribable confusion of angelic trumpets, and the shrieking of the damned, God himself would descend with a great shout to burn up the world, the sea and the dry land?" It made "waking in the still night a painful experience, and a thunder-storm a fearful ordeal, while every sunset brought the inner voice, 'The morning may never come.'"[29]

No wonder then that Millerite and non-Millerite attention focused directly on the predicted time. Himes found that among those who accepted Miller's prediction of 1843, "in *regard to the Time*, they are *more confirmed* as the time *draws* near." They became increasingly impatient with their "faint-hearted" brothers and sisters who would not accept the concept of revealed time, for that not only showed lack of faith but also raised the troublesome possibility that their own commitment to time might be erroneous. Nathaniel Whiting, one skeptic regarding time, suffered abuse from his fellow adventists. "They would not allow the few who like myself did not embrace their views to lecture or even to speak in their meetings. We were completely proscribed. The very things which they had censured in the conduct of the Churches, they now practiced themselves." Furthermore, as adherence to a specific time gained in importance, so did the search for a *definite* time, and the importance of knowing the exact date resulted in heated disagreements.

[28] *Midnight Cry*, June 13, 1844.
[29] Parker, "Little Millerite," 314.

Said Parker, "Private judgment acknowledging no authority contended with private judgment that would be infallible authority."[30]

Ironically, these disagreements occurred as deadlines came and went. Millerites were undergoing a psychological process that Leon Festinger and his colleages call "cognitive dissonance," a peculiar phenomenon noted among apocalyptic groups that as predicted dates for the end of the world passed without the predicted event occurring, belief in both the event and the concept ot a set date increased rather than diminished. This tenacity, Festinger suggests, results from the availability of social support for that commitment. When belief is strong, commitment irreversible, and mutual support reliable, faith increases rather than decreases in the face of absolute disconfirmation.[31]

For Millerism to serve as a test of this theory we would need a great deal more information about adventists than we will ever have—their names, strength of belief and commitment, whether they dropped out of the movement and if so at what point. We do not know whether the least committed dropped out of the movement first leaving an increasingly ardent and frantic core as disappointment mounted. Evidence does suggest that for many the pattern of development was disappointment, strengthening of commitment, rededication to predicted time.

Throughout the crusade, Miller scrupulously avoided specifying his date any more precisely than "sometime in 1843." But when that year had passed, he adjusted his interpretation slightly. He remembered that the prophets would have calculated time according to the Jewish lunar calendar. Accordingly, the prophetic year 1843 would not end until March 21, 1844. Many who were already disappointed were soothed. A. N. Bentley said, "I did not, one year ago, think that I should live to send you a letter dated in 1844, for I then thought with many others, that several months ere this day, we should be shouting glory with all the redeemed." Miller's explanation of the error restored his confidence. "As God has lengthened out our days, I for one, feel thankful that he has also lengthened out my faith, and that it is as strong as it is."[32]

But on March 22, 1844, Millerites faced their first major disconfirmation. Though reports to Miller from across New York assured him that faith was as strong as ever, some fell away. For one, "the first landmark is passed and the vision seems to fail." Jonathan Cole complained bitterly that before March his pastor "was fearlessly proclaiming the Advent doctrine," but now "alas! the time has past by, not a word since, in favor

---

[30] Himes to Miller, January 26, 1841; Nathaniel Whiting to Miller, October 24, 1844; Parker, "Little Millerite," 315.

[31] Leon Festinger, Henry W. Riecken, and Stanley Schlachter, *When Prophecy Fails* (Milwaukee, 1956).

[32] A. N. Bentley, *Midnight Cry*, February 8, 1844.

of the cause, and he is ready to cast reflection on those who remain firm in the faith." The fact that Millerites scolded the "faint, the fearful, the half-resolved" indicates that desertions were probably high. While some urged their compatriots to remain steadfast, others viewed the departure of the weak as a good sign. "God holds the fan in his hand, and will blow out all the chaff, before gathering all of the wheat into his garner." Morale sank low, and calls went out for adventists to "cease their hardness" towards each other that "all of God's children might be all of one heart, one mind, and one understanding."[33]

According to Festinger's theory these initial defectors should have been either the least committed or those who failed to receive adequate support for their beliefs. However, just as likely, low commitment to the set date would have led to low disappointment when the first deadline passed. One adventist who "always considered it a nice point to determine the definite time of the termination of the 2300 days" was not "disappointed because the vision seems to tarry." He was sure the Second Coming of Christ was "at the door" and did not believe that "any adventist will, for a moment, cease watching or sounding the alarm." Judah L. Richmond's response was similar. His rhetoric was millenarian, but despite the fact that he was Olive Maria Rice's brother-in-law, he does not appear to have been an active Millerite. "I have now lived to witness the completion of the time, which according to Wm. Miller, completed the history of this world," he wrote. Christ surely would come, "but whether *today* or *tomorrow*, God only knows."[34] Having staked nothing on the date, these two men, at least, maintained their essential beliefs intact.

Others who were committed to revealed time did profess increased confidence after the first failure. Samuel W. Rhodes, for one, avowed, "My faith has never been stronger in the glorious personal coming of our dear Redeemer than at present." Perhaps group support was what made adventists gathered in a conference at Gerry change their mind, for "a number who had been wavering on time, became fully convinced on this point, and are now rejoicing in the blessed hope of soon seeing the Lord." The same could explain the enthusiasm of adventists who attended probably the largest camp meeting in the movement's history, which occurred after the March debacle. Wrote Martha Spence, "I feel stronger than ever in the hope of the speedy coming of our blessed Jesus." An inability to accept crushing disappointment or to admit error might help to explain this persistence, but popular ridicule, now merciless, surely enforced it. "The

[33] A. H. Tanner to Miller, March 21, 1844; Cole, *Midnight Cry*, September 19, 1844; "State of the Cause," ibid., May 30, 1844; Bentley, ibid., September 5, 1844; Seymour, ibid., August 1, 1844.
[34] H. S. Burchard, *Midnight Cry*, May 9, 1844; Richmond, Diary, April 3, 1844.

World Won't Flummux" wrote the *Chenango Telegraph* in a bold head-
line. "Well, March 21, 1844, has come and passed, so has the period of
'April Fool,' yet no 'bust up!'—What is the inference? Is Miller a dunce, or
have the wheels of time become clogged?" It's all right if "those who have
believed Mr. Miller's theory do not disband," said another paper, "but then
ought they not to frankly admit that this light was *no light*? Why delude
themselves, or others, that what was *false* was *true*?"[35]

Such ridicule caused Millerites to yearn more than ever for vindication. Adventists continued to hold prayer meetings, and lecturers still
roamed from town to town comforting the disappointed. Commitment
and faith remained and awaited but a new suggestion to bring the fires
of enthusiasm once again to full heat.

That August, the spark was struck. Samuel S. Snow was a long-time
adventist who had converted from agnosticism after reading Miller's
book. As early as February he published a personal prediction that the
Lord would not come in March but sometime during the summer. His
expectation failed, but, undaunted, he prepared a new chronology showing that the March "cry" was merely preparatory to the true midnight
cry. The traditional Jewish liturgical calendar placed the Day of Atonement, the day when Jews fasted and contemplated their sins, on the
tenth day of the seventh month. Could there be a more appropriate day
for the Second Coming of Christ than this? Surely this day would mark
the final atonement of all sin! Calculating that in 1844 the tenth day of
the seventh month would fall on October 22, Snow published his views
in the *Midnight Cry* in August. This new date caught fire quickly, and
within a few weeks leading figures in the movement like George W.
Peavey, T. M. Preble, and H. H. Gross all accepted it and were preaching it across the state. By the end of September Himes reported to Miller, "This thing has gone over the country like lightning. Nearly every
lecturer has come into it, and are preaching it with zeal and great success." Indeed, Himes was more interested in its effects than its correctness. Although the new date "was not yet clear to my mind," he wrote,
he found that "the fruits are glorious. . . . It has done away all Fanaticism, and brought those who were given to extravagance into sober dis-
creet state of mind. '43 never made so great, and good an impression as
this has done upon all that have come under its influence. The worldly
minded have been quickened and made alive—and all classes have been
blessed beyond anything we have seen in times past. With this view of
the matter, I dare not oppose it, although I do not yet get the light as to
the *month & day*." He was sure Christ would come in the autumn, and
"for ought I know he may come on the 7th month—& 10th day."

[35] S. W. Rhodes, *Midnight Cry*, August 22, 1844; Himes to Miller, September 30, 1844.

Charles Fitch and Sylvester Bliss accepted the date, too.[36]

The tone of this letter leads one to suspect that Himes was trying to recruit Miller. He had once written, "All depends on Father Miller," and it was still true. The failure of the March deadline had left Miller dispirited, forcing him to acknowledge an error in calculation, although he did not recant his essential beliefs. Now he was reluctant to exert himself in the interests of a new date, especially one that was not his own. He would "never be able again to labor in the vineyard as heretofore." Besides, for years he had truthfully denied predicting a day or hour, and he now publicly affirmed that this new date came "from others, not from him." Yet unbearable pressure was being exerted by colleagues who apparently were determined to get his support. Himes asked him in strong terms to provide written answers to questions regarding the seventh month theory, supposedly "to get the truth for others." In writing such an article, however, Miller would clearly be on the defensive trying to show why the date was incorrect. Bliss wrote to him, too. He was "under the most solemn impressions that the Lord will be here in a few days." Bliss added ominously, "The hand of God must be in this matter. . . . We take our stand that the anniversaries of the seventh month, will bring His glorious appearing. . . . It will be glorious to go into the kingdom so soon; but, O how awful to be left." Illness and disappointment had weakened Miller physically and emotionally, and perhaps his longfelt lack of confidence moved him to hope desperately that others were correct. For whatever reason, his reluctance melted. Just two weeks before the October 22 deadline, Miller wrote to Himes, "I see a glory in the seventh month which I never saw before. Although the Lord had shown me the typical bearing of the seventh month, one year and a half ago, yet I did not realize the force of the types. Now, blessed be the name of the Lord, I see a beauty, a harmony, and an agreement in the Scriptures, for which I have long prayed, but did not see until today. Thank the Lord. I am almost home. Glory! Glory!! Glory!!!" Adventists all across New York who received their October 12 issue of the Cry read Miller's statement, "I am strong in the opinion that the next will be the last Lord's day sinners will ever have in probation; and within ten or fifteen days from thence, they will see Him whom they have hated and despised, to their shame and everlasting contempt."[37]

Fervor mounted as never before. On October 9 Bliss wrote to Miller in a hand so shaking with emotion that the writing is almost illegible,

[36] S. S. Snow, Midnight Cry, May 30, 1844; Spence, ibid., August 1, 1844; Chenango Telegraph, April 3, 1844.

[37] Nichol, 228; Baptist Register, October 25, 1844; Himes to Miller, September 29, 1844, and October 2, 1844; Bliss to Miller, October 3, 1844, Himes Papers; Midnight Cry, October 12, 1844.

"Praise God. Praise God. May we all be ready & meet in the skies. May God grant it." With a particular date on which to focus, Millerites prepared for the great day of wrath. Some looked for even more specific information about the time. C. B. Hotchkiss of Auburn was sure the Great Event would take place in the early hours of the morning, and Judah Richmond heard a Millerite lecturer declare that "'tomorrow, the Heavens (i. e. celestial bodies) would be shaken, & on the 10th day of the 7th month Christ would come the 2d time without sin unto salvation." Reports flowed into the adventist papers of people who confessed old crimes, settled disputes with neighbors, repaid loans, to be ready for the great day. Lydia Maria Child bought some cloth from a merchant and was surprised to have him return 2¢ a yard to her. "The fact is," he explained, "I have been hearing Mr. Miller, and I thought he proved his doctrine clear enough to satisfy any body. If we are all to come to an end so soon, it is best to be pretty moderate and fair in our dealings." In Rochester a hatter opened the doors of his shop and "invited the crowd to come in and help themselves to hats, umbrellas, etc., which they naturally did." Not all activity was so salutary, notwithstanding Himes's statements to that effect. Nathaniel Whiting reported "a tempest of real fanaticism" in his group. "Our poor brethren were deluded into a belief of 'signs & lying wordes' gift of tongues & modern prophecies." In Springwater Valley near Rochester the "deluded ones withdrew entirely and set up for themselves holding meetings, as the time drew near in a private dwelling in the neighborhood night and day, and all night long, neglecting almost wholly their temporal affairs, and in some instances, leaving their little children to take care of themselves, or to be cared for by others less infatuated than their natural guardians." A woman who claimed to be "inspired with authority over the rest" was in charge, and she "would breathe on them the Holy Ghost," accompanying the ritual with "extravagant gesticulations."[38]

In so many ways adventists prepared for the great day, and when it finally arrived, Millerites were not the only ones who watched the skies. Gerritt Smith of Peterboro, well-known lawyer and reformer, was away from home on the 22nd, and he confided to his wife that he regretted having ignored the adventists' warnings. Though he was not convinced their predictions were correct, "I cast myself on his mercy like the thief on the cross. I seek His salvation, though now in the last hour." How many others thus covered their bets? In Rochester a terrible gale buffeted the city and blew down the liberty pole, "frightening many into

[38] Bliss to Miller, October 9, 1844, Himes Papers; C. B. Hotchkiss, *Midnight Cry*, October 11, 1844; Richmond, Diary, October 1844; Child, 236; Parker, "Little Millerite," 316; Whiting to Miller, October 24, 1844; F. W. Conable, *History of the Genesee Conference of the Methodist Episcopal Church* (New York, 1885), 520.

believing that the end of the world had truly come." The factory in
Ithaca where the adventists gathered caught fire in the night, sending
the Saints scurrying from the building. A nonadventist reported waking
from a sound sleep and hearing the cries "Fire!" in the street below his
hotel room. Rushing outside to see what the excitement was all about he
followed the crowd toward "a luminous part of the village, which from
its location had the appearance of being the Millerites' headquarters!"
The startling thought entered his mind that perhaps they were right and
the world was actually burning to a cinder. Soon he was relieved to find
it was "the temple of the Millerites in flames, instead of the world." Now
reader, he concluded, "can you imagine how much I was relieved from a
load of anxiety which for the last few minutes had borne heavily upon
me?"[39] People could laugh at the Millerites, but when the moment
came, many must have had similar secret suspicions that they might be
right after all.

Most information about what Millerites did that day comes from
nonadventists, and therefore it is hard to separate fact from rumor. In
Rochester, according to one witness, the Millerites, "expecting every
moment will be the last," spent the day "hovering around their temple
with upturned eyes and countenances as devoid of life and expression as
marble statues." One of the Springwater enthusiasts walked up the street
claiming "with an air of confidence and triumph, almost defiance, 'Today at twelve o'clock the sun will be darkened!'" These stories have a
ring of truth, but others almost certainly were fables. The Millerites were
said, by so-called eyewitnesses across the state, to have dressed in ascension robes, climbed the highest hills, and sat on the roofs of houses and
barns to be closer to Christ when He appeared. Thus in Rochester "Tall-
man Hall was crowded with believers, dressed in white, and in the countryside whole families greeted the rising sun, from the roofs of barns."
Others placed the action in Rochester on Cobb Hill which was supposedly white with their robes. Jenny Marsh Parker later strongly denied all
these stories. Indeed, it seems probable that the vast majority of Millerites gathered in their usual meeting places or remained at home with
families and friends and waited, praying through the day. Joseph Marsh
had exhausted himself in the days before the climax, and the dawning of
the tenth day "found him too ill to rise from his pillow." Jane was
secretly glad; overwhelmed with terror at the approaching judgment, she
took comfort from his presence. "If anybody was saved," she believed, he
would be, and knowing that her father "would never shake me from his
arms into the fire" as he rose in the air she clung to him desperately,

[39] Gerritt Smith to Ann Smith, October 21–22, 1844, Gerritt Smith Papers, Syracuse University; Parker, "Little Millerite," 316; *Tompkins Democrat*, October 31, 1844.

meaning to have "a firm hold on him when the crisis arrived."[40]

Persecutors, too, were active that day. In Williamsburg, New York, the adventists "were in some danger from the mob" which attacked their meetinghouse. "The mayor however offered to put down the mob with strong hand if a meeting should be held in the evening." Not wishing to jeopardize anyone's safety, the adventists then chose not to gather. In Lewiston town officials were not so cooperative. There, said L. Delos Mansfield, "some lewd fellows of the baser sort" who were furious at him for preaching the Second Coming "jeopardized my life by their plans to execute vengeance upon me." He did not give details, but Mansfield did note that "the magistracy of that town have more sympathy with the lawless mob than their innocent objects, upon which they wished to wreak unprovoked vengeance." In Seneca Falls Millerites were not so passive. A group of "thirty or forty ruffians with blacked faces, and disguised apparel" invaded the schoolhouse where they were meeting. Armed with "clubs, dirks, etc.," the mob seized the lecturer and another leading adventist "with the intention of taking them off by force and injuring them." The Millerites fought back. "The people present thought it time to defend themselves and wresting from the mob some of their clubs, and turning their own weapons against them, they were soon discomfited, and retreated from the house." To his horror, said the reporter, a Methodist preacher had "justified their course" and had said that "the Millerites ought to be taken up; if other means fail, forcibly." Commenting later on this violence against them one adventist said bitterly, "Did our boasted land of liberty ever know so much religious persecution in so short a time?"[41]

Whether surrounded by hecklers and mobs or waiting together quietly and undisturbed, the Millerites watched anxiously for the first signs of the general conflagration. Years of sacrifice and persecution had taken them to a pinnacle of longing for vindication and reward. Hopes and fears, products of their personal religious experience and of centuries of Christian tradition, were concentrated in one day of expectation. Soon, they believed, God would complete the work begun in Genesis. Not only temporal life, but time itself would end as the cosmic calendar reached its last page. During the vigil, the Millerites watched the hours tick by, from morning to evening and on into the night—until a faint glow in the east, for ages the sign of renewal, brought not cheer but despair to the Saints.

[40] Lyndley Gould, Diary, October 22 and 23, 1844, manuscript in the possession of the Rochester Public Library; Conable, 520; Orlo J. Price, "One Hundred Years of Protestantism in Rochester," *Centennial History of Rochester*, III (Rochester, 1893), 284–85; Parker, "Little Millerite," 316.
[41] N. N. Whiting to Miller, October 24, 1844; L. Delos Mansfield, *Voice of Truth*, December 4, 1844; E. R. Pinney, *Voice of Truth*, March 5, 1843; Elizabeth Smith and Jonas Johnson to Miller, December 4, 1844.

Chapter 8
HOW LONG, O LORD?

Disappointment was unbearable, for some unacceptable. Many kept watching the skies from day to day, desperately hoping Miller had made a small mistake in calculation and that Jesus would come today, or tomorrow. Marsh predicted Christ would not tarry beyond 6:00 p.m., October 23; others looked for Him to come on the 24th. Gerritt Smith hoped the delay "may be in mercy to my poor soul," and he listened to adventists who "think that time may probably not end until tomorrow." Thus complete despair was suspended. Lacking absolute disconfirmation of their beliefs, Millerites survived from day to day, week to week. "The seventh month was followed by the eighth, the year went out, and another came in. And still he did not come after the manner the Millerites had fore-told." It must have been with a note of complaint as well as disappointment that adventists now sang, "How long, O Lord, our Saviour,/Wilt thou remain away?/ Our hearts are growing weary,/ With thy so long delay."[1]

Those who still hoped received a shock in November and December when they read published "confessions and apologies" of Millerite leaders. On October 24, Nathaniel Whiting had advised Miller that "all who participated in this mistake" should immediately make a "public acknowledgement of their error. . . . Any shuffling on this point will authorize the community to say that we are not only credulous but absolutely *dishonest*." On November 5, Himes admitted publicly that all reasonable dates were passed "and we have not realized our expectations." They were "near the end," but "the authorities on which we based our calculations cannot be depended upon for *definite time*." The following week George Storrs likewise admitted unjustified reliance on the seventh month, tenth day. "That it was an *error*, to say the least, time has shown." By the end of the month, Galusha and Miller himself had confessed their mistake.[2]

Now even the most ardent realized that something had indeed gone wrong. The shock of failure struck them, drained them emotionally.

---

[1] Gerritt Smith to Ann Smith, op. cit.; Parker, "Little Millerite," 316.
[2] Whiting to Miller, October 24, 1844; *Midnight Cry*, November 7 and 21, December 4, 1844; "Our Confession, Defense of our Course, our Position," ibid., November 21, 1844.

"What shall I do, which way shall I turn?" asked one in despair. Adventists who had "given their all for the sounding of the 'midnight cry'" now found themselves "homeless and penniless when the winter of 1844 came upon them." So serious was this problem that Himes urged Millerites to contribute money to aid the destitute. Added to the bitterness of winter was the abuse which detractors now heaped upon them. Fortunately, preoccupation with the political campaign that year saved Millerites from even harsher treatment than they might otherwise have received. A few newspapers, particularly religious journals, treated these "erring brethren" with pity and understanding. But exclusions of adventists continued, possibly with even greater speed now the danger was past that God would prove their prediction correct. The Hampton Baptists waited until 1845 to disfellowship Miller and his followers, and according to an Allegany County historian, that year the Second Baptist Church of Cuba "was mainly occupied with disciplinary measures consequent upon the Millerite craze, and 45 were dropped from the church lists."[3]

The cumulative effects of disappointment, despair, and disgrace caused more adventists than ever to conclude that Miller's entire theory was wrong. Parker felt these backsliders were "the passive minds as a rule, not the bone and sinew of the movement," but whether true or not, they left the movement in droves. By August of 1845, only a half dozen Millerites remained in Saratoga Springs; in Oswego only fifteen of the estimated one hundred kept the faith; the same was true in Ithaca, Seneca Falls, and elsewhere. Classes reported no new students; lecturers counted no new converts. George Miller, the prophet's son, thought that "there will be but a remnant of those who have professed to be looking for Christ will endure unto the end." Many who fled the movement turned against their former brethren and sisters. "The same ones and many more who were crying for mercy two days before," Miller noted, "were now mixed with the rabble and mocking, scoffing, and threatening in a most blasphemous manner." Subscriptions to the papers fell off sharply, and fearing they would sink, Himes combined the *Signs of the Times* and *Midnight Cry*, changed their names to the *Advent Herald* and *Morning Watch*, and struggled on. Mansfield's journal, the *Voice of Elijah*, went out of business in December of 1844.[4]

But while hundreds fled, others remained. Said one, "Truth . . . is what I have suffered the loss of all things for, that I might win Christ." People like this would not easily give up. Those who confessed an error

3 Elizabeth Smith to Miller, October 24, 1844; *Midnight Cry*, November 7 and 21, December 4, 1844; "Our Confession, Defense of our Course, our Position," ibid., November 21, 1844.
4 Parker, "Little Millerite," 316; George Miller to S. Nichols, November 28, 1844; Miller to I. O. Orr, December 13, 1844; Himes to Miller, November 19, 1844, and January 28, 1845.

regarding time strongly defended their essential beliefs. "Although I have been twice disappointed," wrote Miller, "I am not yet cast down or discouraged. . . . I have now much more evidence that I do believe in God's Word; and although surrounded with enemies and scoffers, yet my mind is perfectly calm, and my hope in the coming of Christ is as strong as ever." Fixed dates had failed, but he looked for Christ "Today, TODAY, and *TODAY*, until He comes, and I see HIM for whom my soul yearns." Himes clung to his "published views relating to the personal reign and kingdom of Christ," and Storrs softened his confession by denying "that it was wrong for me, or anyone else, to preach the strong probability of the Lord's coming at any time." To Galusha, too, "Nothing is more plainly revealed in the word of God, than the second personal coming of Christ." Some light broke through the gloom. A Millerite in Syracuse reported that, contrary to what was happening elsewhere, "there have but three or four sacrificed their hope and gone back to the cold embrace of a guilty and wicked world."[5]

That wicked world's need for renovation sustained the faith of some. Materialistic men were yet "laying schemes of future greatness," oblivious of the day of "horror and dread" still approaching. Alienated from their society, adventists continued to long for their true home. "This wicked and adulterous world has no endearments for me," said a Millerite in 1845. "I have long since laid all upon the altar and my heart, and my all, is in heaven, and I am waiting, and longing, for the . . . 'redemption of my body.'" Derision continued to reinforce feelings of martyrdom for outcasts who "rejoice that we are accounted worthy to suffer for his sake." "Oh, how good it is," said Pinney, "to be under God's wholesome discipline—how much safer than in health and prosperity." The "day of vengeance does not hasteneth greatly," but it was surely coming. Even now, Millerites were leaving the churches voluntarily and establishing "meetings regularly by themselves," and calls went out to refrain from voting lest they "remain in Babylon."[6]

Widespread defections meant fewer lecturers than before, and the common complaint from the still-faithful was, "We have had no visits from lecturing brethren, nor even seen one from abroad." Asked Marsh, "Where are the faithful watchmen who but a few weeks or months since occupied these interesting fields?" To fill the need, resident lecturers became itinerants. Thomas F. Barry, who had worked only in Rochester, now preached also in Buffalo, Leroy, Scottsville, and Syracuse; Augustus

---

[5] Thomas Fish to Miller, February 3, 1847; *Midnight Cry*, December 5, 1844; Joseph Endwell, *Voice of Truth*, December 4, 1844.

[6] E. C. Howe, *Voice of Truth*, April 19, 1845; D. Clow, ibid, August 4, 1845; E. S. Bryant, ibid., May 24, 1846; E. R. Pinney to Miller, October 25, 1847; T. F. Barry, *Voice of Truth*, 1845; B. F. Robbins, ibid., September 19, 1845.

Beach returned to western New York from the Mohawk Valley and served adventists in Fredonia and the Niagara plain. Now, rather than to try to win new converts for the Lord's army, they worked to stop desertions, to get Millerites to reenlist, to "strengthen the things which are ready to perish," to "have minds stirred up by way of remembrance."[7] If the campaign did not result in wholesale return of wayward adventists, it did ensure the survival of the doctrine where it otherwise might have perished.

Those who retained faith in Miller's doctrine now searched for the basic mistake they had made in October of 1844. Explanations varied from the ridiculous to the measured. George Storrs believed "some other mere human influence which I call *Mesmerism*" was responsible for leading Millerites into error. Some "influence not of God" had driven them all "beyond the just bounds of discretion." What the force was, what its purpose, were clear to him. Another believed God had sent disappointment to separate those of weak faith from true Christians and thus ensure their damnation. More astute was Galusha. Adventists' dependence on the October date had been a human error, not devilish trickery or a divine test. The Millerites were correct in their *faith* that Christ would soon return since that faith rested "upon the positive declarations of God's word." But their *belief* that He would come on October 22 was wrong because it "was founded upon an analogical argument, which, though sound and convincing, came short of absolute assurance." Nathaniel Whiting confessed, in addition, that he and too many others accepted the date "because belief in the *tenth day* provided such joyful emotions." Unfortunately, "an *opinion* which is not *true*, may awaken a Christian to prayer and duty." All together, these men now would agree with E. Goodwin of Oswego, "I do not believe the hour was ever intended to be, or ever shall be revealed to man; and we see that even the year has not yet been revealed."[8] For them, revealed time was the principal—the only—doctrinal casualty of the Great Disappointment.

But others would not concede even that much. C. B. Hotchkiss of Auburn pleaded with Miller to hold his ground "which *includes definite time*" and to "hold out to the end," for "the world is to be condemned for rejecting 1843." George Miller, too, rejected his father's idea that "the truths that we have been brought through for the last two or three months is all impression of fancy." Surely, said Miller's son, "the will of God was being done two years ago in preaching the *time* of the Lord's

---

[7] Elisha M. Hickox, *Midnight Cry*, November 12, 1845; *Voice of Truth*, January 15, 1845; John J. Porter to Miller, December 5, 1846.

[8] *Midnight Cry*, November 14, 1844; George W. Burnham to Miller, December 15, 1848; Galusha, *Voice of Truth*, December 19, 1844; Whiting to Miller, October 24, 1844; E. Goodwin, *Voice of Truth*, August 13, 1844.

coming," and in order to purify the world "we must have a specified time." Among these adventists, the search for a new date began immediately after the October 22 disappointment. H. Tanner of Albany believed Christ would come on the "10th day of Nov., for I cannot now be moved (the Lord help and keep me) but one step at a time." Orlando Squires similarly believed that November, and not October, was the seventh month, and he pointed out that the Dark Day of 1780 and the Shower of Stars of 1833 both occurred in mid-November. "It seems as though God has marked and marked and marked right upon *that spot in November* as though he would have his children understand that he *meant* something by it." George Miller believed that time would not continue beyond March of 1845, Marsh focused on the Spring and then the Summer, and others predicted dates in 1846, '47, and '48. Henry H. Gross of Albany was indefatigable. First he predicted the Second Coming for the Spring of 1845; by March he had refined the critical period to April 8 through April 24. Excitement once again mounted in some, and S. S. Snow picked up the date and preached it. Failing once again, Gross recalculated, found another small mistake, and announced "the autumn of 1846 is the *extreme* point for the termination of the 1335 days." Come the winter of 1846 he cancelled his previous statement and preached the end of the world for 1847.[9]

Tenacious clinging to revealed time was only one way to resist acknowledging disconfirmation. Many others believed that on October 22 a momentous event *had* taken place but that it had occurred in an unexpected *manner*. Christ had undertaken a great work spiritually rather than physically. As early as December of 1844, Galusha cautioned, "Above all, beware of mysticism." Ignore any person who "mystifies the word to make it agree with his absuridities. Receive no one's pretended inward revelation, unaccompanied by outward and divine demonstration." Bliss also worried about those who are "so disappointed in the passing of the time that they feel unwilling to believe they can be in any way mistaken, & therefore now sympathize with that class of ultra brethren who are all arrayed with much bitterness against us." These mystics nearly shattered what was left of the movement.

Their spiritualizing assumed two forms. First, many of them believed that Christ had returned to earth spiritually rather than personally on October 22 and that he had separated the saints from the damned. "I am satisfied that the time is correct," wrote one, "that on the tenth day of the seventh month the atonement was finished and Jesus came out and blest his people and all the holy ghost witnessed to was the

9 Hotchkiss to Miller, March 28, 1845, and George Miller to S. Nichols, November 28, 1844; H. Tanner to Miller, November 4, 1844; George Miller to Nichols, op. cit.; "Definite Time Again," *Voice of Truth*, September 24, 1845.

time and not the manner." After all, explained another, "How shall we look for what is not in Existance? His body was given for the life of the world, so how could he take away or come with a body?" Another had actually seen the Lord return in a vision, riding in a "two whealed carriage with two drivers or anciently called a chariot." Truly, "Babylon has fallen." In 1845 Orlando Squires, who had adopted the doctrine, published a new spiritualizing journal called the *Voice of the Shepherd.* Does not this truth create "truly a *new heaven,* compared with the *traditions* hitherto held by us?" Apparently so, for the doctrine attracted support all over the state—Hotchkiss in Auburn, W. D. Cook in Rochester, Mary Seymour, Benjamin F. Bissell, all were disciples, and adventists traveling around New York found spiritualizer groups in Albany, Utica, throughout Chautauqua County, and in Syracuse.[10]

A second variety of spiritualism was similar in doctrine but assumed a harsher tone. These were "shut door adventists" or door-shutters. They believed Christ had not returned to earth but had, in Heaven, judged humanity, separated the wicked from the saved, closed the period of probation for sinners, and "shut the door of mercy." Their views derived from the Biblical parable of the foolish virgins, Matthew 25:1–13. A bridegroom arrives at his wedding feast only to find preparations incomplete. Five foolish virgins had gone out to buy oil for lamps, and while they were gone, the bridegroom closed the door on them and shut them out. This was interpreted as an analog of the Second Coming of Christ, Christ being the bridegroom, the marriage feast representing the resurrection of the saints, and the foolish virgins sinners unprepared for His coming. Door-shutters believed that what had happened on October 22 was that "The foolish virgins and the slothful servants, together with the wicked that do wickedly, are cast or shut out into outer darkness, and their lamps are gone out."[11] Leading advocates of this view in New York were Silas Hawley in Albany, Nathaniel Hitchcock and George W. Peavey of Oswego, and Samuel S. Snow. Like spiritualizers, shut door adventists published newspapers, Snow the *Jubilee Standard,* E. Jacobs the *Day Star* in Cincinnati, Ohio, and John Pearson and Miss E. C. Clemons the *Hope of Israel* in Portland, Maine.

Both groups preached the sanctification of the Elect, in other words of themselves, a view identical to some forms of Perfectionism, and proponents gave themselves over to much of the same behavior. Himes reported that shut door Millerites were neglecting "ploughing and all preparations, planting &c—some are selling off their cattle &c." Even

[10] Elon Galusha, *Midnight Cry,* December 19, 1844; Bliss to Miller, February 11, 1845; C. F. Fenton to Miller, December 10, 1844; C. Swartwout to Miller, November 21, 1845; anonymous to Miller, July 28, 1845; *Voice of the Shepherd,* May 1845.
[11] Matthew, 25:1–13; R. R. Chapin to Miller, October 9, 1847.

worse, they often "live in continual association in exciting, and social meetings, which has degenerated into *fleshly*, and selfish passions." The *Voice of Truth* accused one spiritualizer not only of having accumulated stolen goods but of keeping "a very bad house." And in Collins, spiritual-izers claimed to have become immortal and practiced promiscuity. At a meeting of ultraists in South Westerlo, one of the enthusiasts "bit a person's arm." They reportedly worshipped "in a nude state." One of the most notorious of these rites was "promiscuous feet washing." George Peavey, who loudly justified the ceremony, defended it by citing past precedent in the apostolic church and Christ's commandment, "If I then, your lord and Master, have washed your feet, ye also are to wash one another's feet." But regular Millerites objected to a man washing a woman's feet and *vice versa*. L. Delos Mansfield passed along rumors that Peavey, in washing the sisters' feet, "like all men with whom I have met who advocate these ridiculous, revolting and indecent ceremonies, *selected as his victim* a YOUNG GIRL! Why if his heart is pure, and his desires holy, did he not choose a male, or a matron in the presence of her husband?" Mansfield also condemned the accompanying ritual of "holy kissing." When one woman rebuffed Peavey's efforts to wash her feet, Mansfield claimed, Peavey "approached her, and without giving her any declaration of his intentions, actually gave her a (holy! ah! what mockery!) kiss! If holy kissing is to be tolerated among the sexes, I have yet to learn that it is to be exchanged between a saint and a sinner!" All in all, Mansfield thought Peavey was "a bad and impure man."[12]

Strangest of all was the door-shutter commune in Springwater Val-ley, whose antics we have already encountered. There in 1844 an unmarried black man named Houston, who led the group, his married black companion, a man named Hull Barton and "his *miss*" of Spring-water, and John D. Poor and a Mrs. Green of Marion moved into the large house of a wealthy Springwater Valley family. Houston convinced the others that God had imbued him with the Holy Ghost and that if they were to be saved, they would have to obey his every command. Taking complete charge of the house, he ordered the carpets torn up and furniture broken up for firewood. Practicing spiritual wifery, he had even made "licentious proffers to the woman of the house, as the last *test* of her consecration to God!" This was too much for Poor and the others, who moved out leaving the black couple alone with the owners of the house. The hosts, too, had ordered Houston and his mistress to leave, but when Houston said "the family must consequently go to hell," the fright-ened couple invited them to remain.

[12] Himes to Miller, March 27, 1845; *Voice of Truth*, December 31, 1845, and December 2, 1846; Edwin Burnham, *Midnight Cry*, September 3, 1845; *Voice of Truth*, April 23, 1845; L. Delos Mansfield, *Midnight Cry*, November 19, 1845.

Henry F. Hill and Joseph Marsh visited the commune in September, 1845, to investigate. They received a cold reception from Houston and his mistress, who fastened upon their unexpected visitors "a fiendish look, and demoniac grin." The woman followed Hill "stamping, throwing her arms," while Marsh tried to reason with the self-appointed prophet. But Houston told Marsh that "'God had sent us there to be judged' that 'he was our judge'—that 'Jesus Christ in him was judging the world,' and that 'all that come there and knocked for admittance, and came in, would be judged.'" Undaunted, Marsh warned Houston's impressionable hosts that their "guests" were "fallen, debased characters, having lived together the last summer." Houston acknowledged the truth of the charge and then compounded the sin by admitting that "the night before they had lodged together!" Having done all they could to warn the family, Marsh and Hill left, "earnestly praying that God may open their eyes to their perilous condition and deliver them from this snare of the devil."[13]

In 1846, the commune, now calling itself the Household of Faith and the Household of Judgment, sent Miller a chilling letter telling him what God, "who sits here upon the throne," had revealed to Houston in a vision. "Beloved, these things that I declare unto thee are the words and works of God to thee which thou shall do well if thou take heed. . . . God has undertaken here to bring together and prepare a people to confer upon them the promise of the father even the gift of the Holy Ghost, that they may walk through the earth working the works the father shall give them to do." Specifically, God had commanded Houston to write to all the Millerite leaders that "God's trumpet in muttering tones of thundering peals, will soon wake up thy sleepy powers, to cry behold the Son of God, as this house of Judgment reveals him the King Eternal." In a few days these heavenly trumpets will "gather Gods elect from the four winds into the same liberty and glory and power till the whole body the 144,000 are perfected in God the perfection of beauty." Because they knew Miller would "turn from this and despise my council with the Lord God the King," the prophet's fate was sealed. "But thou shall be slain and thy wisdom perish when my Father's fire shall search after thy soul to consume thee. . . . William Miller has got to die, and the Son of God, only live for this new creation alone hath immortality dwelling a tabernacle for God in the flesh." Now it was up to God to "make his word a fire and William Miller wood, that the fire may consume the wood and stubble, and the Son of God in thee alone be saved in the day of Glory."[14]

Few radicals went so far, but most condemned regular adventists

---

[13] *Voice of Truth*, September 19, 1845.
[14] Houshold of Faith to Miller, May 14, 1846.

with a "denunciatory spirit . . . and in some instances demoniac spirit, exulting over the downfall of their brethren." A female footwasher who had unsuccessfully tried to recruit a fellow adventist had cried out at him, "Bro. E. you have not got the spirit, you are going straight down to hell; and," said he, "I exhult and rejoice over you." Peavey's practice was to advise his followers "to withdraw from the brethren who did not believe in [his] doctrine, and also to discontinue the papers which oppose it." Spiritualists particularly condemned those who published confessions of error. Regulars reacted to them just as hotly. "It is really mortifying to witness the extremes they run into," their system was "as absurd and as little supported by scripture as Mormonism," the closed door theory was "damning in its influence," the "doctrine of devils." Moderates could not forgive their "proscriptive spirit," "the most unsparing reproach . . . I have received from those I have most ardently loved in the Lord." Furthermore, the two radical camps feuded with each other.[15]

Distressing to regulars was the impression that radicals were winning the strongest influence over those who remained in the movement. E. R. Pinney toured New York in the summer of 1845 and reported a sad situation: "Since I left [Auburn], I have visited Syracuse, Albany, Greenville, Troy, Lansingburgh, Middletown, Freehope, New York, and Newark, N. J. I find in almost every place the bands divided, and as a natural consequence, dissensions, evil surmisings, and evil speakings abounding." Moderates were fighting a losing battle. "At Rochester Bro. Barry & between that place and this [Seneca Falls] only one young brother, who believed the door is shut. Crozier at Canandaigua whose preaching commenced with this faith some two years since. Myself here at Seneca Falls, whether they have any lectures there I am not certain.—Then Troy so that from Rochester to Troy I know of no lecturer but myself that stands on the principles of the Advent faith."[16]

The situation in Oswego illustrates the dilemma of moderates. The city is said to have hosted one of the largest Millerite meetings in the state, enlisting almost the entire Baptist Church. Silas Guilford, son of Miller's brother-in-law who had sponsored the advent leader's first lecture in Dresden, had moved to New Haven just east of Oswego in the 1830s and founded a Millerite meeting there. But after the Great Disappointment, George Peavey led that group into shut door adventism and condemned the regulars, thereby causing division and hard feelings. Guilford said it had all started when Peavey first arrived in the city "with the Shut Door and its trimmings, split and divided, scattered them

in every direction. staid here all winter. tried hard for mastery and to
kill off the wicked with his faith with many other such things such as
Praying the Dead out of their Graves, healing the sick, etc. failed in
them all. turned spiritualist. did all the hurt he could do with his new
doctrine." The band was in shambles. "I see them split up into all kinds
of isms from Millerism, to spiritualism, Peaveyism, Shut Door, feet washing, Holy salvation, Praying for the destruction of sinners and many
other sentiments—hardly any two can believe alike." The atmosphere
became so uncomfortable that Guilford and his wife withdrew from the
meeting and were, so far as he knew, the only regular adventists in the
county. Peavey had gone on to Troy, but he recruited two colleagues to
go to Oswego "finishing up the work of destruction."[17] Such evidence
may be factually accurate but still biased. Guilford probably exaggerated
somewhat, particularly if he had been a leader of the band and Peavey's
intervention had diminished his status, yet the appearance of so many
similar stories in the regular Millerite press makes clear that the activities
and influence of the radicals was strong.

The plight of the moderates became critical in February of 1845,
when Miller published a letter implying sympathy with the shut door
position. Disheartened after the Great Disappointment, he would have
liked to escape the bickering among the Millerites, but his brooding lack
of activity brought mild rebukes from colleagues. Himes, for instance,
had written, "I do not wonder at your despairing state of mind about
further labor. And now that you have put of[f] the armour in the hope of
a discharge, it is very hard to think of putting it on again." But, "God
requires it—the world requires it." Though Miller wanted simply to keep
"in my own breast" his personal opinions about the disputes wrecking
Millerism and not to become involved, he could not deny his responsibilities as the crusade's leader. Slowly he began to take sides. In December,
he criticized those who were seeking a new date, saying there was "no
good that can be accomplished by taking a stand for any future period
with less evidence than we had for 1843-4." Then he rejected the theory
of the spiritual return of Christ, for once believers begin to spiritualize
the event, "all the rest must of course be spiritualized in like manner;
and it would make the whole description of the Judgment but a jumble
of nonsense." Having sacrificed more than anyone else for the cause,
however, he was not ready to give up everything. To him "the experience and scenes of Oct. 22" provided evidence that God "by his invisible
angels was separating the two classes of men, the chaff from the wheat."
Something momentous had indeed taken place, he was eager to affirm.
His own son George being a shut door disciple, it was a short step from

[17] Silas Guilford to Miller, March 17, February 23, 1846. (Unfortunately, the records of
the Oswego Baptist Church have never been made available for research.)

believing God had separated the good from the bad to accepting the idea that the door of mercy too had been shut. In December Miller wrote a letter confirming that "the terrifying time from April until October, and the sanctifying influence of the seventh month" represented the "beginning and preparation of the final *cleansing of the sanctuary.*" He was "fully convinced the work has already begun." In February of 1845, a published letter from him in the *Advent Herald* went further. He formed scriptural argument supporting the closing of probation *before* rather than simultaneously with the Second Coming of Christ. He did not openly accept the shut door doctrine in so many words, but there was no mistaking the direction of his thoughts.[18]

Himes and Sylvester Bliss reacted immediately and hotly. "This class of ultraists are now rejoicing that Father Miller is with them and against us," Bliss said. Parroting Miller's own comments, he taunted Miller, "If we begin to spiritualize the coming of the Bridegroom we may spiritualize it all," and he scolded, "I do pray that no souls may fail of salvation from any errors we may inculcate, or from our neglect of faithfully admonishing them to repentance." Himes, who marked his letter "Private, for Father Miller," warned about the ultraists' intentions. "*They will lay all in ruins*, if they have time enough to do it. They are using *your influence*, or your *name* and *letters* to sustain themselves in this new, and visionary movement." Miller must "stand by us, and defend the great principles of the *advent* creed. Nothing but a full, and decided defense of the *doctrine* of the kingdom—and the principle of *time*, as taught in the Bible will save us." The challenge was not entirely theological. Himes's comments show he was at least equally concerned about protecting his leadership role in the movement and retaining subscriptions to the regular papers. Pearson of the *Hope of Israel* and Jacobs of the *Day Star* were raising "havoc with our publications.—If things go on this way long," he complained, "I shall have to shut up both my offices! The persons going into this view are seeking to do what they can to destroy the Herald." For heaven's sake, write no articles for those papers until Jacobs "makes some honest amends for his unrighteous conduct towards me. He has pursued a course the most unchristian, and injurious to me, and to the cause." Salvation of the movement, of the publications, and of Himes's influence all required that Miller now dissociate himself from the radicals. Assuming Miller's need to escape from the radicals'

---

[18] Himes to Miller, November 19, 1844; *Advent Herald*, February 12, 1845; ibid., December 3, 1844; White, 329; reply to N. N. Whiting, *Morning Watch*, March 20, 1845; *Advent Herald*, February 12, 1845. In his letter to S. Nichols, George Miller wrote, "I believe God did in the 7 month a great work among his people which we shall see in a very few days. . . . The Trumpet was blown in the 7 month to make all ready. On the 24th day of the 7th month we were all separated from strangers since which time we have been like Doves of the Valley mourning upon the mountains."

influence, Himes offered to publish any comments he cared to make "to exculpate you, for any sympathy with them in their wild movements."[19]

Under this pressure Miller gave in. Responding to a published letter from N. N. Whiting challenging him to justify the shut door position, Miller admitted that though he sympathized with some of their views, "to say my judgment was fully convinced [the door of probation] was closed, I must say, No." Far from a rejection of this theory, It had the necessary effect. "Your *letter* to Whiting is doing a world of good," said Himes in obvious relief. "It is just what was needed." Radicals who had been rejoicing over Miller's support now called him "a fallen man." Indeed, the *Jubilee Standard* was sad that Miller "has been imposed upon by the misrepresentations and slanders of others, and has thus been induced, unwittingly, to unite with them in the unholy work of smiting their fellow servants. May God forgive him."[20]

The conquest of Miller was the regulars' first victory against radical-ism. Now moderate lecturers itinerated and attacked spiritualizers and door-shutters. Elon Galusha spoke in Geneseo, Copenhagen, Syracuse, Rochester and elsewhere and was so effective in subverting radical influ-ence that Himes said he "has kept things all right at the West. I found things in a much better state than I expected to." Finally the move-ment's leaders announced a conference to be held in Albany the last week of April 1845 to systematize the battle for moderation. Himes must still have suspected Miller of laxness or backsliding, for just before the conference he ordered Miller peremptorily, "Do you go to Albany to lecture. You will go to the *Conference of Course. And No Mistake!!!*"[21]

Regular adventists from across New York and New England attended the conference, but New Yorkers held the most important offices, Galusha as President and O. R. Fassett as Secretary. The goal of the con-ference was to discredit the radicals; the methods were to formalize Adventist faith and practice. Ratifying essential doctrine was fairly easy, for in their earlier confessions to the public, Miller and Himes had outlined the principal tenets of their beliefs. Doctrines of future judg-ment, damnation of the wicked (aimed at the Storrsites), the two resur-rections, now became standard Adventist theology. Deemed unacceptable were visions of a temporal Millennium, return of "carnal Jews" to Pales-tine, and conversion of the world before the Second Advent. The next step was to expel specific groups that believed errors "respecting the state

[19] Bliss to Miller, January 28, 1845; Himes to Miller, March 12, March 31, 1845; Himes to Miller, March 12, March 31, 1845; Himes to Miller, February 13, 1845, June 30, 1845, and n.d.

[20] Himes to Miller, March 15 and 29, 1845; N. N. Whiting to Miller, March 5, 1845; *Advent Herald*, April 7, 1845; Himes to Miller, n. d., *Jubilee Standard*, April 17, 1845.

[21] Himes to Miller, March 22, 1845; ibid., March 31, 1845.

of the dead, or the final state of the wicked, or any other peculiarities, which are no part or parcel of the advent doctrine." Mystic rites were also condemned—"promiscuous feet-washing and the salutation kiss, . . . sitting on the floor as an act of voluntary humility, shaving the head to humble one's self, and acting like children in understanding." Because many of these ceremonies had developed as a result of enthusiastic meetings, the conference advised Adventists to reject the instruments that had most assured the growth of Millerism, revivals and camp meetings. The regulars called for a full-scale assault on radicalism by means of increased lectures, tract distribution, and carefully orchestrated conferences. Finally, in order to create and maintain discipline, the Albany Conference created an Adventist clergy. Error had resulted when persons "who had *called themselves* to the ministry . . . taught errors," so it was imperative that Adventists choose ministers carefully. The first prerequisite was that preachers now be men; they should be *brethren* who "will teach the unadulterated word of God." Examination of candidates and ceremonies of ordination were logical measures to ensure both quality of preachers and control over who should become a minister.[22]

The pietistic dynamic had come full cycle. Antiformalism was dead, apparently, rejected in favor of formalism and institutional self-preservation. Many adventists were quick to point out the obvious contradiction between the work of the Albany Conference and the movement's traditional libertarianism. Needless to say, radicals did not take the conference kindly at all. The *Voice of the Shepherd* advised that the time had not yet come for formalization; the "power of the holy people must be scattered" to evangelize rather than be brought together to tyrannize. Even some regular Millerites were upset. Marsh, who had vacillated in his attitude toward the theological and personal disputes of the last few months, tried to serve as a mediator. "We should labor to see how *near* we are agreed rather than to show how wide we are apart," he editorialized. "If both [sides] keep honest, humble, and persevering for the truth, our differences will soon vanish." Thus he allowed proponents of all views to publish articles in the *Voice of Truth*, even though he rejected spiritualism out of hand and was reserved toward the shut door group. All he succeeded in doing was to earn Himes's suspicions: "*The disaffected ones* are forming in their aid to *sustain him*, which they would not do, if they knew his real views." At one time Himes even classed the *Voice of Truth* as one of the radical papers. But in spite of the difficulties between the two editors, Marsh agreed to attend the Albany Conference, and this reassured Himes that his colleague would "take the same

[22] "Address to the Brethren Scattered Abroad," *Advent Herald*, May 14, 1845; *Voice of Truth*, May 21, 1845, and July 2, 1845. See also *Proceedings of the Mutual Conference of Adventists Held in the City of Albany* (New York, 1845).

ground that we do on *Bible order*, etc." Of this misconception Marsh quickly disabused him. Deciding not to attend after all, he stayed in Rochester and published editorials condemning the whole proceeding. Marsh resented "the declarations, in a few short paragraphs, of what our brethren *do* and *do not* believe." Once a leader of the come-outers, he now condemned formalization of the movement "because human names when connected with churches are all unscriptural." And, he said, no one has a right to decide "by *voting* or *resolving* that a certain doctrine or practice is *true* or *false*." He rejected the Conference's obvious intention of "forming a new sect, under a sectarian name. . . . It looks like laying plans of our devising to be acted upon in the *future*, when we have in our possession the perfect economy of the Lord, by which we should be guided, and when we profess to be looking for his coming every hour." Himes was furious: "You see that *Marsh* did not stay at home for nothing. He is determined to have things go at loose ends—or to go to support *him*, and not the *mutual*, or *general cause*. . . . He has had a good harvest out of the *Herald & Watch* and now he seeks another, by raising the 'cry' of creeds, Bondage, etc."[23]

But who could deny the truth of Marsh's charges? The Albany Conference *did* establish a new Adventist sect, and did so in face of the Millerites' continuing confidence that Christ would come at any moment. One of the most astounding developments in the months following the Great Disappointment was the movement's slide from immediacy to futurism, from a millenarian reliance on divine agency to an almost postmillennial belief in human agency. Himes's change of heart illustrates the trend. "I am still of the opinion that we have more work to do, and that 'this Gospel of the Kingdom' shall be preached in all the world &c—and *then* shall the 'End come.'" God now required the conversion of the world before the end of all things. "*It will be done*," and because it "*has not yet been done*" Adventists have "*no right* therefore to hold our peace *yet*." Bliss also believed the "best way to hasten Christ's return is to labor with all our might in plucking sinners out of the fire; for when he has accomplished the number of his elect, he will descend in glory and power."[24]

Thus formalization of creed and ritual was more than an expedient to isolate and destroy the radicals. It was a means of keeping faith with God, of continuing the work of Adventism in saving souls and disseminating the Truth. Himes had no desire "to bind a brother's conscience,"

---

[23] *Voice of the Shepherd*, May 1845; "Let There be no Strife," *Voice of Truth*, March 5, 1845; *Voice of Truth*, December 19, 1844; Himes to Miller, March 31, March 12, March 22, 1845; *Voice of Truth*, May 23, 1845; Himes to Miller, May 3, 1845.

[24] Himes to Miller, November 19, 1845, January 28, 1845, and February 13, 1845; Bliss to Miller, February 11, 1845.

but he could not see how Adventists could "act together, and apart at the *same time. . . .* Men may cry liberty &c—and live for a time in the distraction they produce, but it cannot be of use to Gods cause, or the world. Neither can it be permanent. it will die—I am glad to have done what we have."[25] Permanence, discipline, and authority were necessary now in the face of error, uncertainty, and disputes over when and how the world would end.

The Albany Conference did not so much create an Adventist sect as give shape and direction to a body that already existed. That sect had grown from the bottom up, in dozens of communities where Millerites had separated from the churches and established their own meetings, built their own "tabernacles," thought and spoke of themselves as Adventists. By recognizing their transformation from a mass movement into a sect, the regulars were able to impose order and prevent the movement from completely fragmenting because of its own libertarianism. Perhaps by formulating a creed and making plans for an extended sojourn in this world they surrendered to profane time, but they also assured that Second Adventism would survive, that Christians would continue to honor Miller's promise to God to "tell it to the world."

The Albany Conference marked a turning point in the history of Adventism. The Conference had provided a rallying point for regular Millerites. Eschewing camp meetings and revivals, they now held local and regional conferences and "union meetings" to solidify fellowship. As early as October of 1845, Marsh reported, "The breaches in Zion have been healing since the Conference in Albany last spring. I think that fanciful and fanatical notions have had their day."[26]

Not all Adventists came to agree on doctrine and practice; far from it. Many still tried to find a specific time for the Second Coming. John Thomas, an English physician, founder of an adventist sect in Virginia (unrelated to the Millerites) called the Christadelphians, toured upstate New York in 1847 and was shocked to find such strong reliance still on revealed time. "They have occupied themselves too exclusively upon *the moment when*," he wrote; "let them examine more minutely *the things which*, so that when time fails them, they may not be taken unawares by events which must surely come to pass before the Lord comes. This will be soon, but not so soon as they imagine." Spiritualizers of both camps still preached their messages, though the Albany conferees undertook a strong counterattack against them, and rumors that Miller accepted the

---

[25] Himes to Miller, May 3, 1845
[26] The only camp meeting advertised was at Caryville in June 1845. Adventists held conferences in 1845 in Syracuse, Constable(ville), Dickinson, Massena, Copenhagen, Union Corners, Springwater, Laona, and Troy. *Voice of Truth*, October 15, 1845, and December 3, 1845.

shut door theory continued to circulate. Peculiar people still wandered
the region trumpeting dire warnings. A man named Sheppard arrived in
Rochester in 1845 with "a little message from the Lord." Marsh met him
and described the millenarist's manner of broadcasting that message:
"He stood in the middle of the street, with his Bible open in one hand,
his hat in the other, his eyes raised to heaven, and repeated in a loud,
clear, distinct, and most solemn tone, the following scripture: 'Behold, he
cometh with clouds; and every eye shall see him, and they also which
pierced him; and all kindreds of the earth shall wail because of him.'"
Sheppard then walked down the street a short way and repeated the
message, continuing in this manner "until he had gone through the city."
From Rochester he intended to itinerate throughout New York, New
England, and even England.[27]

Regulars took delight from the defection of a spiritualist leader, John
Pearson, editor of the *Hope Within the Vail*. Concerned about dissen-
tions among Adventists which spiritualism apparently was causing, Pearson looked to his Bible to find scriptural justification for his beliefs. "As I
began to pray and search for light," he said in a public recantation, "it
became clearer and clearer that we had been believing and promulgat-
ing an error." Remorse sent him to Rochester where he worked with
Marsh to mend some of the damage he felt he had caused. The result,
reportedly, was that a "number who have long been silent and inactive
have been led to acknowledge their backslidings, and engage anew in
the work of the lord."[28]

Apart from declining spiritualism and rising moderation, another
reason for growing stability in Adventist ranks was that the secular world
now ignored them. "Prejudice against the doctrine of the Second Advent
is gradually waning." Increasingly free from ridicule, the movement now
settled into its long sectarian development. New laborers arose to take
the place of the disaffected, their names appearing for the first time in
Adventist journals. Towns which had never before received Advent lectures now hosted conferences. In 1849 the Adventists in Low Hampton
built the first Advent Christian chapel on Miller's farm, and in years to
come the Advent Christian Church, first child of the Albany Conference,
would spread across the Northeast and Midwest.

Former radicals also organized. In the 1850s adherents of several con-
temporary religious movements combined under the preaching of Ellen
Gould White, O. R. L. Crozier, and others to found the Seventh-Day
Adventist Church. This sect combined sabbatarianism (Saturday worship),

27 *Herald of the Future Age*, III (1847), 203; for rumors of Miller having accepted the
shut door theory see O. R. L. Crozier to Miller, April 2, 1847; *Voice of Truth*, May 28,
1845.
28 J. J. Porter, *Voice of Truth*, October 8, 1845.

vegetarianism and food reform, and Adventism. Adventists of all stamps were achieving a respectability that must previously have seemed unattainable. Wrote Nathan Chapman, brother of a well-known Millerite lecturer, "Were it not for the [*Advent*] *Herald* and what I get from my Brother I must have supposed the Denominations were all used up. But it is not so the denomination is gaining in numbers and respectability."29

This progress was largely owing to the work of new people. Few of the most important Millerite leaders in New York had anything to do with the formation of the later churches. L. Delos Mansfield dropped out of sight after 1845, a rare clue to his later activities being a request to William Henry Seward's wife for an endorsement of a girls' school he had built and managed in the Catskills. Calvin Bateman of Seneca County moved to Michigan after 1845, where he reportedly went insane and died in 1852. His former hometown Baptist association eulogized him as "a man of cultivated mind and devoted spirit" but failed to mention he had been one of the most active Millerite lecturers in western New York. Elon Galusha remained with the Adventists for awhile but eventually returned to the Baptist Church and regained much of his lost prestige, his "sins" forgiven. Joseph Marsh continued publishing Adventist newspapers until 1855, when financial difficulties forced him to sell the last of his presses. After that, though he remained an Adventist, abolitionism captured his time and attention. He sent his daughter Jane to an integrated school and became a personal friend of Frederick Douglass. Himes, the Gray Eminence, eventually turned the *Advent Herald* over to new editors, went west to the gold fields of California, and spent the rest of his life in the Rockies and Plains States. Though he never lost his belief in the imminent Second Coming of Christ, he nevertheless converted to the Episcopal Church, became a priest, and by the 1880s was serving as a vicar at a mission in the Dakotas.30

Miller withdrew from public notice. After 1846 he was ill and depressed, continually hoping for the Second Coming of Christ, but now asking others sadly, "Am I a fanatic?" The debate over the effects of the movement he had fathered was still raging. Sharp losses in church membership in 1844 and 1845 terrified churchmen, who saw in it the imminent collapse of Christianity. Many blamed the Millerites for it, ignoring the role of declining revivalism generally and of other vexing political

29 George D. Bradway to Miller, July 17, 1846; for the development of Adventist denominations after 1845 see David Tallmadge Arthur, "'Come Out of Babylon': A Study of Millerite Separatism and Denominationalism, 1840–65," unpublished Ph.D. dissertation, University of Rochester, 1970.

30 L. Delos Mansfield to Francis Adeline Seward and Lazette Miller Worden, March 13, 1858, Seward Papers, University of Rochester; Halsey, 106; Charles Wesley Brooks, *A Century of Baptist Missions in the Empire State* (Philadelphia, 1900), 135; Benedict, 561; Parker, *Rochester*, 254; Cross, 310.

and religious issues that divided the churches. The Troy Methodist Conference, which lost 1,000 members in 1845, claimed that Millerism alone was the cause. "The Second Advent delusion has proved inconceivably the greatest calamity that has befallen us since our organization as a conference." They failed to mention the separation of antislavery Wesleyan Methodists from their conference, probably the single most important cause of Methodist removals. The Baptists fared worse, and they too blamed Millerism for declining numbers. Unquestionably Millerism had caused dissociation of many Baptists but that they had exacerbated the problem by forcing Millerites out of the church was a fact Baptists chose to ignore.[31] Nevertheless, all condemnation must have weighed heavily on Miller's heart and mind.

Adventists, on the other hand, saw in the effects of their movement proof that God had inspired it. "Were I to judge of this work by the mighty effects it has produced," wrote James Battersby, "I should certainly say, it carries with it its own evidences that it is the work of him whose 'Judgments are unsearchable, and his way is past finding out.'" Elon Galusha consoled Miller by pointing to the "thousands of baptists" who have "joyfully submitted to the blessed ordinance" because of Second Advent preaching. "Instead of making infidels, as it was predicted they would, they have *un*made more of that unhappy class (by bringing them to Christ) than all other instrumentalities employed in our country during the same period."[32] The movement had long-range effects as well. Women's preaching in public under the aegis of Millerism did not directly influence women's rights, indeed the religious background of many women's rights activities was Quaker, not Baptist or Adventist, but it did publicize women acting in public service and therefore contributed to the chain of events that led to the Women's Rights Convention of 1848 in Seneca Falls. Miller's preaching drove many Christians to reread their Bibles, and that exercise increased the age's preoccupation with identifying and rooting out sin of all sorts. The quest for ultimate sin accelerated the drive against slavery. It is no mere coincidence that the war hymn of the Union began with the words, "Mine eyes have seen the glory of the coming of the Lord."

Miller could not have contemplated these effects of his crusade, but he did receive occasional word of personal encouragement. Many wrote to assure him he had acted the part of the good and faithful servant. Said Henry Buckley, "I think it would be a hard matter to convince the

---

[31] Henry Buckley to Miller, April 5, 1847; Stephen Parks, *Troy Conference Miscellany* (Albany, 1854), 66; Duane Hamilton Hurd, *History of Clinton and Franklin Counties, New York* (Philadelphia, 1880), 265; P. H. Fowler, *Historical Sketch of Presbyterianism Within the Bounds of the Synod of Central New York* (Utica, 1877), 240–43.

[32] James Battersby, *Midnight Cry*, November 14, 1844; Galusha to Miller, July 4, 1845.

world that you were 'Nothing'—The name of Miller has been sounded from nearly every pulpit, in the land & I might say in the world, & think you the people talk so much about 'nothing.' By the grace of God you are what you are, and I thank him for bestowing so much grace on you, for when I was spiritually blind you opened my eyes to see the glorious things in God's law." Wrote Peavey, former outcast, "Your sacrifices and devotion in that work have ever been convincing proofes of the deep regard which you cherished under a sense of duty to the welfare of others."[33]

Comfort came from God, too. Many years earlier, when Miller was vexed and afraid to preach, God had sent him a dream that had assured him of the Lord's blessing. Now, according to his memoirs, God sent another. In this dream God gave Miller a "curiously wrought chest" filled with jewels and gold and silver. Wishing to share the beautiful treasures with others, Miller placed the chest on a table "and gave out word that all who had a desire might come and see." But the throngs that arrived scattered jewels over the floor and dropped counterfeit coins into the box. Disgusted, Miller struggled to eject the unworthy crowd, but in doing so broke the chest and scattered its contents worse than ever. "I thought wholly discouraged and disheartened, and sat down and wept." Then a stranger entered the room, swept up the dirt and counterfeit coins, and gave him a new chest with even more dazzling treasure. In his joy Miller shouted out, and the shout awakened him. This new treasure reassured him that God had not abandoned the crusade nor its spokesman. "The effect of this on my mind has been extremely consoling and happy."[34]

Thus at times light broke through the gloom, helping to assuage doubts. But constant illness now racked his body, making such periods of sunshine few and brief. Only Himes wrote regularly, though less often than before, generally to tell him the state of the cause, asking for a tub of butter from the farm, once even asking for money. The relationship between the two men had changed. Gone were the abrupt directives from the editor to the spiritual head of the movement. Affection seemed to have been the surviving quality of each man's feeling for the other. Himes, said Miller to one of his sons, was a "stout son in the Gospel" just as William, Jr., was his "stout son in the flesh."[35]

As months passed, Miller's illness lingered, increasing the sixty-eight year old man's yearning for release. Now in 1849, his eyesight gone, he wrote to a friend of his longing "to go home," referring obviously to that

[33] Buckley to Miller, March 12, 1842; Peavey to Miller, October 25, 1848.
[34] Bliss, 360–63.
[35] Himes to Miller, October 9, 1848, January 26, 1848; William S. Miller to Himes, May 14, 1864, Himes Papers.

mansion he had been building in the Kingdom of God. Miller would have agreed with Himes's assessment of life: "This is a world of affliction and toil—who could not rejoice to have Christ come, and put an end to all sorrow, terror and death?" This dream of the ages, to escape the universal condition of humanity, was the dream yet unfulfilled. Continuing to look for the Second Advent of Christ, Miller watched the days pass one after the other until finally, on December 30, 1849, with Himes beside his bed, Miller found the haven so long desired. In the words of a dear friend, "He is now where the wicked cease from troubling and the weary are at rest."[36]

[36] Buckley to Miller, April 5, 1847; Himes to Miller, October 9, 1848; Nichol, 268; Matilda H. Tracy to Himes, January 22, 1850.

EPILOGUE

The task remains for us to assess Millerism in a scholarly context. For decades social scientists in many disciplines—history, religion, sociology, anthropology, mythology, literature, psychology—have investigated apocalyptic movements around the world, past and present. Surprisingly, they have either ignored the most important American example, the Millerites, or have casually accepted contemporary detractors' labels of them as fools or cranks. Perhaps the occurrence of an apocalyptic mass movement in our society is an embarrassment. A seemingly primitive response to the world such as millenarism does not fit well with our image of ourselves as modern, sophisticated, and rational. Yet the period of religious heterodoxy of the 1960s and 1970s through which we have so recently passed ought to make us aware of the continuing role of religion as a vital element of the American character. Rather than ridiculing or ignoring the Millerites, we would do better to try to understand the forces that created Adventism and the results that followed it.

Though my principal purpose until now has been to describe and explain Millerism, at this point it seems useful to draw upon theories of millenarism arrived at by other scholars of apocalyptic to see if they clarify the meaning of this single variegated movement.[1]

One set of theories about the cause of millenarism maintains that visions of universal destruction and subsequent renovation appeal most often to people who are materially or politically deprived. Dispossession may take the form of economic poverty or political tyranny, such as colonialism for example; so one consequently finds millenarism in cargo cults which promise wealth to the saved, in liberation movements, or in social revolutions. This theory sheds little light on Millerism. Most Millerites were not dispossessed either materially or politically; not only is there no evidence of general poverty among adventists, but there are strong clues that most of them were comfortably situated. However, Millerites' pietistic longing for Heaven, their habit of contrasting earthly pain and sorrow with future bliss and union with God, does indicate that they felt spiritually deprived. Millerism also had a liberating tendency that benefited men and especially women who discovered for themselves

---

[1] Historiography is reserved for the bibliographical essay, especially the section labeled "Millennialism," where works are listed that illustrate each of the morphologies of millenarism discussed below.

an active public role through adventism or that freed pious dissenters from the doctrinal authoritarianism of the formalizing sects. But this is far from the kind of social rebellion deprivationists see in millenarism.

Other scholars view millenarism as an attempt to relieve social and psychological tensions. True, many adventists found solace in contemplating imminent release from the world. But in general, apocalypticism is as likely to create tension as to relieve it. By focusing attention on salvation and damnation, it evokes profound terror of being unworthy of Heaven. Millerites feared as much as they yearned. Miller's own experience—public assurance, private doubts, and resulting stress—is a case in point.

Some theorists ignore the relatively narrow questions of sociologists and psychologists and instead inquire into the broad significance of apocalyptic as an element of human experience. Mircea Eliade (whose work has influenced this study) is a comparative mythologist who has found universal themes among cultures separated widely in space and time. He believes that apocalypticism not only promises release from this world but actually places the believer one step into the next. This view neatly defines the Millerite or pietistic temperament, for Millerites kept their eyes focused directly on the New Jerusalem. Moreover, this cosmological approach is particularly suited to illuminating Millerism because it views apocalyptic essentially as a cultural phenomenon rather than narrowly as a product solely of social tension or change.

In this regard, a theory that Anthony F. C. Wallace developed to describe apocalyptic is relevant. He sees millenarism and messianism as products of a process he calls "mazeway formation" in which stable societies that undergo stress for any number of reasons experience "mazeway disintegration," or a decline in traditional values. As individuals find themselves adrift in a new and incomprehensible culture, apocalyptic allows some of them to resynthesize the mazeway, to create a new sense of community and their place in it. Essentially this is what the Millerites did. Rejecting their present world, they created a vision of a new world drawn from popular and formal culture and then endeavored spiritually and psychologically to place themselves in it. Prophecy and biblical precedent provided "dictionaries" useful in defining events and describing their relationships to others in this world. Hence, believers were citizens and compatriots in this new land; scoffers were outsiders. Far from creating a fortress, however, Millerites worked eagerly to find additional citizens for their New Jerusalem, for each convert to adventism justified his or her own beliefs.

This mazeway theory might have led to more specific and fruitful conjecture. If the demographics of adventism were discoverable we might have charted in greater detail the specific social and economic changes that sparked so much animosity toward society. Were complaints about increasing materialism unconsciously a rebellion against changes in values accompanying the industrial revolution? Paul Johnson suggests in *A Shopkeeper's Millenium* that revivals in Rochester from 1826 to 1834 attracted greatest fervor among new industrialists and factory workers, and he suggests that revivalism was the tool new industrialists used to maintain status and moral authority over the new industrial labor class. If this interpretation is correct, would it hold true for Millerism as well? Or did Millerism represent a rural backlash against the industrial revolution? Unfortunately, we cannot tell, for Millerism appeared in all kinds of communities—rural, commercial, and industrial. Perhaps it represented one ethos in industrial communities and a different set of values in rural communities, but no evidence suggests this.

Whitney Cross presents a more productive line of reasoning in his theory that the "burned-over district," a region of special religious fervor and innovation west of Rome, N. Y., resulted from qualities endemic to a maturing Yankee society and culture. The greatest weakness of his work is that he failed to illustrate the process by which this happened. Millerism does. As an antiformal pietistic rebellion against the formalization of the evangelical sects, Millerism was a conservative reaction against social change and formalization (maturation). The fact that the crusade achieved wide support in New England and areas of the nation settled by New Englanders (New York, the Western Reserve of Ohio, Michigan) also supports Cross's description of the burned-over district as a Yankee phenomenon. In fact, the only region of upstate New York where Millerism made no headway was the "Pennsylvania Triangle," those counties in the Southern Tier (Steuben, Schuyler, Chemung) settled by Pennsylvanians who came from a German Lutheran tradition rather than from the New England Calvinist tradition. However, Cross erred in describing the burned-over district in terms of a geographical area. In fact, it was a social process that extended geographically and chronologically far beyond Cross's boundaries. It appeared as early as the 1780s and 1790s in western New England, the cultural home of Miller, Joseph Smith, and founders of the Christian Connexion and Anti-Mission Baptists. Indeed, ultraism in upstate New York in the 1830s and 1840s was probably a continuation of the same religious ferment that churned the Connecticut Valley at the end of the eighteenth century.

The burned-over district moved gradually across this country as people tried to create a new sense of community in their own time, a community in which their status was absolutely clear, a community of traditional pietistic values. Millerism was but one vehicle for achieving the goal. Rooted in formal and popular apocalyptic and millennial traditions, it proffered hope of cosmic renewal and release from profane time. With traditional values disintegrating about them, adventists rejected the world in good pietistic fashion and sought through antiformal libertarianism to place themselves in their New Jerusalem. The

Great Disappointment did not put a permanent end to this process; the burned-over district simply changed locales once again. It went with the Mormons on their trek to the Great Salt Lake, and today we find innovators working in the newest burned-over district, California, rebelling against a changing world which is bewildering and threatening.

Nor did apocalypticism end with the Great Disappointment, for it was a powerful force in the rise of modern Fundamentalism. Its influence can be seen today in the popularity of Hal Lindsay's book, *The Late Great Planet Earth*, in current speculation about global environmental catastrophes, in the dire ticking of the Doomsday Clock. One need not be an Adventist to see apocalyptic as neither primitive nor archaic. In this nuclear age images of Revelation are awesomely believable, for we have seen the great cloud, heard the terrifying thunder, and turned from the blinding light that threatens to bring the end of the world. If our secular catastrophists appear more rational than their religious counterparts they are also more dire, for they cannot match the Millerites' vision of human redemption. By comparison their apocalypse seems the poorer, a vision of the end of time that has dimmed from the image of a shining New Jerusalem to that of a desolate wasteland.

SELECTED BIBLIOGRAPHICAL ESSAY

This bibliographical essay is intended as a guide for interested readers to further information about three areas: Millerism, religion and evangelicalism, and New York State history. Therefore it is organized in three sections, one for each field, and where necessary subdivided for the convenience of the reader. Because the average reader is not interested in research resources, each section proceeds from the general (secondary sources) to the more particular (primary sources) rather than in the more traditional reverse order.

MILLERISM

Until recently histories of the Millerite movement were almost exclusively produced by Adventists, and they often suffered from apologetics. This is particularly true of the standard work, Francis D. Nichol's *The Midnight Cry: A Defense of William Miller and the Millerites* (Washington: Review and Herald, 1944), as the title alone reveals. Leroy Edwin Froom, *The Prophetic Faith of Our Fathers* (4 vols., Washington: Review and Herald, 1946–54) is also hagiographic and its information not always reliable.

On the other hand, Adventists have provided some of the most objective histories of Millerism. The best published account is Isaac C. Wellcome, *History of the Second Advent Message and Mission, Doctrine and People* (Yarmouth, ME: I. C. Wellcome, 1874), but it is difficult to find. L. Richard Conradi, *The Founders of the Seventh-Day Adventist Denomination* (Plainfield, New Jersey: American Sabbath Tract Society, 1939) offers biographies of leaders in the rise of that denomination. A fascinating non-Adventist commentary, really a collection of reminiscences of former Millerites, is Clara Endicott Sears, *Days of Delusion: A Strange Bit of History* (Boston: Houghton Mifflin, 1924). The most recent discussion of Adventism's roots is a series of essays edited by Edwin Scott Caustad, *The Rise of Adventism: Religion and Society in Mid-Nineteenth Century America* (New York, Evanston, San Francisco, London: Harper & Row, 1974). N. Gordon Thomas presents a brief view of Millerism in Ohio in "The Millerite Movement in Ohio," *Ohio History* (Spring, 1972), 95–107.

The movement's best histories appear in unpublished doctoral dissertations. Foremost is Everett Newton Dick's "The Adventist Crisis of

1843–4," University of Wisconsin, 1930. Somewhat less satisfactory but still objective is Reuben Elmore Harkness, "Social Origins of the Millerite Movement," University of Chicago, 1927. The only regional studies are Nathan Gordon Thomas, "The Second Coming in the Third New England: The Millerite Impulse in Michigan, 1830–60," Michigan State University, 1967, and my own "Thunder and Trumpets: The Millerite Movement and Apocalyptic Thought in Upstate New York, 1800–45," University of Virginia, 1974. David Tallmadge Arthur's excellent study, "'Come Out of Babylon': A Study of Millerite Separatism and Denominationalism, 1840–65," University of Rochester, 1970, discusses thoroughly the development of Adventist churches.

Original research must begin with Sylvester Bliss, *Memoirs of William Miller: Generally Known as a Lecturer on the Prophecies, and the Second Coming of Christ* (Boston: Joshua V. Himes, 1853), a recompilation and editing of Miller's own memoirs. This is the only source of information about Miller's early years, and although it partakes of apologetics it is still an invaluable firsthand account for those who wish to read between the lines. The book received a second editing in James White, *Sketches of the Christian Life and Public Labors of William Miller* (Battle Creek, MI: Steam Press, 1874). Miller's principal publications include *Evidence From Scripture and History of the Second Coming of Christ About the Year 1843* published in various editions beginning with the original pamphlet version of 1836. A second principal work is his *Views of the Prophecies and Prophetic Chronology* (Boston: M. A. Dew, 1841). The multivolume set entitled the *Second Advent Library* includes almost all of the pamphlets listed in my notes and may be found in various repositories including the Jenks Adventual Collection at Aurora College, Aurora, Illinois.

Personal reminiscences of Millerites are very instructive. Besides Miller's they include Joseph Bates, *The Autobiography of Elder Joseph Bates: Embracing a Brief Account of the Great Advent Movement of 1840–44* (Battle Creek, MI: Seventh-Day Adventist Publishing Assn., 1868); O. R. Fassett, *The Biography of Mrs. L. E. Fassett, a Devoted Christian, a Useful Life* (Boston: Advent Christian Publication Society, 1885; Jane (Jenny) Marsh Parker, "A Little Millerite," *Century Magazine* XI (November, 1886–April, 1887), 310–17 and additional reminiscences in *Rochester, a Story Historical* (Rochester: Scranton, Wetmore and Co., 1886); and Hiram Munger's colorful autobiography *Life and Religious Experiences of Hiram Munger* (Chicopee Falls, MA, 1861).

Anti-Millerite tracts from the period include John Dowling, *An Exposition of the Prophecies Supposed by William Miller to Predict the Second Coming of Christ in 1843* (Providence: George P. Daniels, 1840); Kittredge Haven, *The World Reprieved: Being a Critical Examination of William Miller's Theory* (Woodstock, VT: Haskell and

Palmer, 1839); and Otis A. Skinner, *The Theory of William Miller Concerning the End of the World in 1843, Utterly Exploded* (Boston: Thomas Whittemore, 1840).

Millerites published many newspapers across the Northeast, and most are available in the original at Aurora College, Andrews University at Barrien Springs, Michigan, the Seventh-Day Adventist Historical Society at Takoma Park, Washington, D. C., and elsewhere. Those I found most relevant were the *Midnight Cry* (New York) and *Signs of the Times* (Boston), their post-1845 successors, respectively the *Advent Herald* and *Morning Watch*, the *Trump of Jubilee* (Seneca Falls), and the *Voice of Truth* (Albany and Rochester). Dissenting Millerite periodicals included the *Voice of Elijah* (Sherbrook, Canada), *Voice of the Shepherd* (Utica), and the *Bible Examiner* (Albany).

The principal archival repository is the Jenks Adventual Collection at Aurora College that includes almost the entire holding of Miller's correspondence as well as newspapers, pamphlets, secondary sources, and artifacts. The William Miller Papers are an invaluable resource not only for studying Millerism but American religion, revivalism, and culture. The Massachusetts Historical Society retains the single largest collection of Himes letters in the Joshua V. Himes Collection. More fugitive manuscript materials appear in private collections across the country, mostly at universities, and I list those in the section on New York State History.

Finally, a word on using these sources is in order here. Assessing objectivity is always a challenge when undertaking any historical research. One must always read contemporary reports skeptically, and Millerite sources are no different. In this book I have relied on these sources for specific information about the geographic distribution of Millerism, evangelical techniques, personal attitudes, and specific events. One cannot evaluate the size of the movement simply by reading adventists' claims of "thousands of converts" and the like, for Millerites relied on numbers to gauge success just as did other revivalists. And every lecturer wanted to be a success! On the other hand, anti-Millerite tracts and publicity were no more objective, and in most cases considerably less so. Once one assumes a reasonable skepticism, though, Millerite materials are truly rich with hidden treasures awaiting the patient prospector.

RELIGION AND EVANGELICALISM

This enormous field provides almost unbounded opportunity for additional reading. Excellent texts include Winthrop S. Hudon, *Religion in America* (New York: Charles Scribner's Sons, 1965 and 1973) and John Wilson, *Religion in American Society: The Effective Presence* (Englewood Cliffs, NJ: Prentice-Hall, 1978), the latter more pointedly sociological in approach. The *American Periodicals Series*, available at many university libraries in microform, is the best source for American religious popular and periodical literature. Journals included in the collection that I found most helpful were the *Christian Journal and Literary Register, Christian's Magazine, Christian Register and Theological Review, Connecticut Evangelical Magazine, National Preacher and Village Pulpit, New-York Missionary Magazine and Repository of Religious Intelligence*. Below are listed specific themes and suggestions for additional reading.

A. Revivalism

American revivalism has received broad treatment in religious historiography. Among the most important general works are William G. McLoughlin, *Revivals, Awakenings, and Reform: An Essay on Religion and Social Change in America* (Chicago and London: University of Chicago, 1978) and his article "Pietism and the American Character," *American Quarterly*, XVII (Summer, 1965), 163–86. Both are valuable guides to the concept of piety and its influence on the whole range of American History. F. Ernest Stoeffler, *The Rise of Evangelical Pietism* (Leiden: E. J. Brill, 1971) presents a good discussion of European pietism and pietistic churches.

There are many studies of nineteenth century revivalism from a variety of perspectives. The best general works are William G. McLoughlin, *Modern Revivalism* (New York: Ronald Press, 1959); John R. Boles, *The Great Revival, 1787–1805* (Lexington, KY: University Press of Kentucky, 1972) which focuses on the South; and, more popular in approach, Bernard Weisberger, *They Gathered at the River: The Story of the Great Revivalists and Their Impact Upon Religion in America* (Chicago: Quadrangle, 1958). Richard Carwardine investigated the interaction between British and American evangelicalism in *Trans-Atlantic Revivalism: Popular Evangelism in Britain and America, 1790–1865* (Westport, CT: Greenwood Press, 1978).

Institutional in approach are T. Scott Miyakawa, *Protestants and Pioneers: Individualism and Conformity on the American Frontier* (Chicago: University of Chicago, 1964 and 1969) and Donald M. Scott, *From Office to Profession: The New England Ministry, 1750–1850* (Philadelphia: University of Pennsylvania, 1978). Both books are indispensable for understanding the changing nature of religion in the developing American frontier.

One vast subfield is the study of evangelicalism's "social ethos," books that posit an evangelical mentality. Principal works are George M. Marsden, *The Evangelical Mind and the New School Presbyterian Experience: A Case Study of Thought and Theology in Nineteenth-Century America* (New Haven: Yale University, 1970); John R. Bodo,

The Protestant Clergy and Public Issues, 1812-48 (Princeton: Princeton University, 1954), Donald G. Mathews, *Religion in the Old South* (Chicago: University of Chicago, 1977); and Charles C. Cole, *The Social Ideals of the Northern Evangelists, 1826–60* (New York: Columbia University, 1954). Again, much of what these writers elucidate as "evangelicalism" I would call "pietism," and in general it would be difficult to find much concensus on social issues among evangelicals or pietists. Two books that describe the relationship between revivalism and social reform are Alice Felt Tyler's encyclopedic *Freedom's Ferment; Phases of American Social History From The Colonial Period to the Outbreak of the Civil War* (Minneapolis: University of Minnesota, 1944) and the more satisfying study by Lewis Perry, *Radical Abolitionism: Anarchy and the Government of God in Antislavery Thought* (Ithaca: Cornell University, 1973). The best regional studies of revivalism's and the Second Great Awakening's social effects in the Northeast are Stephen A. Marini, *Radical Sects of Revolutionary New England* (Cambridge and London: Harvard University, 1982) and David M. Ludlum's pioneering study, *Social Ferment in Vermont, 1791–1850* (New York: Columbia University, 1939), dated but still an informative source.

Evangelical missionary activity needs more careful research. This is particularly true of their attempt to convert Jews. Currently available on this subject are A. E. Thompson, *A Century of Jewish Missions* (Chicago, New York, and Toronto: Fleming H. Revell, 1902) and Isaac Goldberg, *Major Noah: American-Jewish Pioneer* (Philadelphia: Jewish Publication Society of America, 1936). They are both dated but each is superior to the more recent but blatantly anti-evangelical polemic by David Max Eichhorn, *Evangelizing the American Jew* (Middle Village, N. Y.: Jonathan David, 1978). This provides interesting information, but the interpretation is hopelessly flawed by the writer's anti-Christianity.

Contemporary accounts of events and issues surrounding the Second Great Awakening abound. Memoirs that are particularly revealing are Charles Grandison Finney, *Memoirs* (New York: A. B. Barnes, 1876); Thomas S. Sheardown, *Half a Century's Labors in the Gospel* (Philadelphia: O. N. Worden and E. B. Case, 1866); and Charles Giles, *Pioneer: A Narrative of the Nativity, Experience, Travels and Ministerial Labours of Rev. Charles Giles* (New York: G. Lane and P. P. Sandford, 1844). The debate over the nature and extent of atonement can be found in Lewis Cheeseman, *Differences Between Old and New School Presbyterians* (Rochester: Erastus Darrow, 1848); Calvin Colton, *History and Character of American Revivals of Religion* (London: Frederick Westley and A. H. Davis, 1832); and James Wood, *Old and New Theology* (Albany: E. H. Pease, 1838).

B. Denominations

Denominational histories are legion, but many are dated or flawed by apologetics. This is true of the historiography of the Baptist Church, most important for this study of Millerism. A basic work is Albert Henry Newman, *A History of the Baptist Churches in the United States* (New York: Christian Literature Co., 1894). Contemporary commentaries are more useful and colorful. They include David Benedict, *A General History of the Baptist Denomination in America and Other Parts of the World* (New York: Lewis Colby, 1848) and William Cathcart, *The Baptist Encyclopedia* (Philadelphia: Louis H. Everts, 1883). Free-Will Baptists are covered in Norman Allen Baxter, *History of the Free-Will Baptists: A Study in New England Separatism* (Rochester: 1957) and in Marini's study of New England sects. One should also consult W. J. McGlothlin's *Baptist Confessions of Faith* (Philadelphia: American Baptist Publication Soc., 1911). The Baptists in New York State was the focus of Charles Wesley Brooks, *A Century of Missions, as Exhibited by the Work and Growth of the Baptist Missionary Convention of the State of New York* (Philadelphia: American Baptist Publication Soc., 1900). The most important contemporary document is by two pioneers of Baptism in New York State, John Peck and John Lawton, *An Historical Sketch of the Baptist Missionary Convention of the State of New York* (Utica: Bennett and Bright, 1837). Among the many histories of associations and congregations are A. Russell Belden, *History of the Cayuga Baptist Association* (Auburn: Derry and Miller, 1851); Lewis Halsey, *History of the Seneca Baptist Association* (Ithaca: Journal Association, 1879); S. S. Crissey, *Centennial History of the Fredonia Baptist Church, 1808–1908* (Buffalo: Matthews-Northrup Works, n.d.); and Mary Shaw Parker, *History of the Baptist Church of Lockport, New York, 1816–1928* (n.p., n.d.). Newspapers vital for researching the history of New York Baptists are the *Massachusetts Baptist Missionary Magazine*, the *Western New York Baptist Magazine*, *Baptist Advocate*, and the *New York Baptist Register*. Archival resources are rich and available thanks to the American Baptist Historical Society, Crozier-Andover Theological Seminary, Rochester.

Methodist documents are not so well centralized. I found them to be the most difficult to find of all church materials because of the Church's tendency to maintain records locally in conference headquarters. A standard study, though dated, is William Warren Sweet, *Methodism in American History* (Nashville: Abingdon Press, 1954), and I found helpful as background material Bernard Semmel's *The Methodist Revolution* (New York: Basic Books, 1973) that describes the church's British roots. Contemporary and local documents include F. W. Conable, *History of the Genesee Annual Conference of the Methodist Episcopal Church* (second edition, New York: Phillips and Hunt, 1885); Stephen Parks, *Troy Conference Miscellany* (Albany: Conference of the Methodist Episcopal Church, 1854); and *A Collection of Hymns for the Use of the Methodist Episcopal Church* (New York: J. Collard, 1829). The most important journals are the *Methodist Review* and the *Methodist Magazine*. Though archival collections are rare, one important source is the Methodist Collection at Syracuse University.

The Presbyterians have generally fared better. Contemporary histories include the invaluable James H. Hotchkiss, *A History of the Purchase and Settlement of Western New York and . . . of the Presbyterian Church in that Section* (New York: M. W. Dodd, 1848) and P. H. Fowler, *Historical Sketch of Presbyterianism Within the Bounds of the Synod of Central New York* (Utica: Curtiss and Childs, 1877). Two contemporary documents were helpful for delineating Presbyterian dogma, *The Constitution of the Presbyterian Church in the United States* (Philadelphia: Edward Barrington and George D. Haswell, 1834) and *Confession of Faith and Covenant Approved by the Presbytery of Chenango, April 21st, 1830* (Oxford, N. Y.: Mack and Chapman, 1830). Important journals include the *Princeton Review*, *Oberlin Evangelist*, and the *Religious Recorder of Central and Western New York*.

The least satisfying of all denominational historiographies is that of the Christian Connexion. The principal contemporary resource is its journal, the *Christian Palladium*.

Universalism and Unitarianism are the focus of continuing research today. One can discover their Rationalist roots in Herbert Montfort Morais's *Deism in Eighteenth Century America* (New York: Russell and Russell, 1943). Contemporary documents include Stephen Rensselaer Smith's memoir, *Historical Sketches and Incidents Illustrative of the Establishment and Progress of Universalism in the State of New York* (Buffalo: Steele's Press, 1843). The tone of evangelical opposition to Universalism appears in an obscure pamphlet, Robert Scott, *An Antidote to Deism, or Scripture Prophecy Fulfilled* (Pittsfield: Phinehas Allen, 1816). New York State journals are the *Evangelical Magazine and Gospel Advocate*, and *Gospel Inquirer* of Little Falls, the *Herald of Salvation* published in Watertown, and the *Religious Enquirer* of Cooperstown.

C. Millennialism

Millennialism as a specialization has a life of its own in the broad field of religious studies. Excellent guides to the field are David E. Smith, "Millenarian Scholarship in America," *American Quarterly*, XVII (Fall, 1965), 535–49; Marian W. Smith, "Towards a Classification of Cult Movements," *Man* (January, 1959), 8–12; Bryan Wilson, "Millennialism in Comparative Perspective," *Comparative Studies in Society and History*, VI

(October, 1963–July, 1964), 93–114; Yonina Talmon, "Pursuit of the Millennium: The Relation Between Religious and Social Change," *Archives Européennes de Sociologie*, III (1962), 125–48; A. J. F. Köbben, "Prophetic Movements as an Expression of Social Protest," *International Archives of Ethnography*, XLIX (part 1, 1960), 117–61; and C. John Sommerville, "Religious Typologies and Popular Religion in Restoration England," *Church History*, XLV (March, 1976), 32–41.

Studies from particular vantage points have shaped my own approach to Millerism. A standard sociological approach is Peter Worsley, *The Trumpet Shall Sound: A Study of Cargo Cults in Melanesia* (London: McGibbon and Kee, 1957). This book not only fathered a whole "cargo cult" genre but also initiated studies specifically of millenarism in the Third World. Mircea Eliade's cosmological approach is best represented in his books *The Myth of the Eternal Return* (New York: Pantheon, 1954) and *The Sacred and the Profane; The Nature of Religion* (New York: Harcourt, Brace and World, 1959). Social deprivation as a cause of millenarism receives treatment in Vittorio Lanternari, *The Religions of the Oppressed: A Study of Modern Messianic Cults* (London: Knopf, 1965) and Eric J. Hobsbawm, *Primitive Rebels: Studies in Archaic Forms of Social Movement in the 19th and 20th Centuries* (New York: W. W. Norton, 1959). The sociology of sectarianism was the focus of two studies that informed this book, H. Richard Niebuhr's *The Social Sources of Denominationalism (New York: Henry Holt,* 1929) and Ernst Troeltsch, *The Social Teaching of the Christian Churches*, Olive Wyon, trans. (New York: MacMillan, 1949–50). Social implications of millenarism was also the concern of Anthony F. C. Wallace whose mazeway theory has influenced scholars in many fields. Relevant works include "Revitalization Movement," *American Anthropologist*, LVIII (1956), 264–281; "Mazeway Disintegration: The Individual's Perception of Socio-cultural Disorganization," *Human Organization*, XVI (Summer, 1957), 23–27; and "Mazeway Resynthesis: A Biocultural Theory of Religious Inspiration," *Transactions of the New York Academy of Sciences*, second series, XVIII (1956), 626–38. Bryan S. Wilson presents the psychological interpretation of apocalyptic in *Magic and the Millennium* (New York: Harper & Row, 1973), and the conclusion to this book provides a fine discussion of millenialist historiography. Two fascinating case studies of modern millennial movements are Leon Festinger, Henry W. Riecken, and Stanley Schlachter, *When Prophecy Fails: A Social and Psychological Study of a Modern Group that Predicted the Destruction of the World* (Milwaukee: University of Minnesota, 1956) and John Lofland, *Doomsday Cult: A Study of Conversion, Proselytization, and Maintenance of Faith* (Englewood Cliffs, N. J.: Prentice-Hall, 1966). Finally, Michael Barkun traces the relationship between millenarism and cataclysm in *Disaster and the Millennium* (New Haven and London: Yale University, 1974).

Histories of millennialism are numerous. Its role in Western culture has received the attention of Norman Cohn, *Pursuit of the Millennium: Revolutionary Millenarians and Mystical Anarchists of the Middle Ages* (New York: Columbia University, 1979), both of which concern themselves with medieval apocalyptic myth and movements. Post-Reformation millennialism is the field of Peter Toon, *Puritans, the Millennium and the Future of Israel: Puritan Eschatology, 1600–60* (Cambridge: James Clarke, 1970) and Clarke Garrett, *Respectable Folly: Millenarians and the French Revolution in France and England* (Baltimore and London: Johns Hopkins University, 1975). Most valuable for discovering the relationship between apocalyptic and popular culture generally is Keith Thomas's monumental *Religion and the Decline of Magic* (New York: Scribner, 1971), an investigation of British innovative religion in the sixteenth and seventeenth centuries. One can also usefully peruse John Strype's *Annals of the Reformation* (4 volumes, New York: Burt Franklin, 1968) that includes fascinating stories of prophets and seers of England's reformation. Gershon Scholem was the great scholar of Jewish mysticism. See particularly *Sabbatai Sevi: The Mystical Messiah* (Princeton: Princeton University, 1973). An important early cross-cultural study is Sylvia Thrupp, *Millennial Dreams in Action* (The Hague: Mouton, 1962).

Histories of millennialism in America begin with James W. Davidson, "Searching for the Millennium," *New England Quarterly*, XLV (June, 1972), 241–61 and *The Logic of Millennial Thought: Eighteenth Century New England* (New Haven and London: Yale University, 1977). Also valuable are Ernest Lee Tuveson, *Redeemer Nation: The Idea of America's Millennial Role* (Chicago: University of Chicago, 1968); J. F. C. Harrison, *The Second Coming: Popular Millenarianism, 1780–1850* (New Brunswick, N. J.: Rutgers University, 1979). Ernest R. Sandeen in *The Roots of Fundamentalism: British and American Millenarianism, 1800–1930* (Chicago: University of Chicago, 1970), emphasizes millenarism's role in the rise of Fundamentalism, and Timothy P. Weber offers a fine history of post-Millerite millenarism in *Living in the Shadow of the Second Coming: American Premillennialism, 1875–1925* (New York and Oxford: Oxford University, 1979).

A study of early nineteenth century millennial exegesis must include Moses Stuart, *Hints on the Interpretation of Prophecy* (second edition, Andover: Allen, Morrill and Wardwell, 1942) and the works of the day's most noted premillennialist, George Duffield, Jr., especially *Dissertations on the Prophecies* (New York: Dayton and Newman, 1842). Pamphlets, many of them appearing in the Second Advent Library, include Henry Dana Ward, *History and Doctrine of the Millennium* (Boston: n.p., 1840); Eliphalet Nott, *A Discourse Delivered in the North Dutch Church (Albany: Charles R. and George r* Webster, 1804) and *A Sermon Preached Before the General Assembly* in *Miscellaneous Works* (New

York: Ryer Schermerhorn, 1810); J. W. Olmstead, *Millennial Observation* (Utica: Sennett, Backus and Hawley, 1841); Richard Chamberlin, *New Discoveries concerning the Millennium* (Poughkeepsie: Mitchell and Bush, 1805); A. L. Crandall, *A Brief Explanation of the Book of Revelations [sic]* (Troy: James M. Stevenson, 1841); John T. Matthews, *A Key to the Old and New Testaments* (New York: n.p., 1842).

Contemporary comments on the period's deep millennial speculation were also frequent. The most interesting articles are Orestes Brownson, "Come Outerism; or the Radical Tendency of the Day," *Brownson's Quarterly Review*, I (1844), 370–79 and James K. Paulding, "The End of the World, a Vision," *Graham's Magazine*, XXII (March, 1843), 145–49. Finally, two newspapers carried millenarism to the general public, *The American Millenarian*, and *Hierophont; or Monthly Journal of Sacred Symbols and Prophecy*.

NEW YORK STATE
A. State and Local Histories

The standard text on New York State history is David Ellis, *New York: State and City* (Ithaca: Cornell University, 1979). Of value too, is Ruth Loring Higgins, *Expansion in New York* (Columbus: Ohio State University, 1931) which discusses early periods of migration into the upstate region.

Specialized histories exist for almost every county and most cities and villages. Many date from America's Centennial. Though they are old and, in the eyes of some, unsophisticated, these histories contain enormous information unavailable anywhere else. Some contain published reminiscences of early settlers, perhaps the first widespread use of oral history. While only a relative handful are mentioned here, these few hopefully can represent the work of all the dedicated and too seldom noticed local historians who for decades have worked tirelessly and without pay to preserve the heritage of their hometowns. Works that dealt particularly with areas of my interest include John S. Minard, *Allegany County and Its People* (Alfred, N. Y.: John A. Ferguson and Co., 1896); Duane Hamilton Hurd, *History of Clinton and Franklin Counties, New York*, III (Rochester: Historical Society 1933); W. M. Beauchamp, "Notes of Other Days in Skaneateles," *Annual Volume of the Onondaga Historical Association, 1914* (Syracuse: Dehler Press, 1914); *History and Biography of Washington County and the Town of Queensbury* (Chicago: Gresham Publishing Co., 1894); Allen Corey, *Gazetteer of the County of Washington, New York* (Schuylerville, N. Y.: n.p., 1850).

B. Burned-over District

The history of religion in upstate New York begins with Whitney R. Cross, *Burned-Over District: The Social and Intellectual History of Enthusiastic Religion in Western New York, 1820–60* (Ithaca: Cornell University, 1950). An interesting addition to the literature is Paul Johnson, *A Shopkeeper's Millennium: Society and Revivals in Rochester, New York, 1815–1837* (New York: Hill and Wang, 1978).

Particular religious movements have received some attention. Edward Deming Andrews has written a standard history of the Shakers, *The People Called Shakers: A Search for the Perfect Society* (New York: Oxford University, 1953). Useful contemporary documents on this sect are Frederick William Evans, *Autobiography of a Shaker and Revelation of the Apocalypse* (n. p.: Charles Van Benthuysen, 1869); *A Concise Statement of the Principles of the Only True Church* (Bennington: Haswell and Russell, 1790); and Seth Y. Wells, Shakerism's most important publicist, *Testimonies Concerning the Character and Ministry of Mother Ann Lee* (Albany: Packard and Van Benthuysen, 1827). This last includes fascinating testimony by original Shakers, those who joined the sect in the 1770s. Distinct from but similar to Shakerism was Jemima Wilkinson's sect, described in Herbert Andrew Wisbey, *Pioneer Prophetess: Jemima Wilkinson, the Publick Universal Friend* (Ithaca: Cornell University, 1964).

Of all upstate New York sects, the Mormons have received the most extensive treatment. Fawn Brodie's *No Man Knows My History: The Life of Joseph Smith the Mormon Prophet* (New York: Alfred A. Knopf, 1946) is controversial, but it first introduced me to the direct link between innovative religion and popular culture. A second good biography is Stanley P. Hirschson, *The Lion of the Lord: A Biography of Brigham Young* (New York: Alfred A. Knopf, 1969).

C. General Source Materials

I have relied greatly on local newspapers for comments and attitudes about Millerism (though not for *news* about them) and for revelations about popular culture. Interested readers can find a valuable list of extant upstate New York newspapers and where they are located in *New York History* throughout 1972. Papers I found particularly revealing were: *Advocate for the People* (Auburn), *Albany Argus*, *Albany Evening Journal*, *Angelica Reporter*, *Antimasonic Enquirer* (Rochester), *Bath Constitutionalist*, *Cayuga Republican* (Auburn), *Chenango Telegraph* (Norwich), *Cortland Advocate*, *Exeter News Letter*, *Jamestown Journal*, *Monroe Republican* (Rochester), *New York Herald*, *Oswego Palladium*, *Plattsburgh Republican*, *Republican Monitor* (Cazenovia),

Rochester Daily Advertiser, Rochester Daily Democrat, Rochester Tele-graph, Seneca Falls Democrat, Schenectady Reflector, Skaneateles Columbian, Steuben Democrat (Bath), *Tompkins Democrat* (Ithaca), *Tompkins Volunteer* (Ithaca).

Archival resources are rich and varied. Of significance is the recently-completed "Burned-over District Collection" housed in the Local and Regional History Collection, Cornell University. This merely adds to an archive that was already one of the most important for local New York history. Some of the collections there I found most helpful were the Abell Family Papers, James Boorman Fisher Papers, Judah L. Richmond Diary, Benjamin Russell Diary and Autobiography, George A. Throop Papers. At the Rochester Public Library I viewed the Diary and Account Book of Lindley E. Gould, 1817-1853, and the University of Rochester made the William Henry Seward Papers available to me. The archives at Syracuse University include the Brockway Family Papers, Spalding Family Papers and Lyman A. Spalding Journals, Chapman Family Papers, Gerritt Smith Papers, and the Susan Bibbins Fox Memorial Book.

INDEX

Abolition, 34, 42, 91–92
Adrian, J., 42
Advent Christian Church, 156
adventism: anticlericalism, 79–80; antiformal pietism, 72 and passim,
    89–93, 109, 130, 153; apocalyptic rhetoric, 21, 60–61, 66–67;
    Baptist Church, 22, 25, 35; Christian Union movement, 87; cities,
    hostility to, 41; come outerism, 115–18; conversion of the Jews, 120;
    cosmic time, 125; dissenters, 100–101, 123, 130; divine agency,
    91–93; effects of, 158; historicism, 67–68; insanity (comments re), 2,
    40, 104–5, 124; interdenominationalism, 99, 119; Judaizers, 130;
    martyrdom (feelings of), 113–14; materialism (opposition to), 51;
    meeting places, 46; Mormons, 105, 149; numbers of followers,
    47–48; opponents (re), 113–15, 143; orthodoxy of, 51, 67–68, 79,
    96n; ostracism of, 109, 142, 157–58; Perfectionism, 146–47; politics
    (opposition to), 77; preachers, 124; propagation (methods), 40,
    43–45, 49; reform, 34, 91–92; sectarians, opposition to, 78–79,
    89–90; religious liberty, 120–21; revivalism, 24–26, 48–49; sacrifice
    and commitment, 26, 123–25, 137; set time, 119, 121, 132–37,
    144–45, 155–56; thefts from movement, 105; volunteerism, 45–46,
    47, 123; women activists, 126–29
adventist(s): activities, ix–x, 93, 123; beliefs, ix–x, 152–53; chronology,
    67; fanaticism, 63, 94, 101 and passim, 137, 145, 149–50; camp
    meetings (use of), 41, 46–47; conferences (use of), 35, 36, 41;
    preachers, 18–19, 20, 99; publications, 23, 29, 33, 37, 38, 45, 142;
    social status, 106–7
Adventist denominations, 95, ix (note) (see also Advent Christian Church
    and Seventh-Day Adventist Church)
Adventist historiography, x
Albany, NY, 36, 119, 122, 146
Albany Conference, 152–53
Allen, Ethan, 5
American Antislavery Society, 91
American Millenarian, 98
Andrews, Emerson, 22
Angier, Aaron, 27
annihilationism, 121, 130

Anti-Masonry, 18, 19, 20, 34, 38, 84
Anti-Mission Baptists, 49, 88–89, 163
Antichrist, 78, 88, 98, 115
Apocalypse, 11–13, 52, 54–57, 91
apocalypticism, 57–62, 164
ascension robes, ix, 102, 138
Attica, NY, 37
Auburn, NY, 44

Badger, Joseph, 28–29, 86
Baptist Church: anti-Catholicism, 78; apocalypticism, 57; associational
    authority, 84–85; clergy, 20, 81–84; formalization of, 80–85;
    growth, 80; laity versus clergy, 83–84; missions, 87–88; pietism, 75
    and passim; pietistic dynamic, 74, 80–85; tenets, 81
Baptist Education Society, 81
Baptist Register, 96, 97, 101
Barry, Thomas F., 39, 143, 149
Barton, Hull, 147–48
Barton, Michael H., 63, 101
Bateman, Calvin, 157
Bates, Joseph, 91
Battersby, James, 158
Beach, Augustus, 38, 45, 143–44
Bentley, A. N., 133
Bible Examiner, 121
Bible prophecy, 11–12, 57, 58, 67–68, 97
Biblicism, 44, 79
Binghamton, NY, 47
Bissell, Benjamin F., 146
Bliss, Sylvester, 122, 136, 145, 151, 154
Boston, 31
Brisbin, Robert, 84
Brockport, NY, 44
Brownson, Orestes, 112
Buckley, Henry, 158–59
Buffalo, NY, 39, 40, 44, 46, 55
Burned-over district, x–xi, 163–64
Burnham, W. S., 105
Bush, George, 54
Busti, NY, 119

C., A. E., 54
Calvinism, 4, 6
Camp meetings (Millerite), 41, 46, 47, 129

messianism, 51, 62–63
Methodist Church, 57, 74, 89
Methodist Magazine, 107
Midnight Cry, 34, 38, 42, 47, 61
millenarism (*see* premillennialism)
Millennial Harbinger, 107
millennialists (lack of consistency), 53–54
Millennium, 2, 12, 15, 28–29, 52, 56, 69, 96 (*see also* premillennialism
    and postmillennialism)
Miller, Elisha, 3
Miller, George, 144, 145
Miller, Lucy Smith, 4, 7
Miller, Paulina Phelps, 6, 8, 9
Miller, William, Sr., 3–4, 6, 8–9
Miller, William, ix, 35, 84, 148, 162: and New School revivalism, 17–18,
    25; as a Baptist, 1, 3–4, 9, 15; as a father, 7, 9–10, 16; as
    abolitionist, 91–92; as antiformalist, 117–18; as Biblist, 11, 13, 79; as
    reluctant prophet, 1, 14, 17, 20, 28; confession, 142; conversion, 10;
    Deism, 5–6, 9; dreams, 14–15, 159; early life, 1, 3; education, 4, 8;
    eschatology, 1–2, 10–14, 98–99, 121; fear of death, 6–7; financial
    contributions to movement, 107; Great Disappointment, 141;
    hermeneutics, 10–11, 98; Himes, relationship with, 33–34, 159;
    hypnotism, 101; in western New York, 40, 43; last years and death,
    157–60; marriage, 4; Masonry, 15n, 18; on annihilationism, 121,
    122–23; Catholic Church, 24; on cities, 76–77; on divine agency,
    92; on Nature, 60; on necessity of action, 123; on October 22 date,
    136; on opponents, 114–15; on history, 68; on religious liberty, 131;
    on the Jews, 98–99, 120; on sectarianism, 90; on separatism, 115,
    117; on set date, 12, 67, 120, 121, 133; on shut door, 150–52;
    opposition to, 18–19, 26, 27, 114–15; orthodoxy of, 17–18, 26;
    personality, 11–13, 27, 124; physical condition, 40, 124; political
    career, 1, 5; publications, 19; Rationalist, 1; rumors re, 108; social
    status, 1, 5, 106; War of 1812, service in, 7
Millerism (problems of definition), 48
Millerite movement (*see* adventism)
missions, 55–56, 87–88
mobility, 73–74, 82
mobs, 110
Mooer's Forks, NY, 21
Moorstown, NY, 21
Moriah, NY, 21
Mormons, 49, 63, 72, 105
Munger, Hiram, 104, 110

DATE DUE

HIGHSMITH   #LO-45220